KISS M

SLÁINE THE W/
THE SECRET HISTORY

PAT MILLS

MILLSVERSE
BOOKS

Cover art by Alex Ronald
Cover design by Lisa Mills

Edited and formatted by Lisa Mills

Millsverse Books
2042 Davenport House
261 Bolton Road
Bury
Lancashire BL8 2NZ
www.millsverse.com

❀ Created with Vellum

Dedicated to the memory of
Jack 'The Lad' Mills, the very best of my three dads.

INTRODUCTION

Writing *Sláine* began as a personal quest for me to make sense of my Irish roots and turned into an incredible quest to explore and dramatise Celtic magic, myths and mysteries. Sláine would emerge from them as a unique hero who stands apart from all other sword and sorcery warriors. But I barely appreciated what this meant at the time, and its profound implications. Thus I didn't realise a quest to discover more about my ancestors and my own paternity would become a magical quest of its own.

I didn't know about a little understood and often denied esoteric rule: if you take an interest in magic, it will take an interest in *you*. Anyone who has looked at magic in any detail will know just how true and how real this is.

But Celtic magic is not the magic of elites; of wizards who would disempower us with their 'superior' learning, Latin and 'libers'. It's the magic of peasants, of ordinary people who have embedded the mysteries of the past in their folk traditions and tales. I wanted to draw on that real life magic, which is still all around us today in Ireland, Wales, Scotland and England. Thus megalithic tombs in the west of Ireland date back five thousand years, older than the pyramids; their significance and meaning barely understood and still a matter for speculation.

But this was not my magical quest alone. It was also the artists' quest, and the story had a profound and magical effect on many of them. They, too, seemed as driven as myself, even if their vision for *Sláine* was sometimes at variance with my own. They were passionate about the character as never before on their previous works. They drew and painted works of wonder that could not be the products of my descriptions alone and were beyond anything they had hitherto illustrated.

Kiss My Axe! is about all the creators' search for inspiration from those ancient stones and sagas of long ago to produce *Sláine* for *2000AD*. It's about how the character survived against considerable odds – primarily the unthinking and unwise interference of its various 'alien' editors – to become an international success.

It's a celebration of all that's most exciting, fantastic and humorous in Celtic myths and legends.

It's a celebration of our ancestors who are renowned as role models and inspiration for rebellion and challenging injustice.

It's the story of the author and the incredibly talented artists who drew this best-selling comic – and the people who nearly destroyed it.

PART I
SLÁINE THE WANDERER

THE FIRST PUNK

When I started researching the ancient Celts for my *Sláine* saga, they seemed absolutely insane to me. They charged into battle stark naked to show the enemy they had no fear. They tore open their wounds to make them bigger to impress other warriors. They were headhunters. They kept their favourite 'brainballs' in boxes to show off to their friends. They drank each other's blood. They fought to the death over which of them should get the biggest piece of meat in a banquet: the 'Champion's Portion'. They wore trousers with different patterns on each leg. They spiked up their hair in three different colours: brown, white and red.

And, according to the monk Gerald of Wales, they were an unstable race who wallowed in vice, didn't pay their taxes, and lived in sin. So what was so bad about them?

Gerald also noted:

'From an ancient and wicked custom, they always carry an axe in their hands instead of a staff that they may be ready promptly to execute whatever iniquity their minds suggest. Wherever they go, they carry this weapon with them and watching their opportunity as occasion offers, it has not to be unsheathed like a sword, nor bent like a bow, or thrust out like a spear. Raised a little, without any preparation, it deals a deadly blow. They have, therefore, always at hand, nay, in their hands, that which is sufficient to inflict death. From these axes there is no security: while you fancy yourself secure, you will feel the axe. You put yourself heedlessly in danger, if you permit the axe and omit to take precautions for your security.'

The Normans called for a total ban on Irish axe-ownership. I'm sure we can all understand why.

Their myths and legends were equally weird and also sometimes incomprehensible. I'd read them and be baffled by their logic, or lack of it. They didn't seem to make sense: fantasy and reality merged into each other in a way that seems strange to our modern eyes.

A popular YouTube video attempts to deal with this very problem: *Why isn't Irish Mythology more popular?*

It isn't just the Irish Celts: distinguished academic W. F. Skene spent a lifetime translating *The Four Ancient Books of Wales* and, once he had completed his meisterwork, concluded he had failed miserably as he realized they were still largely unintelligible. Having read the poems many times over, I know just what he means.

Similarly, when I looked at Scottish writer James Macpherson's translation of the Ossian cycle of epic poems, they felt strange and distant to me. This is because, although the stories 'are of endless battles and unhappy loves', the enemies and causes of strife are given little explanation and context.

Hence a producer at the Irish Film Board who, some six years ago, after reading *Sláine*, commissioned me to write a screenplay on Cuchulain, Ireland's greatest warrior. But he warned me with a wry smile that he had shelves full of past abortive screenplays on Cuchulain that had tried and failed to make sense of the Hound of Ulster's life. He was right to warn me, because my screenplay, too, would eventually join them.

In my view, only *Excalibur* and *Braveheart* have captured the elusive Celtic dream on the big screen.

Yet my personal quest to make sense of my Irish ancestry urged me on to make sense of my fragmentary understanding of the Ireland of the Celts. Officially, I was half Irish, half English, but the Irish side always seemed to predominate. I was well read on modern Irish history, but knew little about its pre-Christian past.

But I was attracted intuitively to anything I could read about the ancient Celts. I loved the few *Wulf the Briton* strips I discovered in *Express Weekly* comic, beautifully illustrated by Ron Embleton, because Wulf was a rebel fighting for freedom against the Roman oppressors. I even read schoolmaster Henry Treece's anti-Celtic, pro-Roman classic *Legions of the Eagle*, despite hating his calculated establishment propaganda that the Celts needed the civilising influence of the Romans.

But I was unaware of Cuchulain, or the Tribes of the Earth Goddess, or Ossian, or the great Welsh bard Taliesin or any other Celtic myths and legends.

Instead, I was given Charles Kingsley's *The Heroes*, covering the ubiquitous Greek legends. Yet his popular stories about Jason and the Argonauts, Theseus and the Minotaur, and the Centaur, exciting as they are to most young readers, left me absolutely cold. They still do, even though it seems irrational and unfair.

But I'm glad about my dislike, because in 1860 Kingsley describes visiting Ireland during one of its Great Hungers:

'I am haunted by the human chimpanzees I saw along that hundred miles of horrible country ... to see white chimpanzees is dreadful; if they were black, one would not see it so much.'

Even before I knew about Kingsley's racism, somehow I had sensed he was the enemy. He was one of numerous propaganda voices of the establishment, just like Treece. I couldn't bring myself to watch *Clash of the Titans* (1981), or later versions, despite the genius of Ray Harryhausen. Back then, I didn't really know why Greek legends didn't interest me. But now I realise it's because they are *not* the legends of our ancestors and there's rather more to it than that.

Of course there are movies about King Arthur and William Wallace, but Celtic heroic fantasy films are still thin on the ground. The implication is that they're not as enthralling as Beowulf or Jason and the Argonauts. The *Sláine* stories have always aimed to challenge this with stories based on similar legends that are in the public domain. Thus there's my saga of Scota, the runaway pharaoh's daughter, whom Scotland is named after. Or the story of the Trojan Brutus, who has wiped out the giants of Albion and created the magical maze of legendary London, but who is challenged by rebels like Sláine.

The absence of such movies is no oversight. Nor is it bad luck. Or because directors can't be bothered. And neither is it pro-Celtic paranoia to think so.

Something else is going on.

It's the result of a long-standing, subtle form of censorship and propaganda that falls outside the remit of this book to consider in comprehensive detail. It's *deliberate* and that's why I see those who play a role in it as cultural enemies, because they are consciously eroding our heritage by ignoring it and promoting imperial alternatives. With mainstream publishers – to my personal knowledge – rejecting any heroes that would challenge the status quo and 'agreed' versions of historical events.

It was an awareness of this propaganda at the very outset that was a key inspiration for creating Sláine, who I felt might act as a counterweight to establishment heroes.

If you look around, you will find the propaganda everywhere. Thus today the school houses of the prestigious Sherborne preparatory school are named Normans, Romans, Greeks and Trojans, in admiration for imperial invaders. Not Celts, Picts, Gauls and Iceni, to honour our past. They would be far too unruly, far too rebellious to act as role models for children who need, above their academic studies, to be taught obedience to authority and admiration for empires who civilised (and exploited) the 'savages'.

Or there's *The Eagle* (2011) starring Channing Tatum, where a Roman hero defeats the barbarian Caledonians. Once again, the Celts needed a good thrashing by those 'civilised' Romans. The subtext is not accidental. It's pure propaganda. It was from the novel *The Eagle of the Ninth* by Rosemary Sutcliff, a contemporary of Treece. I realise now why I always consciously avoided her popular books as a kid when there were rows and rows of them on the library shelves and I was absolutely desperate to find novels to feed my history habit. Somehow, I knew they were establishment propaganda and were, most emphatically, off limits to me.

It was my intuition, rather than intelligence, that made me ignore them. Intuition is a quality we all have that we are conditioned to discount or over-ride, usually by teachers, clerics or parents who, supposedly, know so much better than our own divinity. Bordering on the esoteric, our innate and primal wisdom can also be referred to as the muse. It must have been my muse: she just didn't like the look of Sutcliff's books. More on my muse later.

As a boy, the ancient Celts, such as the heroic but maniacal Cuchulain and the seductive Queen Medb, were excluded from my reading curriculum and were never spoken of, doubtless because they were so pagan and 'uncivilised' in their outlook. Otherwise my muse would have enthusiastically endorsed them. Queen Medb, determined to possess the legendary Brown Bull of Cooley, offers its owner, 'A portion of the Plain of Aí the equal to his own lands, and a chariot worth seven times three bondsmaids, and my own friendly thighs on top of that.' Not really suitable reading matter for a good Catholic boy.

The establishment even tries to erode the very identity of the Celts with supposedly learned articles and books that claim this recognisable people and culture never really existed as such. It's a hard proposition, as we have to ignore the evidence of our own eyes with visual similarities in the artefacts they left behind from Turkey to Ireland. Academics will, of course, have a flimsy explanation for this. Furthermore, they suggest the Celts were actually diverse Neolithic, or Pictish, or Basque, or Beaker, or whatever, who had little in common with each other; *anything* to cast doubt on the sense of a Celtic identity.

Against this culturally deprived background, I concentrated on Irish modern history to understand my heritage. With my Irish mother's active encouragement, I had read everything I could find on Irish history: Daniel O'Connell, the crimes of Oliver Cromwell, Wolf Tone, Parnell, Michael Collins, The Easter Rising, the Black and Tans, the Treaty and Eamon De Valera. My middle name is Eamon, in his honour.

It's no surprise, therefore, that the first 'Dickensian' comic serial I submitted to the girls' comic *Sandie,* in 1972, was about the Irish Great Hunger, filled with grim details I'd researched from academic documents I read in Dundee University library. These portrayed the British occupying army and landlords in a negative light, something that's often disputed today. 'Most of the British did their best for the poor and destitute,' seems to be the preferred view now. I also scripted the first episode with my writing partner John Wagner, and the Scottish managing editor of IPC girls' comics, John Purdie, bought the serial. He said it was excellent, although rather depressing (!), and potentially controversial, given that it was the 1970s and the 'Troubles' had started. So he had the Irish Great Hunger changed to the Scottish Highland Clearances. Meanwhile, he wanted John Wagner and I to work on another more important story he had devised: *Anne's Animal Sanctuary*, which I at least was supremely unqualified to write. The golden rule for authors, 'write what you know about', was never applied. My detailed outline on the Great Hunger was forgotten about and later passed to another Australian writer to script. Things like that happened in comics, I'm afraid.

I mention this to show you just how challenging it was to produce a popular but purist story like *Sláine* in such a barren climate. Aesthetics were frowned upon as an indulgence. Research was definitely a dirty word in many quarters and even seen as a form of intellectual arrogance. 'It's just a comic', 'kids won't care', were the mantras that comic editors and publishers all too often lived by. Speed was everything – the faster a writer was, the more he was rated and respected. 'Overthinking' was seen as detrimental to a story: the faster it was written, the more likely it was to be a quick, ephemeral, smooth read. At least, that's what John Purdie told me at the time.

Nearly ten years after my Irish Great Hunger story, very little had changed when I decided to produce a barbarian hero story for *2000AD*, illustrated by my then wife, Angela Kincaid. And so I set about researching it. At this early stage I wasn't sure if my barbarian should be Irish or not. Initially, I thought he might be half Irish, half English, reflecting my own background and thus drawing on all my roots for ideas.

I had no idea that the process of developing, refining and changing the story and the art would actually take *two years*. And that's just until it appeared in print. Something that I believe is unheard of in British comics, but would be perfectly normal in European comics where creators own the rights to their creations. It would still be frowned upon today in Britain because it highlights how unworkable and unethical the continuing system of buying all rights to a story really is. If anything, the 'fast food culture' of comics is probably faster than ever today, with the inevitable danger that, just as fast food is all too often junk food, so fast comics can become junk comics. No amount of spin can ever justify our current, antique British comics model.

But, blissfully unaware of the monumental task ahead of me, I looked at fictional and dramatic templates for inspiration and began weeks of reading. Naturally I started with *Conan the Barbarian*, and I enjoyed the stories by Robert E. Howard, but they didn't resonate with me personally for reasons I only understood quite recently. It was then I discovered Howard was hugely influenced by the founder of modern fantasy, Lord Dunsany, of whom more anon.

I didn't know at the time that Howard had been on a similar journey of self-discovery. To quote Wikipedia:

'Howard's "Celtic phase" began in 1930, during which he became fascinated by Celtic themes and his own Irish ancestry [...] Howard taught himself a little Gaelic, examined the Irish parts of his family history and began writing about Irish characters.'

I felt the same way about *Elric* and *Corum* by Michael Moorcock. They were superb, but they didn't feed my soul. Even before I knew who he was, I knew my hero would be an anti-hero with a bad attitude to authority and these great fantasy characters were just not extreme enough for me.

My hero had to be a punk.

Then, as I read *Celtic Myths and Legends* by Charles Squire, it dawned on me that Howard and Moorcock were drawing on these legends for their material. Thus, Conan is the name of a Fomorian sea devil, the monsters from Ireland's Tory Island. 'By Crom!', Conan's favourite exclamation, originates from the terrifying Irish worm god Crom Cruach. The *Corum* series features 'Medhbh', Amergin and other Celtic characters.

With these two great writers as an example, I decided to take a closer look at Celtic legends. In this I was greatly aided by Jim Fitz-patrick's *Book of Conquests,* a beautifully illustrated vision of the various Celtic invaders of Ireland, with a well-researched bibliography at the end, which I avidly investigated.

One of the first sources it led me to was Lady Gregory's *Cuchulain of Muirthemne*: her interpretation of the Cuchulain cycle of stories, with a unique prose style that I found quite hard going. 'I will make my doings be spoken of among the great doings of heroes in their strength,' swears the hero. This inspired a simpler line I would later use in *Sláine*: 'I will do things they'll talk about forever.'

I was struck by the words in the dedication at the beginning of Lady Gregory's book: 'I left out a good deal I thought you would not care about for one reason or another.' I found myself wondering just what it was that her Ladyship had left out and why her readers would not care for it.

I came across similar censorship in the Irish *Cycle of the Kings*, where the translator had deleted 'long bombastic sections of prose'. I realised that the Celtic legends were being consciously 'cleaned up' by some academics, and I longed to find the original sources.

Eventually, I tracked down *The Tain* by Thomas Kinsella, a poet's interpretation of the Cuchulain saga, with astonishing brush drawings by Louis le Brocquy that wonderfully compliment the text. Originally published in 1969, by 1981 it had been reprinted numerous times. It was clearly a favourite among students. It has the earthiness, grittiness, wildness and *truth* that I'm sure the original accounts contained. It is best summed up by the final paragraph. Kinsella translated the words of the Christian monk who had copied the pagan saga:

'I who have copied down this story, or more accurately
fantasy, do not credit the details of the story, or fantasy. Some
things in it are devilish lies, and some poetical figments;

some seem possible and others not; some are for the enjoyment of idiots.'

That monk had my number, all right.

With *The Tain* to guide me, I knew I could make a story work
about a Celtic punk. A hero like Cuchulain, but following a rather
different path. Three other books were invaluable because they too
showed an 'alternative' view of the Celts.

Sex and Marriage in Ancient Ireland by Patrick Power (by a happy
coincidence, the uncle of *Sláine* artist, Dermot Power). How could I
avoid a book with such a great title? This slim volume describes the
(relatively) liberal pre-Christian Brehon laws that governed ancient
Ireland. It relates how trial marriages of a year and a day were
permitted, showing a generosity of spirit and humanity noticeably
missing from the theocracy that controlled Ireland until recent
times.

Then there was the beautifully illustrated *Celtic Mysteries* by
John Sharkey. This would later prove to be a fantastic source of
references for artists, in particular for its stunning photo of the
Celtic Wickerman.

And finally *The Celts* by Jean Markale. An academic and a poet,
his exciting work is loathed by establishment academics, so, naturally, I was attracted to it. His books convey a controversial, passionately written evocation of the magical nature of the Celts.

The hero's name was the next challenge. According to legends,
the first High King of Ireland was called Sláine. That *had* to be my
hero. In Ireland, there's the Hill of Slane famed in stories of St
Patrick, Slane Castle and the River Slaney, all clearly named after
this legendary hero. But Sláine was how he was named in the sagas,
so that was how it had to be written. I never thought about the
accent or anticipated a time where the character would be so
successful that I'd be asked how to pronounce it. At first, I hadn't a

clue. Being Anglo-Irish, I lazily pronounced it 'Slain', rather than the correct 'Slawnyeh.'

So I had my hero's name and my 'bible', *The Tain*. However, I was still concerned that I'd run out of suitable story material in Celtic legends. They would need considerable adapting to work in comic terms. If you look at straight comic adaptions of Irish legends elsewhere, they're often reaching a specialist or arthouse audience, rather than a mainstream one. And I was still unsure how my personal quest fitted in, being half-Irish, half-English.

Accordingly, I decided that if I ran out of material, I'd move onto the mythologies of other countries. With this in mind, I originally made Sláine half-Celtic, half-Viking, drawing on my own Anglo-Irish identity. And Ukko, his dwarf, was to be half-Russian, half-Finnish.

All my stories, right through to the end of Mike McMahon's *Sky Chariots* (many months into the serial), were originally written with appropriate references to Sláine's half-Viking and Ukko's half-Russian origins. For example, there's a scene in *Sky Chariots* where a Viking roars at Sláine, 'Hear me, Stranger! You fight well enough to be my own son! Join us! Let's share the plunder together!'

Sláine replies, 'My parentage is none of your concern ... it was not an old goat like you that sired me!'

The Viking charges forward, snarling, 'I meant my offer well, but you took it ill! So be it ... *Whoever your father is,* he loses his son today!'

Originally, the Viking had actually said that Sláine had the features of a Norseman — he could even be his own son. I subsequently deleted any such suggestion.

But the mystery of Sláine's father, and my own, was always in the back of my mind. More on this later.

Ukko was actually the God of thunder in Finnish mythology. I even read *The Kalevala*, the Finnish national epic, in anticipation that my protagonists would one day end up in the realm of ice and snow. And *Bogatyr* was a term used to describe heroes in Russian legends. It means literally 'God Warrior', so 'the Bogs' are 'the Gods'. Thus, Ukko is constantly exclaiming in my original *Sláine* scripts, 'By the Bogs!' and calling Sláine 'bogatyr'.

Certainly, Sláine *is* a bogatyr, a god warrior. However, the more I delved into Celtic myths, the more I became enamoured of them. This was Sláine's complex mystical world and I would only dilute it if I introduced another mythos or three. At least, that's what I told myself. Looking back, I think it was more a case of a subconscious need to confirm my own roots. Accordingly, on one of my numerous drafts, I finally cut out all references to Sláine and Ukko being connected to Vikings, Finns and Russians.

From a Celtic perspective, it was the right thing to do, but I still miss Ukko's Russo-Finnish origins. I think it was a mistake to delete them. It's great *Blackadder*-style humour. Had I included them, I'm sure 'By the Bogs!' would be as popular an expression today as 'Kiss My Axe', especially amongst younger readers. It's too late now, of course, but I later featured Ukko's origins in a one-off story *The Bogatyr* drawn by Chris Weston in 2018.

The early *2000AD* was especially renowned for its punk values and now Sláine was personifying them. But why was this so important to me? The answer, of course, lies in my own roots.

2

THE MASKS OF SLÁINE

The best way to create a protagonist is always to base them on some aspect of yourself. Just as comic artists often use an 'artist's mirror', clipped to their drawing board to get the right expression and feeling for a hero, so I use a 'writer's mirror', turning it on myself, asking myself how the hero would react in each dramatic situation.

The premise of *Sláine* is that the ancient Celts were eternal rebels, punks for all ages. They break the laws of their oppressors and they believe passionately in freedom and justice.

These are concepts I can readily identify with, so I decided to use my own story as a role model and plot for *Sláine*. It's why he is thrown out of his tribe at age 16 and wanders the Land of the Young with Ukko, mirroring my own experiences.

Probably Sláine's rebellious nature had been formed by various events years before he is expelled at 16. Certainly mine had.

A friend from my primary school days recently reminded me what I was like when I was around seven years old:

'I seem to remember, during our time with the nuns at St. Mary's, that you always had a strong sense of natural justice and fair play. It seems a bit vague now, but I'm not sure this didn't occasionally get you into a bit of conflict with The Little Sisters of Absolute Misery (or whoever they were) when you spoke up in some poor wretch's defence. In our little gang, there was the perception that you were brave and would put yourself at risk (unwisely, we thought; we were all scared of penguin power) by speaking up if you saw something that was unjust. It was not unusual for 'Paddy to be in trouble' again but it was never for poor schoolwork, so what was it? I have, in my mind's eye, an image of Paddy Mills being occasionally withdrawn from class 'to be spoken to'; this memory is strong and indicates to me that this sort of thing happened several times.'

I never learnt to stay silent when faced with injustice. The same thing happened at my secondary school: St Joseph's College in Ipswich. But the Catholic Church deals aggressively with 'trouble-makers' who challenge them. Here's an old boy from a similar Catholic school describing to a government enquiry what can happen to troublemakers. Like me, he was a high-achiever. 'In a nutshell, I'd say that boys like me who resisted could look forward to having their educations derailed and wrecked.'

Thus, I found myself leaving school at fifteen, and leaving home at sixteen. Just in time to enjoy the freedom of the 1960s in all its hedonistic, psychedelic and free-love splendour. If I'd kept my mouth shut, things would have been very different. Today, according to my old history master, I'd be a historian or 'have a job in the Foreign Office.' That seems most unlikely, but it's an indication of my passion for history that was so intense, it was noted at the time. But, rather than being an instrument of the establishment, I've since put my talent to far better use with my anti-war saga *Charley's War*, with *Ragtime Soldier* (a Scottish *Charley's War*), *Sláine* and various historical stories. So it was clearly meant to be.

All this easily translated into Sláine being a rebel, with a bad attitude to authority, who was thrown out of his tribe when he was

16. He then meets up with Ukko. As the scheming dwarf relates, 'Sláine needed someone who'd keep him out of trouble ... someone who'd be a good influence on him ... someone like ... me.'

After four hedonistic years of wandering around the Land of the Young and being led astray by Ukko, the youthful Sláine learns his king is dead. The crops had failed, so he was dropped off a cliff. It's therefore safe for Sláine to return to the bosom of his tribe and this is the position at the end of the very first episode of the story.

Similarly, I was twenty years old when I, with much greater reluctance, decided I'd better renew my relationship with my own Irish tribe.

So who was Ukko in my world? I'd probably put my own name at the top of a long list. The 1960s were the perfect time to be led astray and I only regret I was not led astray more often.

With my own background to draw on, it meant my hero had an essential flaw, something that's often missing from comic book characters, from Clark Kent downwards. As my text relates at the outset, Sláine is a mercenary, a cattle-rustler, a thief, a battle-smiter and maybe one day ... a hero. But characters need flaws to hold a reader's attention, to see if the protagonist will overcome them and achieve greatness.

In Sláine's case, his flaw is his criminal and hedonistic nature, externalised by Ukko. In episode one, as part of Ukko's 'cunning plan', Sláine throws a toad in a monster's mouth. 'For when a toad is swallowed, it inflates itself and sticks in an attacker's throat.' Thanks to this dirty trick, Sláine is able to easily kill the monster and collect the prize money. This leads to a fight with the punters, and the 'cops' – the sinister Skull Swords – are summoned. It's time for the pair to make a quick exit via a dung boat, the dung symbolising the kind of deep shit Ukko is always getting Sláine into.

My commercial templates – the necessary archetypes to ensure the story had structure, pace and comedy – came not from heroic fantasy, but rather from two TV series: *Minder* and *Steptoe and Son*. In

Minder, the Dennis Waterman character is always being exploited by used car salesman Arthur Daley. This is similar to Sláine and Ukko, only Minder doesn't really fight back when he's ripped off. Sláine does. Minder's not a smart guy: Sláine is.

In *Steptoe and Son*, Steptoe Senior desperately holds onto his son Harold whenever he plans to leave. We see Ukko behaving in a similar way in episode one, clinging onto his meal ticket's leg. So these were the real and fictional characters behind the mask of Sláine that were used to make the story work.

Just as Baldric in *Blackadder* has his 'cunning plans', so Ukko has his criminal plans that end in equal disaster. There was great comedy potential in him.

So, sometime in 1981, I sent *2000AD* my episode one, although it was not the final version. I would subsequently change the dialogue several times as I discovered more about the Celts.

But the story was only half the job of creating *Sláine*. Angela had to visualise the character and draw episode one. The most daunting task lay ahead.

3

KISS MY EX

Increasingly, in the account I'm about to relate, the chronology of events would become important: exactly who drew what and when. So at the end of this book there is an Appendix: *A Timeline of Skull Duggery*. It gives a summary of the main events with approximate dates in order to tally with others' accounts of this period of *2000AD's* history.

Why did Angela and I create *Sláine*? Looking back, we must have been nuts. It involved us doing an extraordinary amount of work and research, which cost us financially and which we could ill afford. We spent months creating the character of Sláine and producing episode one. For next to nothing.

And, in the course of those months, to our dismay, we found ourselves on the receiving end of a wave of negativity, of passive-aggression and skulduggery that shocked us both and came very close to destroying *Sláine*.

But working together on a story had seemed like a good and indeed, harmless idea at the time. Why not? It could be fun. Although Angela had never drawn a comic strip before, she was of course very familiar with the genre and her figure work and her inking were good. She is a successful children's book and birthday card illustrator, with an art college training, after all.

She also thought it might be cool to join 2000AD's social circle. There was an inner circle of British artists who regularly spent time chatting, gossiping, showing each other artwork and encouraging each other. On the phone, at conventions, or in the pub where they might be joined by Tharg and his editorial team. Freelancing can be a lonely profession, and this is rarely acknowledged. Imagine working long hours all week and barely speaking to another person. I know of at least three comic artists where loneliness became a serious issue, threatening their wellbeing. I'm sure there were many more. So having a support network of fellow artists can really make a difference.

This was important to Angela, who was far more sociable than I was. Frankly, I was indifferent. After all, I had spent a year creating 2000AD, mainly in isolation, lost in my own creative world, where – as any writer will tell you – you're never alone; you've always got your characters to talk to. And I was still wary of the minefield that was 2000AD. Social interaction is something artists seem to need more than writers, and Angela was no exception.

But that was all in the future. Meanwhile, we were having fun. We shared a love of nature and fantasy. Angela drew some great T. rexes and other dinosaurs, which I absolutely loved. For a while, we talked seriously about maybe doing a new *Flesh* story together (my 2000AD serial where twenty-third century time travellers go back in time to farm dinosaurs for food). But that seemed overly ambitious and too science fiction-orientated for her style. We both rated books like Brian Froud's *Faeries* and David Larkin's *Giants*, and realised that similar fantasy images would look great in 2000AD. In particular, we were impressed by Brian Froud's beautiful pencil illustrations of the legendary Irish warriors, the Tuatha Dé Danann. They were the Tribes of the Earth Goddess Danu, who later became the faerie folk.

A comic saga about one of these warriors appealed to both of us, and so I began my research.

While the story developed, we were cycling out into the countryside every day, seeing all the fantasy potential in rivers and forests, and we talked excitedly about how we could bring them into our story. How Angela could make nature look magical and create a sense of wonder to rival the spaceships of *Dan Dare* or the starscrapers of *Judge Dredd's* Mega-City One.

We decided right from the beginning that Jack Nicholson should be our inspiration, our role model for Sláine. This was shortly after *The Shining* and the memorable axe-wielding scene that culminates in 'Here's Johnny!' Who could possibly compete with the handsome but cruel star of *The Shining*? Even though I originally thought Sláine should wear a helmet, it would not have concealed his face. Eventually, we would even buy a special Japanese photo book with endless colour images of Nicholson for Angela's reference.

I can still see a Jack Nicholson vibe in Angela's work and, later on, in Glenn Fabry's. It's no coincidence that these two representations of Sláine's face are the most popular with readers and I believe it's because they are true to the original Nicholson template. Other later versions of Sláine sometimes have an 'uncanny valley' effect on the audience where the character doesn't look quite right to them. By comparison, Judge Dredd rarely veers away from the Clint Eastwood role model still inside that helmet somewhere, and this strong continuity helps his success. With hindsight, maybe I should have been stricter, insisting on the same strong facial continuity, rather than allowing artists to turn the warped warrior into themselves, when their facial features were often rather different.

Physique-wise, we based Sláine on the 'King Mod' of Bury St Edmunds we both remembered and liked from our teenage years. Ray Morgenson was very different to the super-cool 'King Mod' who Sting brilliantly portrays in the film *Quadrophenia*. A nineteen-year-old who worked on a building site, Ray was a handsome, powerful, hard but friendly guy, with a great energy about him. It was his gleaming chrome scooter that led the Bury St Edmunds mod pack. He had as many chrome accessories on it as Sláine has Celtic jewellery. Thanks to carrying hods of bricks up and down ladders all day, Ray was stronger and more muscular than your average skinny teenager (e.g., me). And he was *nothing like* the questionable body-builder look often seen in *Conan* and elsewhere in heroic fantasy.

Our distinctive and very different working class look really comes over in episode one where Sláine is about to throw a toad into the T. Rex's mouth. Now *that's* a guy who looks more at home lugging bricks than hanging out in a gym pumping iron. It's an important and subtle visual difference that I think only Angela, of all the *Sláine* artists, really understood. But it's how we both figured our Celtic warriors must have looked: straight off a building site. Replace the brick hod over his shoulder with a similar sized axe, and he's in business.

Now I just had to find a way to convey how Celts like Sláine were terrifying headhunters. They often kept their favourite heads in boxes and took them out to show them off to their guests. So I suggested to Angela that Sláine has his two favourite demon skulls hanging from his belt. Initially, she tried three skulls, but that seemed too much. I think his trophy still works rather well. It was mirrored a few years later when Marshal Law has the mask of one of his superhero victims hanging from his belt.

And finally there was Sláine's helmet. I was convinced he *had* to wear one. At that time, helmets or masks were obligatory for *2000AD* heroes: Dredd; Strontium Dog; ABC Warriors; Torque-mada; Rogue Trooper and so on, they all had them. Clint Eastwood may be under Dredd's helmet, but it's the *helmet* that makes the character. Helmets were so important for the comic's heroes that today there is even a *Helmets of 2000AD* Facebook group.

I suggested a range of possibilities to Angela, which she patiently designed to my exacting specifications. I didn't want anything cool like the Strontium Dog's helmet, or authoritarian like Dredd's or evil like Torquemada's. I wanted a different kind of helmet that suggested Sláine's 'punk', *rebellious*, 'Jack Nicholson' nature, like he didn't give a damn about anything.

So she tried various battered metal helmets and even one with a rusty hole in it, as if Sláine had salvaged it from a rubbish dump. Thus you'll see one of Sláine's attackers in her episode one is wearing a helmet with a pair of horns crudely knotted on the front: that was actually one of her original designs for Sláine, which she was able to use on the minor character. I'll admit Angela spent a week designing helmets, but I have an uneasy and guilty feeling it may have been much longer.

Initially, I decided her rusty helmet with the hole in it and the horns tied on it was right for Sláine. You will see a character very similar to Sláine wearing the exact same helmet in the *Sláine Diceman* story *Ring of Danu*. It's well-drawn by Mike Collins, based closely on Angela's original design, which we sent to him. He looks like a mysterious, barbarian Man With No Name. I'm quite sure if we'd gone with this design, it would have been equally popular with the readers. Perhaps even *more* popular, at a time when our readers expected their heroes to wear helmets.

But then I felt intuitively that it wasn't Celtic enough. And it wasn't *challenging* us. If characters wear helmets all the time, we don't have to characterize them to the same degree, because their feelings can easily be concealed by their helmets. They don't have the same potential range of expressions as a character that is bareheaded.

So I looked over at Angela's drawing board, at her cool Man With No Name, and said, 'Hmm ... you know what? Maybe he'd better *without* a helmet? With Celtic spiky hair – like a *punk*. If he's not wearing a helmet, we can really focus on his Jack Nicholson menace. Hey – that could look *really* cool! What do you think?'

Conveniently for me, I don't recall Angela's reaction, but I do remember she promptly sketched out a headshot of Sláine, almost certainly with the help of a Jack Nicholson reference. Her response is all there in that iconic headshot of the character staring out at us as he says, 'Kiss my axe'.

As always, a picture says a thousand words.

'That's the look!' I said, excitedly. 'Perfect!'

Like many visual aspects of her episode one, *that* look has never been beaten, undoubtedly because she really meant it! I would often refer to it with artists when I wanted Sláine to react in a cool and menacing way.

I *also* thought to myself: 'Actually, his hair could be a *little* bit more spiky, to really emphasise his Celtic origins. And... I wonder what it would look like in black and white if his hair was dyed three colours?' But I rightly feared Angela's response would be even spikier, so I sensibly kept my thoughts to myself. Sometimes you've got to know when to stop!

The face she drew is the face of a 20-year-old *hard man*, which I recognised only too well from when I had met them during my misspent youth. It sums up his whole persona, something that doesn't happen enough in comics. Invariably, comic faces and expressions are 'off the peg'. But this was 'made to measure'.

And his words are also uniquely Celtic: the ancient sagas are full of warriors responding in that menacing, deadpan, laconic way.

Not only does Angela's Sláine have expression; he's also handsome. Yet another reason for the prevalence of the helmet in 2000AD is that it often absolves the artist of the responsibility of having to draw a handsome hero. In fact, some artists cannot do it and don't believe it's important. Maybe it's because they feel uncomfortable drawing what they might see as 'male models'. Whatever the reason, they are wrong. The good-looking hero is as essential to the majority of comics as it is to the majority of movies. We all want to fantasise we're James Bond or Dirty Harry or Braveheart.

The rest of the designs were easy by comparison. Ukko was spot on from the beginning. Angela loved Ukko – you can see that in every picture. She is influenced by Froud, but also by the expressions of chimpanzees in *National Geographic*, and she's brought something all of her own to the character. Especially in that iconic opening scene where Ukko first appears, which cries out for a caption like: 'Would you buy a used chariot from this dwarf?'

But there was much more for her to create. No wonder it took her so long. Martial arts, like the salmon leap where our hero could jump onto the boss of an enemy's shield. The Celtic logos and special credit box. The map of Sláine's world. The megalithic magic. The sinister urban criminal underworld. The skull swords. And the Drune Lords. They were all uniquely and painstakingly designed by Angela and featured in her episode one, either in the story or on the cover she drew to go with the episode. They provide a reference resource that is invaluable to me and to the artists to this day, 40 years later.

In particular, Angela created several full-page, fully inked images of fabulous and unspeakably evil Drune Lords, with their foul, stinking fur robes that you could almost smell from the way she drew them. Frustratingly, I couldn't major on them in episode one (or, indeed, on her love of nature). Instead, they were passed on to subsequent *Sláine* artists Mike McMahon and Belardinelli as references, and both drew closely on them. They can, however, be seen as small figures on page one and there's also a close-up of one on Angela's cover.

Angela's various designs were approved by Tharg McManus (I wasn't aware anyone else being involved in his decision-making), and I took that as an endorsement of her style and her representation of the characters. I already knew they were great, but if there was a problem, this was the time to speak up. McManus, however, seemed enthusiastic, so that was validation for Angela and encouragement for her to continue.

It soon became common knowledge in the *2000AD* artist

community that she was drawing my new strip. I think Angela and I were vaguely aware of a cool reaction. Correction: there was no reaction at all. In a community where everyone literally lives, talks and breathes comics, her work was never mentioned by my peers, and that's still the case through to the present day. Or at least, never in my earshot. Angela's creation of *Sláine* was and remains a gorilla in the corner that is never spoken of. Needless to say, that did not endear me to those concerned.

At the time, the two of us were far too caught up with her episode one, and so excited by the exciting images she was producing, that we didn't notice what was happening or that it would eventually become a problem for us. If I had noticed, I'd have probably reassured Angela, 'Oh, the guys are just being a bit weird. They'll get used to the idea of you being a *2000AD* artist in time, and come around.' Of course that is not how jealous and over-competitive people behave. They *never* come around.

My bad for not realising we were just about to enter that minefield. Again.

I knew that Angela would need other artists to also draw her character. That was the norm in those days. I discussed possibilities with Tharg, and Belardinelli and Mike McMahon were agreed upon as the artists. I decided Belardinelli should draw episode two, directly following Angela's work because he would give it the illustrative look I wanted. I had no real idea what style Mike would adopt. Nor did anyone else either at that time, probably including himself. But I knew it wouldn't matter, that it would be brilliant, and that contrasting styles had worked on so many *2000AD* stories in the past. *The Cursed Earth* being a prime example.

I was aware that Mike wasn't happy with what he was currently doing for *2000AD* and was looking for a new direction: a story he could make his own. Probably he was drawing *Judge Dredd* after *ABC Warriors* ended. I was also told he played historic battle strategy games and was knowledgeable about the Celts. My peers said he was made for a story like *Sláine*. 'It's his dream', one of them told me.

That was good enough for me. Meanwhile, I needed to focus on the artist's 'bible' Angela and I had chosen to inspire her style on episode I. This was *Conquering Armies* by Dionnet and Gal.

Here's what publishers' Humanoids have to say about it today:

> 'Jean-Pierre Dionnet, one of the founders of "*Metal Hurlant*," started a new genre in comics when he collaborated with artist Jean-Claude Gal ("Diosamante") in the late 1970s: Heroic Fantasy. It shortly thereafter gained the favor of the public and has since grown immensely. This is the occasion for all lovers of the genre to return to its roots.'

Conquering Armies was yet another story from *Metal Hurlant* that had hugely influenced me when I created *2000AD*. It blew Angela and I away. There's a new colour edition retitled *'Armies'*, from Humanoids, but it's worth Googling the black and white original, too. I still regard it as a work of genius. It's a celebration of black and white art; perfect as a guide on how to capture the magnificence and the glory of the Celtic world: the detail of their jewellery; their weaponry; their great round halls. Everything I wanted to write about, and artists to draw. It was especially important as *2000AD* was still printed on crude bog paper, so it needed this 'luxury look' to disguise that fact. Belardinelli's art has a similar 'luxury look' in those early *2000AD* progs.

I didn't make this choice lightly. There was a lot of consulting with Angela and with those in the industry whose opinion I valued. All my experience of what readers liked went into my choice. But that choice, even though I was the writer of *Sláine*, and had three commercially successful comics under my belt, was to be endlessly challenged and undermined. Even in the face of all the evidence to the contrary. My big mistake, as you will see, was putting ordinary readers first and fan tastes last. This didn't suit the forces of fandom, who were increasingly controlling 2000AD's destiny and who thought they knew so much better than the French – the world leaders in comics, after Manga.

The art style in *Conquering Armies* was totally unique, like nothing I had ever seen before. It was noticeably free from comic book devices, such as action lines. It was deliberately and unashamedly illustrative, with an impressive and detailed use of strong blacks, quite different to other masters of black and white art. I talked openly and enthusiastically about it, saying *this* was how *Sláine* was going to look.

And that was our undoing.

In simplistic terms – and it has to be this way or we will stray too far from our story – there are two basic art styles in comics: an illustrated style and a comic book style.

Frank Hampson (*Dan Dare*), Don Lawrence (*Trigan Empire* and *Storm*) Gal, and any number of great French artists could be described as having an illustrative style. Frank Miller (*Batman*), Mike Mignola (*Hellboy*) and Carlos Ezquerra (*Judge Dredd*) could be said to have a comic book style.

Of course there are endless hybrids, and both styles have their strengths and weaknesses. There is no one 'orthodox' way. Or at least that's what I thought.

Generally, my peers on 2000AD rated a comic book style.

Consequently, when I told them about my choice, I discovered they disliked *Conquering Armies*, at least as passionately as I liked it. For instance, Nick Landau, publisher of Titan Books, closely associated with 2000AD back then, and whom I also consulted, thought it was 'stiff and too illustrative'. His opinion had considerable weight, because he was already 2000AD's unofficial kingmaker: he decided which stories were published as reprint editions and which ones were not. I don't recall Mike expressing an opinion on *Conquering*

Armies, but, in any event, I was looking forward to his own unique take on the Celts.

What did it matter if they disagreed, you may ask? Why didn't you and Angela just do your own thing: you're the creators, and never mind what anyone else thought? Who cares?

We didn't care – at first. When I started *2000AD*, I always ignored the considerable opposition and passive-aggression of my peers (described in my book *Be Pure! Be Vigilant! Behave! 2000AD & Judge Dredd: The Secret History*). Now history was repeating itself. In starting *Sláine*, I once again ignored surprisingly similar opposition and passive-aggression.

Then the penny slowly began to drop.

The more they enthusiastically talked up Mike's *Sláine*, the more I became aware of the deafening silence on Angela's *Sláine*.

The first rule of passive-aggression? Nothing is ever said to your face. So you have to figure it out for yourself. If you challenge the aggressor, it's denied, you're gaslit, and you start believing you're being paranoid.

As I always believe in confronting passive-aggression, I'm going to fill that silence with the most likely explanation, which has been confirmed by the events that followed:

I had the effrontery and the nepotism to choose to create my next *2000AD* serial for my wife: an outsider; not one of the team; an unknown artist who had never drawn a comic strip before. She was going to draw it in a style that was not only loathed by *2000AD's* 'inner circle', but was radically different to the usual *2000AD* art styles. My exciting new story about a Celtic barbarian was thus surely doomed for failure. Certainly in fandom, (which is what really mattered to the inner circle) and probably for the majority of younger and mainstream general readers, too. They wouldn't like Angela's art either. But, fortunately, Mike was there to take the story over from Angela and rescue *Sláine* from disaster and make the creation his own, a creation he was born to draw. I would have to radically change my story to suit Mike's very different view of the character.

(Belardinelli, like Angela, was also *never* mentioned. He was not seen as relevant to the future of *Sláine*, only Mike. He was a 'fill-in' who would be tolerated in between Mike's amazing and ground-breaking episodes.)

Once again you might ask, why would it matter if a number of your peers and an outside publisher didn't like what you were doing? Or if they had their own favourite candidate to draw *Sláine*? Surely Tharg McManus was in charge, not them?

I'll leave that question on the table for the time being, and continue.

I began to ruminate on just what was going on behind the scenes and how I should deal with it. Was this *really* about my possible nepotism? Was it jealousy? Competitiveness?

To give you some idea of how competitive *2000AD* artists were at this time, here's an example. Artist A was the established *2000AD* artist. Artist B was the exciting, ambitious newcomer. Artist B asked Artist A: 'On a scale of one to ten, where would you position me in the *2000AD* top artist league table?' Clearly, he was expecting a position towards the top of the league. After a pause for reflection, Artist A replied: 'Er ... ten.'

Angela and I had no such league table in our heads — we just wanted to enjoy working on a story together that we were both passionate about. For me, as a writer, it was a unique opportunity to work closely with an artist as never before. I loved every moment of it. I think it's also very healthy for a couple to have a shared objective. It never occurred to us that others would be jealous of a successful husband-wife team.

Just how dumb could I be?

But to deter any accusations of nepotism, I was determined that we *must* have a hit, so I made sure every picture Angela drew was absolutely spot on. This of course made it tougher for Angela, and ran the risk of her art stiffening up. That's what happens when an artist is nervous. An artist's visual flow comes with confidence, not with someone breathing down their neck and asking them to endlessly 'tweak' things. In fact, Angela coped admirably well. Her art is not as refined as Conquering Armies: it's actually looser.

Because we were having fun.

It was an exciting and enjoyable working relationship, especially as the art developed, and Angela rightly asserted her co-creator's view on the story.

Example:

Me: 'You've got Sláine smiling in the bar scene where he's telling the bad guys to back off. You can't have that!'
Angela: 'Why not?'
Me: '2000AD heroes *never, ever* smile. It's a rule.'
Angela: 'Well, it's a *stupid* rule. I think it suits him. He's just relaxed after killing a T. rex, he's having a beer, and he's hoping to score with that barmaid later.'
Me: 'You're right. He *should* smile. Forget the rule.'

Check it out and you'll see that, up to this date, 2000AD heroes invariably went around with clenched teeth and a constipated glare on their face. They never smiled. This was actually more of an artist's short cut; it meant no different facial expressions were required, which some 2000AD artists could not easily draw at this time.

It may seem strange now, but at that time, having a 2000AD hero smile was a *big* deal. Angela was the first artist on 2000AD to give her hero a smile.

By now, Mike had seen Angela's concept art and improved one of Angela's original two Celtic logos by tightening it up. He also tweaked the belt on Angela's version of Sláine's 'waist mat', and it's all the better for it. And he asked for Sláine's axe 'Brainbiter', to be a single blade weapon, which he felt was more realistic. Angela was happy to change it from our original double-headed axe.

In fact, I far preferred her double-headed axe, because this is fantasy, not a history lesson, and I reverted back to it as soon as I could. It's now an iconic image that's been made into merchandise. In fact, there is some evidence that double-headed axes were used by the Celts. But as with their roads, their great halls, their unique and bizarre martial arts feats and their druid technology, this is usually denied or denigrated by establishment historians.

Angela completed her pencils and I was thrilled for her. All my judgment in assessing past artists for the comic told me she had produced something very special.

The negativity we had already experienced strangely worked *for* us, just as it did when I started *2000AD*, because it made both of us try harder. My peers had actually done us a favour!

So in the spring of 1982 she confidently sent her pencilled pages into the Nerve Centre and we looked forward to the Mighty One's reaction.

4

CELTOMANIA!

To set the scene on what happened next, I should introduce the relevant personnel properly. Tharg was Steve McManus; and his art editor was Robin Smith.

Steve was an easy-going guy, well-liked by the creators he'd go down the pub with. If I wasn't involved with him business-wise, I'm sure he would make the perfect drinking companion. But 'being a nice guy' can also be a front, as would become apparent to me on several occasions, some of which I've previously described (see *Be Pure!*). Other creators have noted the same problem and at least one of them has talked about it elsewhere. In any event, it's not really what being an editor is all about. The mark of a good editor is to have a strong and successful creative vision or the ability to sustain your predecessor's creative vision. It's also what you actually achieve on a practical level. I'd previously had a hugely ambitious story, *ABC Warriors*, destroyed by his poor planning and I'd sworn to Angela at the time, 'I cannot put up with any more of these artist cock-ups. Don't let me ever work for this guy again.' That's the censored version of what I actually said.

But for reasons I can only speculate on, the premature demise of *ABC Warriors* seemed to suit Steve. He actively discouraged its return and it took a huge effort on my part to get it back in the comic some time later. So the warning signs were there for me to see. Freelancers rely on their gut instincts to survive, and we avoid problem editors like the plague, so once again, I only have myself to blame.

Describing Robin and his role on *2000AD* will take a little longer.

It was the norm in British comics for decisions about artwork to be the sole province of the editor – and it still is today. The editor would make his choices, including the covers, usually with little reference to his art editor. This certainly applied to all the comics I've worked on, such as *Tammy*, *Battle* and *Action*. And in particular, when I edited *2000AD*. The hugely talented Doug Church, who designed *Action* and *2000AD* for me was – uniquely – an art *supremo* with a roving brief over all the adventure comics, but he was not an art editor. The art editor was typically a backroom figure, primarily concerned with production, logos, lettering and so forth, who rarely interacted with writers or artists, except on covers on odd occasions.

Thus today, I couldn't tell you who the art editor of *2000AD* is, or indeed if they even *have* an official art editor. I'm sure whoever they are, they're talented, but I've never heard from them or their predecessors in all the years of writing *Sláine* and choosing artists. This is the editor's concern alone.

But on *2000AD*, at the time *Sláine* was created, this was to change during the era when Robin Smith was art editor. There seems to have been a power vacuum in Tharg's 'Nerve Centre' and Robin, with his strongly held views and assertive character, easily filled that vacuum – as others would do later. Perhaps he saw himself as another Doug Church, and was keen to make his mark on the comic.

Foolishly, I ignored the power politics inside *2000AD*, although I was vaguely aware – from numerous incidents – that Robin was hostile to me for some reason. Possibly he thought I had too much influence on the comic and needed cutting down to size. For example, he gleefully told artist Kevin O'Neill that our *Nemesis The Warlock* Great Uncle Baal story was very unpopular with the readers and the story was dropping in the vote charts. If you find such negativity a little weird, let me assure you it was commonplace if creators were deemed to be 'too big for their boots'. *2000AD* editorial would chortle over writers and artists' setbacks, back then and all the way through to the late 1990s. At that time Tharg Bishop and his assistant editor memorably 'high-fived' each other when a rival comic book, drawn by an ex-*2000AD* artist, was delayed in production. That would cut the artist down to size and serve him right for leaving *2000AD*!

But I was under the impression I only had to deal with Steve, so who cared about anyone else? That was a mistake. Robin played a key role in Angela's decision to walk away from her character. He also tried to stop future *Sláine* artists Glenn Fabry and David Pugh getting into *2000AD*, as I will describe later.

If I'd realized just how important Robin Smith was on *2000AD* at that time, I would never *ever* have gone ahead with creating *Sláine*. I would have stopped work immediately. Editorial may well have sensed this and kept him in the background.

This is not freelance paranoia. Some years later, a BBC script editor wisely advised me at a writers' workshop I once attended: if you encounter an editor who has a hostile agenda towards you, no matter what the reason, you are fucked. Do *not* hang on in there, just give up and *walk away*. Profound advice I urge all creatives to follow, especially myself!

Even without a proper understanding of the *éminence grise* pulling Tharg's strings, I was still apprehensive when I got Steve's response to Angela's pencils. Disappointingly, he had no comment on her work, positive or negative, and said he was passing her artwork over to Robin for him to deal with. That did indeed set alarm bells ringing.

But to my relief, Robin's subsequent letter was brief, courteous and professional. Like Steve, he had *absolutely no comment* on the art, other than to want one important picture changed. He sent Angela an overlay with the change he required and his own drawing of Sláine on the overlay that he wanted her to copy.

It was the large scene on page four. We had intended it to be Angela's *pièce de résistance*; the 'money shot'; the climax to the adventure; the visual pay-off.

After Sláine has done his salmon leap in the air, he brings Brainbiter down on his opponent's head, and then swings him around in a circle on the end of his axe, the blade still embedded in his head! It's one of those ideas that it takes a writer 10 seconds to describe, and an artist at least ten hours to draw and make it work.

Angela made it work. I can still see it in my mind's eye. It was an astonishing achievement that most artists would flunk.

It was violent, funny *and* anatomically correct. Funny, because you cannot possibly take a scene like that seriously. I remember laughing out loud when she drew it!

It's exactly how our insane Celtic ancestors described their battles. So it's going right to the very *core* of what Sláine is all about. This makes it *the single most important picture* in the opening episode. I wish I still had the original to show you, but, as you've already gathered, I am hopeless at holding onto memorabilia for posterity.

It's telling the readers: *this* is what you can expect in *Sláine*. *This* is where it will be different from *Conan* and any other traditional, conservative sword and sorcery serials you have ever seen. This is what you can expect in a *2000AD* sword and sorcery saga.

This is *Celtomania!*

But, without explanation, Robin redrew the image on the overlay so the victim is flying off the end of the axe at an angle towards us, rather than still going round in a circle with the axe embedded in him. Only the victim's head is significantly changed, but the figure of Sláine needed redrawing to rationalise the modification and there were other alterations to make this significantly different pose work.

Thus, Ukko had been originally swinging on the cauldron, rather than in a static position and the spear thrower was positioned better.

As a splash image, Robin's revised version is fine, but it was emphatically not the important pay-off scene we had planned.

But there's another important point here: he had made his revision of Angela's work without consulting with her first. It's fair enough for him to have a problem with a particular panel. But the way to deal with it is to explain the problem (censorship fears; anatomical error, etc.) and *ask the artist to redraw it*. Only if this is not possible, for whatever reason, would it then fall to the art editor or someone else to change it.

A disappointed Angela and I wondered why it had been altered and toned down. We decided it had to be the 'violence'. In this we almost certainly were correct, because later the extreme censorship on Sláine's axe would become truly ludicrous, leading me to be forced to change his weaponry, as I will relate in Part II.

We talked it over and decided not to challenge Robin or Steve. Why didn't I fight our corner? I should have done. After all, this scene was designed to be the *highlight* of the episode. But I was confused by the far-from-clear power structure and also concerned I'd already put Angela through more than enough by immersing her in my increasingly hostile, weird and unprofessional comics world.

Today, I can still see that slight difference in the style where Angela is copying Robin's amended *Sláine*. It's a mark of her professionalism, *and* the quality of Robin's figure work, that you'd have to look carefully to pick up the vibe of a different artist. But the holistic *soul* and composition of her original is marred. It looks like typical comic book heroic fantasy now. It's not quite *Sláine* anymore. It's *Conan*. Or even sub-*Conan*. At the beginning of any serial, setting up the template for the future, all these things *matter*. Every detail counts.

The small cauldron picture that follows doesn't make sense now, because the figure was originally spun round in a circle to then fly off the axe and fall into the cauldron. Now, he flies off at angle *away from* the cauldron. Robin hadn't thought it through. But we decided not to bring it to his attention in case he wanted that changed, too, which would have led to extensive further alterations to Angela's art.

It was around this time that Angela very calmly and with no anger or tears said to me, 'This is not really working out. I think I'm going to leave it at just drawing episode one.'

Angela has always had far greater perception than me. She has always been able to see through people's masks and their bullshit, sense trouble ahead and take the necessary steps to avoid it, whereas I just keep on going, come hell or high water. Usually both.

Aware of the cold shoulder she was getting from fellow professionals that she knew personally, and from her editor and art editor, this major art alteration, without explanation, was the last straw for her. She instinctively knew that BBC script editor's advice was the right one: *walk away.*

She had spent months researching and developing the character and drawing episode one, which, whatever the pleasure of creating it, made it an economic disaster. Plus, she was selling all her rights to her character with no influence on its future and little financial benefit.

I was gutted, but I also felt – with my 'never give up' attitude to life – that she could be persuaded back *later.* Creators regularly walked away from 2000AD and its numerous disasters, and were invariably persuaded to return. Myself included. All it would take, I felt, was a little editorial persuading from Steve, telling her that her work was still really valued, and she would change her mind. That usually worked for most of us. After all, look how often *I* had returned to the minefield.

But now one of those mines was going to predictably explode. I say 'predictably' because screw-ups were a way of life on 2000AD at this time. They were the norm. This particular mine was called *Zarjaz.*

5

AXE TO GRIND

The mine exploded when I learnt that Mike had been commissioned to do a *Sláine* cover for a new adult version of *2000AD* entitled *Zarjaz*. Mike also talked about *his* Sláine in a fan interview and the *Zarjaz* cover was 'publicly displayed at a comic event', according to the chronology of official *2000AD* historian Dave Bishop.

It's a truly excellent cover and is based on Angela's page one where Sláine confronts a T. rex.

It was produced *ahead* of Angela's episode one appearing in print. Before she'd even completed inking her creation.

But first, my thoughts on *Zarjaz* itself (Named after one of Tharg's popular phrases, it's not to be confused with the current fanzine with the same name). It illustrates just how out of touch editorial were *already* becoming with younger and mainstream readers, and who would ultimately decide *Sláine's* future.

And decide *2000AD's* future, too. The continual emphasis on older/fan-orientated readers would, in the course of time, provably result in a huge drop in circulation. This is yet another gorilla in the corner that is rarely talked about because it doesn't fit what many concerned would still prefer to believe.

In fact, they would probably say something similar to what I once heard said about French arthouse cinema: *The smaller the audience, the better the movie.* Who needs all those annoying kids, anyway? It's adult fandom that really matters.

Zarjaz was the first of endless failed attempts to 'go beyond' what *2000AD* stands for. The comic I began was aimed at and attracted a wide mainstream younger audience. But fans in the industry, who increasingly called the shots, wanted to 'rise above them' and appeal to those elusive, older, purist fans instead, who they were convinced were out there in sufficient numbers to make a more 'prestigious' comic viable.

Despite the overwhelming evidence – over 40 years now – that comics for adults have regularly failed to sell in significant quantities, industry fans *still* persist with their dream, confident that one day, somehow, they'll find a way: one day they'll have a success.

Zarjaz was probably put together by the end of 1982. I understand it was Robin Smith's concept in conjunction with McManus and his assistant Richard Burton, and had been 'prompted' by *Warrior* magazine.

Excellent as *Warrior* was, thanks to the love bestowed on it by its editor and publisher Dez Skinn, and its great writers and artists, it only ran for 26 issues.

According to Wikipedia,

'Despite a strong launch and critical acclaim, sales were not strong and for much of its run the magazine was subsidised from the profits of Skinn's comic shop, Quality Comics.'

A pity, and that it lasted that long is a tribute to the vision, the talent, and the determination of the editor and the creatives concerned. It is still rightly remembered with enormous affection today. *Zarjaz*, by comparison, seemed to be some kind of copycat, doubtless hoping to trade on its success, get similar Eagle awards, prestige and fan acclaim that *Warrior* had *rightly* received. I have no evidence that *Zarjaz* had any of the love, vision and talent of the original.

You'd assume that editorial would have sent me a copy of the cover, given that *Sláine* was appearing in it. They did not. Instead, I remember hearing on the grapevine, rather than officially, that Mike was doing a *Sláine* cover for a new adult *2000AD*.

This prompted me, understandably, to ring Tharg McManus up and ask just what the hell was going on?

'It's only a dummy,' was his guarded and *extremely* nervous response. His nervousness immediately rang more alarm bells.

That he had wanted Mike to do the painted cover was not the problem. There was no way Angela could do such a cover, or would even want to. After all, Mike was one of the greatest comic cover artists of all time.

What did I say in reply? I wish I could remember exactly. I know I was furious. My problem was that purist fans, my peers, and *2000AD* editorial had all backed Mike's version of *Sláine* in *Zarjaz* without the knowledge of, without reference to, and at the expense of the creators of *Sláine*. Our very personal creation was literally hijacked.

I said something along the lines of,

'This is *not* about the cover of a dummy. What is going on here, Steve? Angela does all the heavy lifting, all the character designs, that have taken her *months* because that's what a new serial needs and they're absolutely amazing! And now it feels like someone else is taking over, building on her work, her designs, and it's no longer her creation. And her episode one hasn't even appeared in print yet! You and everyone else connected with *2000AD* have pushed her out by not supporting her. By cold shouldering her and making it so fucking miserable for her, she doesn't want to draw her own story anymore. Don't you think Angela and I, the true creators of *Sláine*, are entitled to more respect? Shame on you, you–!'

Something like that. But less coherent and with a lot more swear words, of course.

McManus recalls Angela crying in the background while I was on the phone to him. I don't remember that, myself. *Swearing,* more like.

In fact, it doesn't sound like Angela, at all. I recall she once ferociously – and at some length – tongue-lashed someone closely involved with 2000AD because she felt, quite rightly, he was exploiting me. I should have stood up for myself and I didn't. So Angela stood up for me instead. My bad. But Angela crying, of course, makes for a better, sexist stereotype story.

Steve was very lucky he didn't get a similar tongue-lashing from Angela. Otherwise I might have heard *him* sobbing in the background.

In retrospect, the whole thing feels even more suspicious than it did at the time. Back then, I tried very hard to forget about it and put it behind me. Both Angela and I just wanted closure on the whole unpleasant business. But today, the questions come thick and fast. Why pick *Sláine*, of all the available 2000AD characters, for *Zarjaz*? Surely they would choose an established character, not an unknown? Why not *Judge Dredd*? *Strontium Dog*? That would make far more sense. Particularly as sword and sorcery was an *untested* fantasy sub-genre at this time that had no track record of success.

And why were we not consulted if our character was appearing in it? Would they use our *Sláine* story, which was clearly aimed at younger readers? Or would they commission a new adult *Sláine* story? And who would write and draw it? Or did they not have a clue what they were doing, and were just winging it and hoping for the best?

I suspect that was it. They actually didn't have a clue.

The official reason for the cover is that *Zarjaz* was 'European' and a barbarian on the front would work best. *Really?* 'European' as in Moebius, Druillet, Bilal, and so on? *2000AD* was influenced by these fantastic creators, but it was only to inspire a very British and *mainstream* interpretation, *never* a specialist magazine.

It would seem they were trying to appeal to a minority adult fan audience that was into *Metal Hurlant* and *Pilote*, usually available only in English translation in *Heavy Metal* or in collected translated editions from publishers like *Dragon's Dream*. There is no way a European-look, adult comic would sell significantly in the UK. And I'm the biggest supporter of European comics, being the only *2000AD* creator to ever write for them.

But let's turn to something more cheerful and focus on Mike's cover. Regardless of *when* I saw it, I absolutely loved it. It's a triumph. It's based closely on Angela's Sláine and his 'outfit' is identical. It also included her T. rex. The hero is handsome and heroic. The composition is so good, it must have been art-directed. So full marks to Robin. For me, this image hits probably the highest note in *Sláine* art by *all* the artists over the years. It is truly iconic!

I believed this was Mike's first *Sláine* art, although according to Bishop's chronology it was done *after* he had started *Sky Chariots*. I doubt it. The Sláine of Mike's *Sky Chariots* is rugged and not handsome, unlike this version.

The Zarjaz T. rex cover was later used in the interior of a *2000AD* 1985 annual and also as a Titan cover. That same annual actually features *another* colour Sláine cover image by Mike.

It is very different, more rugged and not handsome at all, which bears out my feeling this wonderful image came *first* and Bishop got it wrong.

However, Bishop is the comic historian, so I must be mistaken. Whatever the order of events, it does indicate Mike's gradual change of direction on *Sláine*.

Mike was moving him away from handsome art-directed hero (*Zarjaz*), to rugged hero (*Sky Chariots*), to ultimately ugly hero (prequels to *Sky Chariots*), which led to a serious negative reader response to his work, as I'll relate later.

But my immediate concern was that by promoting Mike's *Zarjaz Sláine*, Robin's and/or Tharg's objective was to diminish Angela's role as creator and elevate Mike McMahon to de facto art co-creator or at the least, for him to share the art-creator laurels.

I believe they genuinely felt that I was mistaken in giving such a perfect story to my wife – a newcomer to comics, and they were doing their best to gently 'correct' things. This involved some adroit behind-the-scenes manoeuvring to 'softly softly' bring it about, given the delicacy of the situation: namely that I was married to the artist they wanted to get rid of. *Zarjaz* was part of that process. Never mind the issue of copyright, as Angela had not yet been paid and therefore had not signed away her rights to the *Sláine* design that was featured on the cover.

My peers were talking about Mike in a similar vein. They would constantly remind me that Mike was a natural for *Sláine*: they told me over and over that it was his dream story, to such an extent that I finally – finally – began to wonder why on Earth they kept harping on about it? *Duh!* His cheerleaders endlessly enthused over the *Zarjaz* cover, and later over *Sky Chariots*, long before it appeared. Because they had decided it was *their* job to fulfil Mike's dream. At another artist's expense.

They were absolutely convinced it was going to be a smash hit, and it would make Mike the mega-star of *Sláine*.

Angela, as I've said, was invisible to them and was never mentioned. A *woman* couldn't possibly be more successful than one of the lads and, in any event, fulfilling another artist's dream – one of their colleagues – was far more important to them.

If you are thinking that my response to all this skulduggery seems suspiciously restrained and civilised, you would be absolutely right. I can't recall exactly when I twigged and when I reacted to the axe they were grinding (pun intended), because I was trying desperately hard to avoid conflict with my friends. So the subject was often off limits. But when they pushed their cheerleading just that bit too hard, I did finally explode. I know I had very 'over the top' words to say to at least two of them and, consequently, we didn't speak again for some months. The only words I can share even now are 'It's the fucking anti-Christ.' I'll explain that in its context later.

Returning to *Zarjaz*, the publisher John Sanders shared my views about the commercial realities of adult comics selling in significant quantities. It's hardly rocket science. They're a non-starter, a wish fulfilment fantasy by a vocal minority. Apparently he also disliked *Zarjaz*, and the dummy was cancelled.

If Sanders had given *Zarjaz* the green light, things would undoubtedly have been more problematic for Angela and I in establishing our *exclusive* title to our creation.

But the *Zarjaz* move had been made. It had alerted me to danger and now I had to make a counter-move.

I had deliberately ensured that all the key elements: the Drune Lords; the magical megalith and so on, these visual components of *Sláine*, were present in her episode one, so it could not be challenged later. That it was unequivocally her creation. If you look over episode one, you may see just how obvious and calculated this was on my part. Those small, token Drunes on top of the megalith, for example? They were added *after* Steve and Robin had made their *Zarjaz* move.

Massimo Belardinelli's work was always going to run after Angela's, but I remember thinking long and hard about *Bride of Crom*, the Wickerman story, and whether it should go to Mike or Massimo. It was so visual, like *Sky Chariots*, I knew it would undoubtedly make any artist who drew it the star of *Sláine*.

Aware that it could also be used in a creative coup d'état, I decided it was safer for it to go to Belardinelli. The scripts were therefore written with him in mind. And Mike's story would come later when there was no longer a risk of a coup. I do remember wondering if McManus would realise my strategy, and being rather pleased with myself when he didn't.

Meanwhile, Angela, a total professional, was quietly inking her pages. And I loved what she was doing. She was effortlessly using a brush, rather than a pen, which the Obi-Wan Kenobi of 2000AD, art supremo Doug Church, would have been delighted to see.

When I started 2000AD, I would consult Doug about artists and he would explain why many British artists' work often looked stiff by comparison with European artists, and how I should persuade them to change:

> 'See, Pat, the reason a lot of British artists work is so stiff is 'cos they use a pen. No, no, no. It's no good! *It's no good!* Get them to use a brush! The pen is the problem. It's too scratchy. Too tight. That's why your Spanish and your Italian artists' inking is so smooth and flowing: 'cos they use a brush, see?'

The *Conquering Armies* style was working out brilliantly for our episode one. All too often such finer details have been missing from some later *Sláine* stories, and they're the poorer for it. For example, there's Angela's atmospheric, shadowy stairway in the city of Gabala, where thieves and muggers are hard at work. You're unlikely to see such engrossing details in many later *Sláine*s, because they're just too time-consuming for artists to draw. Yet it's those fantastic 'extras' in the background that all of us love in comics. I could still stare at scenes like Angela's Gabala for hours and lose myself in imagining the rest of her city. *That* is what comics should be about.

Her final page is very dark, and I don't think that's the fault of reproduction, but rather of Angela's style. Even so, it still works for me to this day. Given that there are *nine* pictures on a page, there's surprising detail in her atmospheric slums of Gabala, which she based on Gustav Dore's *London*. For example, her cat hissing at the pursuing Skull Swords. So cute! Their authentic Celtic helmets. The triskele of the villains that still endures as the sign of evil in *Sláine* to the very last episode.

This chase sequence, in particular, shows just how much story can be told in a single page. And how important backgrounds are to create a strong sense of place.

Angela duly completed her pages and the cover, and sent them in.

Once again, her pages were accepted *without a single word of comment* by Tharg McManus and Robin Smith.

I don't recall if we saw the lettered version ahead of time, I very much doubt it. But the lettering by Tom Frame seems a fraction small, notably when Sláine says, 'Kiss My Axe'. Otherwise, it's first-class. But the 'Kiss My Axe' balloon really needs re-lettering *today* – it's dismally inadequate for a great slogan and that should have been bleeding obvious to editorial, who would already know of fantastic captions like 'Laugh this off, Twinkletoes' (From *Invasion!*), that rely on bold bash lettering.

Working with Bishop's dates, there now seems to be a long delay of many months before it finally appeared in print, which is probably not correct, but it doesn't really matter as it's the order of events that count.

Finally, our first episode was about to go to press and it was time to see who was right: Me and Angela with our *creators'* vision of the Warped Warrior, or the *2000AD* editor and art editor, and my peers, all of whom had decided they knew so much better than we did.

The readers would decide.

6

CHARIOTS OF FIRE

Angela's episode one of *Sláine* appeared in *2000AD* in Prog 330, on 20 August 1983. It went straight to number one in the readers' vote charts – the first time since the rise of *Judge Dredd* that *any* story had ever beaten the Mega-City lawman.

As no *2000AD* professional, then or now, has *ever* had the good grace to congratulate her on her achievement, or has ever beaten the drum for her work, you'll forgive me if I do so once again. It was truly incredible that an unknown artist – an absolute beginner – *who had never drawn a comic story before*, should have a number one hit story in the Galaxy's Greatest Comic.

She had achieved something that all her highly competitive artist peers had been unable to do then and have been unable to do in all the decades since: create a serial to beat *Judge Dredd*.

It was a real 'Chariots of Fire' moment. Straight out of a traditional comic or movie. The underdog, the outsider, despite the formidable establishment forces and fan-boy prejudices ranged against her, had persevered and come through to win. All the heartache, the agonising, the laughter and the tears we'd shed had been worthwhile.

Was I surprised? I'm not going to pretend I was. I was delighted and relieved by the good news, especially for Angela, but never surprised. I always knew she had the talent and the potential. My job was to bring it out, as I've done with many other artists. And I knew she had succeeded because she had followed the rules of appealing to ordinary readers of all ages who are regularly ignored and sneered at *to this day.*

Her debut episode's astonishing popularity cannot be dismissed as a 'fluke', or due to my story alone, much as I know her critics would dearly like to do. The readers loved Angela's *art* as much as they loved my story. Actually, more so, because Massimo Belardinelli's subsequent art on *Sláine* was also popular, but immediately *dropped to number two* in the charts.

And Mike McMahon's later version, whilst being critically acclaimed, I'm sad to say did not work for the majority of the readers, as I will describe in a later chapter.

Glenn Fabry and David Pugh's work was *hugely* popular, but only Simon Bisley's *The Horned God* had a comparable impact on the readers.

For those who may still try to spin it otherwise, here's what some of the readers have to say today:

Steve Viner: 'Loved that first Angie Mills artwork ... Shame she didn't do more episodes. That particular episode started a life long love of the character.'

'Dave Heeley: Angie's work on *Sláine* was incredible. In more enlightened times she would definitely have become a mainstay of *2000AD*.'

Jules Boyle: 'Until Glenn Fabry came along, Angie was my favourite *2000AD* artist on the strength of that one episode alone. Her art didn't look like anyone else's in comics. I'd have loved to see her continue on it or come back to it. The city looked really interesting and dangerous, it was a shame not to see more of it.'

Chris Wright:'I was about twelve when *Sláine* appeared in the Prog. I just accepted Angela's art as being as good as my then faves. I had no idea she was a newcomer to comics. I was also surprised to learn later that her art had proved unpopular with certain elements of the nerve centre.'

Alan Holloway: 'I always liked Angie's *Sláine* and it was a shame she never carried on. I'm glad, though, that it gave her the co-creator credit she deserved.'

Stewart Moore (artist on *Defoe*): 'She did a terrific job. Particularly surprising since she hadn't drawn comics before.'

Dave Kendall (artist on *Pyschokiller* and *Deadworld*): 'I was disappointed to see Belardinelli take over after the first episode and I loved Massimo's work. Loved the rich shadows and details of Angie's first episode. Such a pity she was given the cold shoulder. Would have loved to have seen more.'

Her story appeared at a time when those famous vote charts were still an accurate assessment, a precise barometer, of the readers' opinions.

They could not be conveniently dismissed, as they regularly were later with the self-serving view that the readers votes didn't really count and that they were holding us all back, and it's the *fans'* opinion that matters. The unspoken subtext of this was, '*Those* readers are just kids. It's the older, cooler comic fans we hang out with in comic shops and conventions who *really* matter.' Those readers' views were held in such low-esteem that the votes were even falsified on at least one occasion in order to keep Dredd in the comic.

Well, it's *those* readers that have always mattered to me. So thank you all. Your support, both back then and today, means a great deal to me.

Despite Angela producing a number one story, Tharg McManus never tried to persuade her to return to her creation.

If we had beaten *Dredd* once, it's reasonable to assume we would have built on our success and done so again. And again.

If Steve had made the effort, I know he could have got her to come back, because, like all artists, what Angela was really looking for was positive feedback and encouragement, rather than the negativity I've described. With all the long and painstaking process of creating characters was behind her, she would have speeded up, especially with the readers' vote of confidence in her work.

Instead, McManus just told me the news, *in passing*, over the phone. I was so relieved, I didn't do what I should have done, which would have been to say, 'Well why don't you tell her the news yourself?'

It's also standard procedure when a comic has a hit story with a hit artist, for the editor to capitalise on it and do everything in their power to ensure the same winning team continues. In fact, if a publisher knew about it, the editor would be *ordered* to. It happened to me on *Battle* when John Wagner and I were ordered to continue with *D. Day Dawson*, written by Gerry Finley-Day, because the readers loved the story so much.

It never happened with *Sláine*.

Possibly, Steve and Robin thought that Mike – who they clearly saw as the true *Sláine* artist – would somehow take *Sláine* to even greater heights of popularity. Angela was still surplus to requirements.

Or, in the very Dreddcentric world of *2000AD*, creating a serious rival to the Judge was not a priority, and may even have been seen as a threat.

Or, despite the clear evidence of the readers' votes to the contrary, Steve *still* shared the negative views of his art editor and my peers about Angela's work.

Or perhaps he was embarrassed by her success.

Take your pick.

Whatever his reason, Angela was driven out in a typical, blood-less, no fuss, 'Very 2000AD coup'. I say 'typical' coup because there were other such 2000AD coups, and that was how it was usually done.

But the cold-shouldering was not over. It continued with Angela and Belardinelli's work not being reprinted by Titan Books. I was told by Titan, in no uncertain terms, that neither of them had 'fan appeal'. It would be *two decades* before they were both finally reprinted by Rebellion.

In all this, you may be wondering what were Angela's feelings about these shenanigans. After all, she was already a successful, professional artist who had never encountered such unprofessional behaviour elsewhere. This only happened to her on 2000AD. Not, for example, on *Misty*, where she happily illustrated text stories for an annual and designed the horoscope for the weekly comic.

She certainly had a low opinion of those concerned, but I would be betraying her confidence if I said more. Her departure was a huge loss to the story. Don't ever assume that the version of *Sláine* we have today is the best possible one.

It's not.

That bears repeating: *it's not.* If we'd worked on *Sláine* together, it would have been rather like Joe Colquhoun and myself working on *Charley's War.* A potential golden era. She would have speeded up and her episodes would have set the style for an accompanying second artist. Because she understood exactly what I was looking for in a story, not just because we were husband and wife, but because it was *her* co-creation, *her* vision as well as mine. And *her* sense of humour that is very British. We would have to wait until Glenn Fabry and David Pugh before we saw that British sense of humour in full force again. That's a long time to wait.

It's why I asked Joe Colquhoun if he would like to draw *Sláine* after Charley's adventures in World War One came to a close: his sense of comedy and also his characterisation. Joe told me he didn't have the imagination to draw *Sláine*, which is not true, of course, but I couldn't convince him.

I've also exampled how Angela had challenged my preconceptions about comics. That would have continued as she brought some much needed female energy and insights into the often male desert that was *2000AD*. Thus, on at least one occasion I had to supply numerous female references for a *2000AD* artist because otherwise the women would not have been drawn properly.

Consequently, *Sláine* would have been a more personal, balanced, sharper, authentic, emotional, funnier, *better* story if Angela had continued to draw it. Developing and improving her style, challenging and improving my ideas and contributing her own: what *she* would like to see happening to *her* characters. In this, I'm not being partisan: the evidence for it is all there in her episode one.

That loss to *Sláine* is incalculable, which is why I'm so unforgiving on the creative damage done to our character by Steve McManus and his cohorts in its opening year.

I know Angela would genuinely appreciate all the great feedback about her work today. On her behalf, I thank you all for your kind and encouraging words about *her* creation of *Sláine*, *her* fantastic Celtic hero.

Ultimately, it's my fault rather than Steve's. He was simply acting in character, being himself, and I should have known this and stayed away. I had also greatly underestimated the strength of the opposition against us. I'd introduced her to a world of deviousness and unprofessionalism that she didn't need or deserve. So, rather than being her creative debut, *Sláine* became a creative debacle. And it was soon to get even worse.

A few years later, Angela briefly returned to comics when I desperately needed an artist on *Third World War* for *Crisis*, when she drew an episode just to help me out. Once again, I have positive recollections of her work and so do many readers. Once again, she was invisible to her artist peers.

Then, on *Finn* – the principle character in *Third World War* – my co-writer Tony Skinner and I needed a 'techno-pagan' helmet for the character's development. 'It's based on a gas mask but the tubes are like rams' horns', we told her. She duly came up with what has since become an iconic design. It was subsequently used in all the versions of *Finn*, as drawn by Liam Sharpe, Jim Elston and Paul Staples.

Angela finally had that helmet design approved!

Later, we created *The Butterfly Children* together: a successful series for young children with books, calendars, figurines, and a musical show that started at Wimbledon theatre and went on tour throughout the UK. It did very well for her financially, far better than her year of working as a thankless serf on a comic plantation. She also got the creative respect due to her. I was the junior partner in this enterprise and I therefore assigned all my rights to her. I've been told recently there are plans to revive *The Butterfly Children*; I hope so, she deserves it. Shortly after, we went our separate ways and built new lives. Angela is now married to Eric Kincaid, an internationally acclaimed children's book illustrator. I, in turn, am married to Lisa, who is my publisher.

Like many creators, Angela has distanced herself from her creation and I totally understand why. She's far from being alone in this. Steve Ditko, artist-creator of *Spiderman*, has similarly kept his distance from his character. Gerry Finley-Day, the writer-creator of *Rogue Trooper*, never gives interviews about the many fantastic stories he produced for 2000AD, stories that are still avidly plundered by other writers. Publishers and writers love it when a vulnerable creator moves on, as they know they can feed on his legacy of work if they 'lack clout' and a fan following. It's why Alan Moore and myself are relatively safe. *Relatively.* Publishers know there would be a considerable outcry from readers. But you can never be sure in a world where money, not creativity, is the force that drives them.

So Angela, Gerry and many others have moved on. And under the current 'all rights' system, there is little financial reward for Angela on *Sláine*. So why open those old wounds? If she's lucky, she'll receive maybe *ten quid* every time they reprint her episode one, the foundation stone on which an iconic character was built that's lasted 40 years.

But the debt that I, and current publishers Rebellion, owe Angela is huge.

Was sexism really a factor in the negative response to Angela from 2000AD and my peers? Like the passive-aggression we encountered, sexism can be hard, if not impossible, to prove. It's *so* cowardly and *so* easy to deny.

Certainly Angela was only too aware of 2000AD's sexism and fought against it. She thought my peers saw her as 'The little wifey,' as the following example shows.

Memorably, she had painted some acclaimed and unique watercolours on John Hicklenton's *Third World War* episodes. He delayed paying her share of the foreign royalties after their work was published in three European countries. The percentages in those days were significant and fairer, far superior to the royalties paid today in the Rebellion era. Probably it was an oversight on Johnny's part. Rightly or wrongly, she felt this was because she was 'just Pat's wife' and therefore her unique contribution didn't count and she was being ignored. *Again.* She rang Johnny up and forcefully explained her point of view.

I recall her words well: 'I am *not* the little wifey, John, who puts up with shit! You *know* the difference my colouring made to your work. You owe me that money.' This is, of course, the expletive deleted version. She received a cheque from him within days.

Much of the subsequent sexism on the comic falls outside this story of *Sláine*.

But I know (presumably making up for lost time) there was the all-female creator *2000AD* Summer Special 2018. And there have been other female artists on the comic in recent years.

But three years ago, *2000AD* proudly announced: 'Next week's *2000AD* Prog 2074 is a landmark issue as artist Emily Zeinner becomes only the second woman to draw a cover for the Galaxy's Greatest Comic – out 28th March.'

Angela, of course, being the first one, *back in 1983*. Personally, I would have cringed with embarrassment. I don't think it's something to draw attention to or to be proud of and proclaim with a roll of drums. Only *two 2000AD* covers have been drawn by women in all these years?

I rest my case.

7

WARP-OUT!

It always struck me that Massimo Belardinelli's work for *Battle* and *Action* – on *Rat Pack* and *Green's Grudge War* – had stronger anatomy than his later stories for *2000AD*. I never really figured out why. But I was told that he was once the last artist in an Italian comic art assembly line: the guy who did the inks and this was why his inking was so beautiful and his figure work a bit stiff. Despite this, the readers still loved his *Sláine*, which debuted with *The Beast in the Broch*.

In it, we discover, in flashback, Sláine's crime that led to him being thrown out of his tribe. It was based on the Irish legend of Deirdre. King Grudnew has been keeping the beautiful Niamh locked away until she was old enough to be his bride, so she's never seen another man. Then Sláine turns up. The two teenagers are discovered together in flagrante: he's imprisoned and faces the death penalty for making love to Niamh, but manages to escape.

Now Sláine is looking forward to getting back together with his first love. In the midst of his pleasant reveries, Ukko arrives and tells him he's just bought a prison with their prize money. He assures Sláine it will be a highly profitable business. Ukko is unaware that there's a monster lurking in the dungeons and *that's* why the jailer has sold him the business cheap.

Now, this really isn't the kind of thing one could imagine serious heroes like Corum, Conan or Elric ever getting mixed up in. Or a sequence in a flashback where Sláine holds up a mead wagon, samples its wares and ends up too drunk to move, so he's arrested and narrowly escapes death. It's this kind of juvenile delinquent behaviour that is the hallmark of *Sláine* in the early years of the saga. I remember film director Duncan Jones talking to artist Clint Langley about it and they both agreed this was much of the appeal of the character when they were growing up.

But it's the warp-spasm, featured in *Beast in the Broch,* which was the key reason why I chose Belardinelli as the *Sláine* artist.

The most famous warped warrior was Cuchulain and he was my role model for Sláine. But other Celtic warriors appear to have similar battle rages. For example, Congal, Murdach (who even turns up later in *Sláine*) and King Arthur. Thus in one saga it relates how:

> 'Arthur went berserk ... He drew his sword Caliburn and rushed forward at full speed into the thickest ranks of the enemy. Every man whom he struck he killed at a single blow. He did not slacken his onslaught until he had dispatched *four hundred and seventy men.*'

He didn't think it too many.

I remember reading the original description of Cuchulain's warp-out in *The Tain*, and thinking this was surely beyond any comic artist's ability to replicate, except possibly for one: Massimo. I just knew his warp-out would be more sensational than any Incredible Hulk metamorphosis. And indeed it was. In comics, only Belardinelli has done total justice to it. Other *Sláine* artists have come very close: notably Simon Davis, Clint Langley and David Pugh, but Belardinelli's monstrous fury is still in a class of its own. There's a *relish* to his work, an *enjoyment* of the grotesque, which other artists don't quite have.

So you can imagine my delight when Belardinelli delivered as I imagined. Actually more horrible that I imagined! It was a relief after the events I've described where I came close to warping out myself.

The next *Sláine* story Belardinelli illustrated was *The Bride of Crom*, featuring the Wickerman.

It introduces the Lord Weird Slough Feg, a master villain so popular he would end up having an American heavy metal band named after him. He is closely based on the Sorcerer of Trois-Frères, a Stone Age cave in the Pyrenees, and Massimo does a masterful job of depicting his Cave of Beasts where it's estimated that it was a cathedral of worship for 20,000 years! The sorcerer's looks were originally bizarre rather than hideous, but Massimo, like the artists who followed him, preferred to show him as grotesque.

As I told all the *Sláine* artists, I think evil can be far more creepy and threatening if it's strange, low-key, and even absurd, rather than 'in your face'. In real life, the most evil characters often don't look evil at all (consider some of our prime ministers). But I found no takers; I've never convinced any of them, alas. It's a male comic artist thing, I'm afraid, that is not so prevalent in female comics or with female artists. In the fantasy genre, artists like villains to be rather too arch for my taste and, in the end, I had to concede. I believe if Angela had drawn Feg, she would have captured and sustained the *mysterious* look of the original cave drawing. And this is the kind of characterisation where I would often miss her creativity. However, it was not to be, and Feg still makes for a nightmare villain.

But back to the *Bride of Crom*. A teenage girl, Medb, has been twisted by Feg into becoming one of his priestesses. Consequently she is looking forward to being sacrificed at the top of the Wickerman as the Bride of Crom. Sláine and Ukko's job is to rescue her, only they are discovered, and they join the criminal scum inside the

Wickerman who are to be burned alive as Medb's dowry to Crom. Amongst the desperadoes looking fearfully out of the 'bone-fire' is Massimo himself!

As Julius Caesar explains:

> '(The Celts) build gigantic wickerwork figures the limbs of which are filled with living men. They are then set on fire and the victims burnt. They think the Gods prefer the deaths of thieves, outlaws and other criminals. But when they run short, they do not hesitate to make up with innocent men.'

One of these outlaws is the drunkard Roth Bellyshaker, whom it transpires is Sláine's father. We discover in flashback that he was a distinguished Knight of the Red Branch but his drunken boasts led to his wife Macha being forced to enter a chariot race on foot and being run down by the King's chariot. The young Sláine sees his mother dying in the dirt.

Subsequently, Roth was thrown out of his tribe, just like his son. He became a criminal too, and now together, they face incineration in the Wickerman.

This is the inciting incident in the saga.

The tragedy has a uniquely crazy *Celtic* quality and is also very *2000AD* and British. It's not for British comics the 'traditional', safe death of parents Thomas and Martha Wayne in front of young Bruce that turns him into the avenging Batman. The benign tycoon and his wife killed by low-life criminal scum. Or the death of Peter Parker's Uncle Ben at the hands of – once again – low-life criminal scum, which inspired him to become Spider-Man.

Sláine's origins are darker, quirkier and strongly suggestive of real-life family dysfunction, which I'll explore in more detail in the next chapter. But for now, I doubt traditional comics or fiction would be keen on a drunken criminal oaf as the father of a legendary hero. And that's *why* I chose him. Because we have to start breaking the odious stereotypes perpetuated by the establishment. The good tycoon (Batman) or the good aristocrat (Scarlet Pimpernel) or the good Etonian (James Bond) or the good University genius (Sherlock Holmes) are the rule in popular culture and that is no accident. Okay, we get the message, it's rammed down our throats often enough: the rich are the real and true heroes and the poor are low-life scum who need to know their place.

Sláine leads a break out from the Wickerman (with his fellow low-life scum), rescues an ungrateful Medb and warps out. Meanwhile, Slough Feg's spell causes Roth to turn a sword on himself and die, while Sláine 'cools off' with a shower under a waterfall; one of the most beautiful nature scenes *ever* to be rendered in comics. This was the kind of scene Angela was so looking forward to drawing: showing the fantasy side of nature. I know she would have drawn something quite beautiful, but nothing compares with this masterpiece.

It's in this sequence that my approach of basing my hero on my own family background runs into trouble, because it misses an important emotional beat. It's so important that a vigilant script editor would have picked up on it and asked me to amend the curiously abrupt demise of Roth.

Because, whether we acknowledge it or not (we may not even be aware of it consciously) most writers base such a key emotional sequence on a bereavement of someone close to them. Thus it's said that *Superman* co-creator Jerry Siegel may have come up with the character because his dad died after an armed raid. He wanted to create an invulnerable avenger. So in his first adventure, Superman rescues a bound and gagged shopkeeper who is being held up by a gunman. Author and researcher Brad Meltzer claims, 'America got *Superman* because a boy lost his father'.

Something a little similar applies to me where Roth is concerned, although I was on safer ground with the death of Macha. That's why the scene of her death is longer and more emotional. I made an almost obsessive point of stressing to Massimo that Macha needs to be reaching out and appealing to the readers for help, and that comes through in the art.

Although, just to make it clear, my mum was *not* run over by the King's chariot. But her life could be described as the life of a risk-taker like Macha, who broke the rules, and who was not treated well by men, and all this is there in the chariot scene. It's a theme I return to and develop much later in the saga. Neither Macha's nor my mum's life plans worked out, so I knew exactly how the young Sláine would react. That whole sequence rings as true today as when I wrote it all those years ago.

But the subsequent death of the father scene is nowhere near as emotionally satisfying. Yes, Sláine's earlier coldness and anger towards his father feels real: his drunken boasts led to Macha's death, after all. I had *something* to go on there. But his father's death *is barely acknowledged* by our hero, which is astonishing!

Missing a major emotional beat like this, I told myself at the time, was because Sláine responding to his death would break the action flow.

'Oh, come on, Pat!' I tell myself now. Any script editor worth his salt will tell you it was a huge missed opportunity. There could have been a powerful scene with Roth dying in Sláine's arms and the son forgiving the father the terrible wrong he had done his family.

Compare it, for instance, with my very emotional death of Judge Dredd's clone brother Rico: 'He ain't heavy, he's my brother.'

The best Sláine can come up with when Ukko tells him his father is dead, is a curt, 'Roth died better than he lived.' Then he quickly gets onto other business *within* the same dialogue balloon!

But the real reason why such an obvious scene is missing is because, at the time, my mind was a blank. I just didn't know *how* Sláine would react to his dad's death, because I had limited recollections of my legal father, step-father or family 'friend' I was basing him on. They were the three contenders for my paternity. I didn't know which one was my real father. In fact my memories were often so hazy, I even merged two of them together for a while!

So I ducked it.

It was also probably a painful subject, so dealing with it in that cursory manner is a typical shut down, rather male way of handling the bad stuff. An important digression is necessary, therefore, concerning my *three* possible role models for Roth, because they progressively drive the saga. The quest for my Celtic roots would eventually turn into the quest for my real father's identity.

It is also the archetypal Hero's Quest that drives countless novels.

8

THE HERO'S QUEST

The archetypal Hero's Quest was popularised by the books of Joseph Campbell. I drew on his *Masks of God* when I was writing early episodes of *Sláine*, including a vivid description of Slough Feg's Cave of Beasts, based on the Cave of Trois-Frères.

George Lucas is on record as saying he was hugely influenced by Campbell and the Hero's Quest in creating *Star Wars*. The Quest is the search for the father and this influences not just *Star Wars,* with Luke Skywalker discovering Darth Vader is his father, but numerous other films, novels and comic books.

Thus in *Blade Runner*, the replicant, Roy Batty, meets and kills his father Eldon Tyrell.

In my *ABC Warriors*, the robots ultimately come face to face with their creator: Howard Quartz.

And in *Requiem: Vampire Knight,* in the concluding volume, he will face his 'father': Dracula.

It would similarly and subconsciously influence Sláine, although I didn't know it *yet*.

To quote Wikipedia:

'The hero must confront and be initiated by whatever holds the ultimate power in his life. In many myths and stories, this is the father or a father figure who has life and death power. This is the centre point of the journey. All the previous steps have been moving into this place.'

Before introducing my three possible fathers, I should make another aside. This is not a 'poor me' story and neither is it a 'stoic' story. I don't subscribe to either approach. Particularly not the stoics' way of dealing with life's challenges. I've seen too many stoics drink or drug themselves to death. Or turn themselves into hermits. Their stiff upper lip simply doesn't work. They just end up wearing more armour than the knights in *Excalibur*.

There's a third way. My preferred strategy for dealing with bad people and bad stuff is 'retaliation', through words or deeds. Not only is this cathartic, but it often gets tangible results, I'm pleased to say. However, a writer also *needs* such material for stories. Without false bravado, I say it's a useful way of turning lead into gold, shit into champagne, and misery into money. In fact, it's *so* commonplace for authors to use aggro for ammunition, I don't need to give you examples. So I have no complaints about my rather tangled youth.

There's an esoteric dimension, too, but I want to keep this account firmly grounded as far as possible.

Therefore I will only refer to my own story in the context of how it inspired and overlaps with Sláine's. If I'm somewhat brief in places, this is because it's Sláine's story, not mine.

There are three paternal contenders:

Firstly, there was Jack Mills, my legal father, a train driver, born and bred in East Anglia, who died of polio when I was two. I loved him dearly as far as it is possible to love someone whose character has been deliberately erased and censored out of existence. Thus if you were to ask me for one family anecdote about him, I couldn't come up with a single tale! *Not one.* All my questions about him were evaded or answered with rehearsed, monosyllabic responses. This was designed to thwart my curiosity, but, of course, like many kids, it actually made me more nosy.

The best I could squeeze out of my family was that he was a shy, quiet, rather dull introvert who liked gardening. But it became obvious to me from a few overheard conversations, and a lack of physical resemblance that, sadly, he may not be my biological father.

Then, remarkably, as I was completing this book I was given some photos of Jack that showed a new and startlingly different side to him. A picture says a thousand words and these photos were very revealing. In them he is extrovert, confident, ultra-fashionable: a 'Jack the Lad'. In a family photo, wearing a cool suit, and carefully posed, he is the focus of attention. I have included that image of him in the dedication at the start of this book.

So his true personality had been knowingly erased and replaced with a cipher.

The photos can't tell me why, but they do confirm what I had always suspected, that my family had lied about him. That there was a 'problem'. And there's a limited number of rather obvious reasons what that 'problem' could be and why he could not be properly remembered. So let's move onto that 'problem'.

The second contender was a Knight of St Columba, at that time a secret neo-Masonic order with misogynistic and psychologically damaging rituals that are a matter of record. As a teenager, I was present at one such offensive and theatrical ritual that was more rugby club than *Eyes Wide Shut,* but could not be dismissed as a harmless 'male bonding exercise', either. I believe this second contender was important in that Order: some kind of 'fixer', although I doubt he was Grand Master, much as he'd loved to have been. Alongside the De La Salle brothers who taught me, he was the inspiration for my fictional villain Torquemada, the sinister enemy of Nemesis. So I will refer to him from here on as 'Torquemada'.

Then and now, there is something unhealthy about people who want to be Knights. And I'm not referring here to the proto-Knights of Cuchulain's Red Branch, also featured in *Sláine*, although I'm sure they're not above criticism.

Rather, I'm referring to the Knights of chivalry, based on the genocidal Crusaders and the sinister, Masonic Knights Templar. These are the basis for all the modern-day establishment's orders of Knighthood and many more imitative orders such as the Knights of St Columba. Elite soldiers in the UK and US are similarly obsessed with copying the Knights Templar and are often associated with white supremacy. All these varieties of Knights are on a massive ego trip and seem to think they're specially chosen to do God's work and endlessly preen themselves as being in the tradition of chivalry and the Christian Knights of old. Chivalry and doing good deeds, like everything involving Knights, is a calculated fraud, designed to boost their sense of superiority over us peasants. Jimmy Savile, who raised so much money for charity, was a Catholic Knight. 'But he does so much good work for charity,' is the oldest trick in the book, yet it still fools most of the people most of the time.

The aim of modern Knights is identical to the Knights of yore. It's so much more than theatrical cosplay. They require our admiration, obedience and a recognition of their supposed superiority and power.

This particular 'noble' Knight was born in Glasgow. The son of a mill worker, a working-class man made good, he married a well-off school teacher, and moved in higher social circles. Most of his fellow Knights were either in the professions, or were businessmen or priests.

When a family has a 'problem', the good Knights back then *and even today*, I'm afraid, are called in to help and have recently 'crossed boundaries', to my certain knowledge.

In the 1940s, the pressure by the Church on Catholic women to procreate was unbelievable. Frequent births were expected and, if they were not forthcoming, women would be sternly interrogated to ensure they weren't using birth control. Bearing children was their function and duty. So if there was a 'problem' in that direction, the Knights were deputised by the priest to 'fix it'. Just how they helped a young married woman desperate to have a child, I can only speculate. But there is evidence to suggest boundaries were crossed and 'Torquemada' was in some kind of relationship with my mother. For example, my expensive college education was mysteriously financed by the Knights for no reason whatsoever.

So 'Torquemada' was the second possibility for my biological father.

The third contender I will nickname 'Braveheart' and describe later. Just briefly here: he was Irish, in a long-term 'unofficial' romantic relationship with my mother, and was fond of Buckfast tonic wine. Despite his faults, I adored him. His son was my best friend. We were inseparable and we called each other 'cousins', even though we were not – officially at least – blood relatives.

Roth, Sláine's dad, partly fits both 'Jack the Lad' and 'Braveheart'. Jack was an outcast, like Roth, but there the resemblance ends. 'Braveheart' was a drinker like Roth but, once again, there the resemblance ends.

The intense hatred Sláine feels for Roth for killing his mother is almost certainly drawing on my hatred for 'Torquemada' and his domestic violence. I also had to keep on the right side of him because he could pull the plug on my school fees at any time, and I'd be out. Given my rebellious nature, I did eventually cross him – and was out.

Bad dad? Good dad? Or lost dad? I hadn't a clue who was the real one.

Thus when I was ten years old, I tried writing a fantasy novel about my father. It was a typical child's search for identity. I used the 'outside in' writing method (disapproved of by writing gurus). This is where you start writing, inspiration comes to you, and then the words just flow across the pages, without any forward planning or plotting. It had worked for me before, so I looked forward to finally understanding who my dad really was.

I gave up on page two.

This time it would be different.

9

SKY CHARIOTS AND SHOGGEY BEASTS

I wanted Celtic *fantasy* for *Sláine*; I definitely did not want the authentic 'mud huts' realism that Mike McMahon preferred. This was the polar opposite of the sinister and fantastic streets of Gabala Angela had created in episode one. Mike and I had several friendly debates on the subject in which we singularly failed to convince the other of the validity of our case. We both wanted something rather different to each other, but we agreed to disagree.

All the wretched nonsense with Tharg and co. had nothing to do with Mike, who I know played no role in their unpleasant power games.

The two of us always kept things strictly professional when chatting over storylines, and we never discussed 'office politics', because we valued our working relationship too much. But, of course, as time passed, he must have realized there was some kind of battle going on between his supporters and myself. And it must have impacted on him in ways I can't imagine.

I felt that with Mike's talent and impressive track record, he might yet find a way of making harsh reality look fantastic, because I had absolutely no idea how he was going to draw it. If I had seen the brilliant *Zarjaz* cover, I would certainly have been reassured because, although it is in colour, it would still translate into a heroic and handsome black and white hero. But my recollection is that I was shown it after I'd seen *Sky Chariots*.

However, our polar opposite views on *Sláine* are central to the character and the problems that subsequently arose with the readers, so it's important to go into them further. This is, more or less, what I would have said to Mike at the time:

Firstly, I think archaeologists who earnestly promote a 'mud huts' interpretation of the Celts are actually wrong. Whether it's because they're looking purely at post-holes in the ground, and not a lot else, I can't say. Because there is actually physical evidence the Celts lived in a far more sophisticated world than they would have us believe. You only have to look at their rich and complex jewellery. They also had extensive wooden roads for their chariots that the Romans later appropriated for their roads (see Peter Berresford Ellis's *The Celts*) and sophisticated methods of communication (see Graham Robb's *The Ancient Paths: Discovering the Lost Map of Celtic Europe*). Many archaeologists would disagree with both of these books. But, in any event, *Sláine* is meant to be a fantasy comic strip – it's not an Iron Age reconstruction by 'Time Team'.

Secondly, the Celts themselves describe living in a fantasy world in their sagas with chariots covered in more spikes than a porcupine, vast, richly furnished drinking halls, martial arts that would have challenged Bruce Lee, and fantasy weapons like the gae-bolga: a lethal, multi-spiked spear, thrown by the foot.

The ancient fantastic descriptions are usually rationalised into insignificance by academics. So the final result is rather like the factual but rather dreary 'Living in the Past' series on the Celts. The book of the TV series was another reference source for me at the time: it describes how modern day people tried living as they did in the Iron Age. It may well be authentic, but I don't see how amazing legends, like the stunningly beautiful and elegantly dressed Cuchulain, could possibly have emerged from such a downbeat and harsh world of Iron Age 'crusties'. The considerable disparity between archaeology and ancient accounts is a nettle that establishment historians and archaeologists choose not to grasp.

However, I can understand and appreciate the attraction of the 'crusty' approach to Mike. It's a desire for realism, a kind of punk reaction to the phoney extravagance usually associated with Hollywood sword and sandals versions of ancient times. As they are usually set in Greece, Rome or Egypt, I'm not a huge fan of them either, so I sympathise with him. But what Mike really wanted to draw was another barbarian story altogether, rather different to *Sláine*. Of course, *Sláine* could not be turned into that other story for him, despite this being his supporters' fervent wish.

Thirdly, there's the esoteric Celtic interpretation of Jean Markale, who elevates our ancestors into a truly magical and mythical race. Consequently, he is loathed by his conservative peers for his allegedly 'creative' use of scholarship. Visionary authors, notably Markale and later Robert Graves with *The White Goddess,* were also my inspiration.

I had no real idea what to expect from Mike when, probably in the early summer of 1983, Tharg sent me copies of the complete *Sky Chariots*, his debut *Sláine* strip. My recollection is the art was on 'tracing paper' overlays with pencils beneath. How this was technically possible for copies, I don't know, but that's my recollection. Maybe they made some special copies for me.

Julius Howe confirms the overlays were the real thing:

'I saw some of the originals in *Comic Showcase* in the early 90s – they had been inked on tracing paper which had been taped over the pencils. I understand it was because Mick was unsure of the effect he wanted for this new style.'

When I saw it, I did a double take. It was not 'illustrative', but it was not 'comic book' either. It fell into neither camp. In fact, it was like nothing I had ever seen before.

It looked historically authentic; his unique style gave it a vibe of antiquity. Even a touch of historical 'wood-cut' drawings, as well. There were also plenty of mud huts. But the story subject matter – flying long boats engaged in aerial battle – lifted it high in the sky above the mundane world of 'Living in the Past'. It was fantastic! The storytelling was excellent and there were extra images added. It was a triumph of sequential art.

The hero, Sláine, was something of an acquired taste – he was more rugged than Mike's *Zarjaz* cover, but still definitely heroic. It was just about consistent with Angela and Belardinelli's interpretation.

But I knew, even as I looked through the pages, that my audience would have to *adjust* to the art, not the other way around, which is how mainstream comics work. It's invariably the reverse with adult or fan-orientated comics. There the reader does the adjusting. So *this* was what my peers had been raving about as the ultimate, groundbreaking sword and sorcery art. Finally, all was revealed!

Grounded in harsh commercial realities, I wasn't sure. Despite its excellence, it was the polar opposite of *Conquering Armies*, my art bible. No wonder my peers had been so negative about my bible.

So I took the pages along to Angela for a second opinion.

'Is this *too* far-out?' I asked her nervously.

Angela lit a cigarette and looked slowly and thoughtfully through the uncompromising, grungy-looking, 'punk'-like pages. She was always supportive of and interested in the work of all the artists that followed her. After all, her legacy continued through their work as they featured her creations, such as her sinister Drune Lords. Briefly shown in her own episode, they were now the starring villains of Mike's *Sky Chariots* who stared evilly out at her.

I waited apprehensively as she drew on her cigarette, exhaled, and finally, after a further pause, gave her verdict.

'This *is* absolutely brilliant,' she said. 'I've never seen anything like it before. I *love* it. I'm sure the readers will, too.'

If it was good enough for the artist co-creator of *Sláine*, it was good enough for me.

It is also a mark of her professionalism that she could look so positively on work that editorial had used in their coup to freeze her out.

Impressed by Angela's – and everybody else's – enthusiasm for this amazing art, I decided it was *so* important, I would build up to it with a number of prequel stories: a warm-up act, if you like, a roll of drums before the main event.

Big mistake, as I'll explain a little later.

These were the prequel stories I accordingly wrote for Mike: *Warrior's Dawn,* featuring Sláine's first warp-out; *Beltain Giant*; *Heroes Blood* and *The Shoggey Beast*. Followed ultimately by Mike's masterpiece, *Sky Chariots*.

So they would appear in the opposite order to which they were drawn; they were produced 'back to front', if you like. If it's good enough for George Lucas, it's good enough for me.

I won't go into all of Mike's stories, just the two that really struck a chord with me: *Sky Chariots* and *The Shoggey Beast*.

Looking again through *Sky Chariots,* I have to say I admire Mike's purism and desire for authenticity. For example, you won't see any alien fauna or flora in his depiction of Sláine's world, the Land of the Young, later to become Ireland and Britain. He meticulously checked that the trees he drew were correct. Everything is depicted exactly how it would have been back then. So there's no Canada geese, no grey squirrels and certainly no cedars of Lebanon here.

I'd already worked out a complex Neolithic magical science, inspired by John Michell's vision in his groundbreaking *View Over Atlantis* and numerous other books of earth mysteries. This science was already established on the opening page of Angela's episode one, where the megalith is seen as a time gate through which the T. rex has emerged.

Now Mike brought that science splendidly to life in *Sky Chariots*.

The story begins in the village of Gavra. The locals are starving, as the power of a giant dolmen draws all the magic from the earth, turning it into sour land. Sláine arrives and gives the villagers his mammoth; but that night, as they feast on it, Slough Throt and his Skull Swords kill the son of the village headman.

It's a dark and superbly sinister scene, followed by Sláine saving the villagers from the Skull Swords' automatic crossbows by ramming a massive table into them. This impressive image was based on a Gustav Dore reference from *Orlando Furioso*, an excellent artist resource that I still use to this day.

Slough Throt needs a battle-smiter, a personal bodyguard, and Sláine reluctantly agrees to take the job in order to save Gavra from the Skull Swords. They fly north in a sky chariot, levitated by earth power.

I remember agonising over the whole concept of magical megaliths being responsible for ancient flight, because it had never been done before and it could so easily have looked wrong. Or stupid! I worked out every detail to ensure it carried absolute conviction. This is reflected in the impressive art, too, where you can see that Mike has spent long hours working out the visual complexity of the skyport and the sky chariot.

Aware that he has an invisible enemy pursuing him, Slough Throt sacrifices a crewman. He is eaten alive by crows. Once again, this was a scene inspired by *Orlando Furioso*. Sláine discovers Slough Throt's enemy is the Lord Weird Slough Feg and he is caught in a battle of sorcerers as the cargo of bulls on board escapes and he has to wrestle one of the animals to the ground and kill it.

Then Viking sky pirates attack in spectacular aerial ship-to-ship action. Disaster is partly averted by Sláine releasing a cage full of half dead zombies onto the Norseman's ship. Then Slough Throt sacrifices a paying passenger in order to cause a volcano to erupt, destroying the Viking ships. Sláine manages to crash-land the sky chariot.

Throughout these enthralling scenes, Mike increasingly adds extra little pictures to pace the story, to make it truly cinematic, and shows the natural world in the shape of eagles, squirrels, wild cats and bears. This culminates in a view of a sinister forest that is still chilling to this day.

The unseen Slough Feg has invoked Carnun, Lord of the Beasts, and the deity's animals close in on Slough Throt. To prevent them tearing him apart, the 'traitor' Throt forms a protective magical circle around him. Throt tells Sláine that he has stolen Feg's plans to destroy their world. He intends to show them to the 'good' Druids who oppose the Drune Lords and stop this madness. But Feg's power is too great, worms thrust up through the earth and consume him as the beasts of the forest look on.

The wizard, who is part of the conspiracy to destroy nature through the megaliths, is finally destroyed by it.

It's a very satisfying story on every level. Originally superbly published by Titan Books with only Mike's artwork, it was reprinted by Rebellion as *Warriors Dawn* with Angela and Massimo's work included.

The reproduction was poor in places, which may have been because there were technical problems at that time or because of Mike's unusual page presentation. The new Hachette edition is *much* better; notably on the full-page scene where the sky pirates attack Sláine's ship. It's much darker now. Even so, there's still some faintness on some of the other smaller pictures.

I think there's now a strong case for a stand-alone, deluxe, collector's edition of *just Sky Chariots*, in recognition of a strong story, superbly drawn by one of the world's most talented comic artists. Perhaps oversize, like the *Conquering Armies* softback edition I originally fell in love with.

Facebook commenter 'German Ponce' gives his view:

'Oversize, but *not white paper*...this great comic should look beautiful in light sepia paperboard, as the French and Spanish edition of *Le Chasseur Deprimee*, by Moebius.'

He could well be right. The texture and paper colour are important on *Sky Chariots*, which, due to its sensitive inking style, is particularly vulnerable and requires specialist reproduction.

Or at least it should be printed like the larger size European editions, so we can really see and appreciate all Mike's intricate detail. And in my view, have *no other stories* with it. This is very important. Not Belardinelli's work, and especially *not* Mike's one-off *Sláine* stories that appear earlier but were drawn in his later more challenging style. Nothing should distract the eye from the unique quality of *this* story.

Otherwise it would be like going to the cinema and seeing four movies one after the other, all jumbled up together. *Sky Chariots* needs its own space. I'd hate this very special saga to be 'diluted' in any way.

Chris Wright speaks for many readers:

'*Sky Chariots*. I think the top of my young head blew on first reading the story. How could this Mick McMahon be the same guy who beautifully illustrated *Dredd* only a short time before? Yet it was Mick. He had evolved and produced something I hadn't seen before. Weird, otherworldly, yet also completely in sync with your words. Mick just seemed to know what would work, and he went for it. I still get a thrill every time I revisit *Sky Chariots*.'

Duncan J Smith:

'I never appreciated how good Mike McMahon was when I was a kid. Looking back, he's awesome.'

Alan Holloway:

'I didn't like it at the time, but reading it last week in the new collection, I was really able to reappraise it. A brave, innovative style.'

Jorge Rodriguez sums up its appeal:

'*Sky Chariots* somehow reminds me of John Ford's *Stagecoach*, in the sense that a bunch of characters that hate each other must collaborate to survive.'

Myself, I see *Sky Chariots* as the *Blade Runner* of British comics. It didn't open well, because the audience had to adjust to it, but is now recognised as a classic. However we are still waiting for the 'director's cut' to show it off to full advantage, rather than it being poorly reprinted, in a small size, and lumped together with other stories.

Turning now to *The Shoggey Beast*, this story was also perfect for Mike. I doubt Massimo or Angela could have given it the same surly quality! Late one night, in the pouring rain, Sláine and Ukko knock on the door of a remote house where the shoggey beast is lurking. The scowling owner comes to the door.

Owner: Yes?
Sláine: Have you shelter for two tired, drenched travellers?
Owner: No.
Sláine: Two tired, drenched *bad-tempered* travellers?
Owner: I see.
He sees Sláine's mammoth eating his thatched roof and comments: Hmm.

Then with a terse 'Sorry', starts to close the door in Sláine's face, which, needless to say, our hero doesn't stand for.

The owner subsequently turns out to be the shoggey beast and is killed by Sláine, leaving his mother lamenting. 'Murderer! You killed my son! You killed my shoggey boy!'

Another memorable scene comes earlier in the same story when Sláine is caught up in a spear-throwing duel. He outwits his opponent, who is speared by the terrifying gae-bolga, the 'bellows spear' with thirty barbs.

Opponent: I played that ... badly.
Sláine: You did.
Opponent: I'll ... die... now...
Sláine: You will.

Those kind of unsympathetic responses greatly amused me and Mike. They reflected something punk in both of us, and I still chuckle and think of Mike when I write similar lines for Sláine today.

I had thought all the difficulties were behind us now, at least where Mike's work was concerned, but I was so wrong.

Sláine was about to hit the rocks. *Again.*

10

NO WINNERS

The prequel stories were drawn in the same style as *Sky Chariots*, but with an increasingly 'wood-cut' look to them, the shading giving it an almost fan-art feeling. The hero is more rugged and ultimately ugly and almost caricatured in some pictures. The characters and monsters are interesting, there are some great facial expressions, and the scenes are atmospheric and well executed. But the conservative layouts mean that every picture has the same weight. So the overall first impression is deadpan, downbeat and disappointing. Sláine's warp spasms are particularly disappointing, especially after Belardinelli's.

It's only if you really look into the pictures that you can appreciate the style. Then you can sense the care and the love that has gone into them. But that's a big 'ask' for mainstream readers – and for many comic fans – to appreciate the subtle quality of the art. 2000AD art – whatever the various artists' styles – was always 'in your face'. Readers look for the 'wow' factor. There are no big dramatic images, as in *Sky Chariots*: there's a certain excitement missing and even a minimalist, sketchy flavour to some of the scenes, especially towards the end of the run.

For these reasons, the prequels alienated many of the readers, which led to *Sky Chariots* not being appreciated as the masterpiece it truly is. *All* Mike's episodes flopped with the readers. My plan had spectacularly backfired. I was gutted. For me, for the character, and for Mike.

I knew that the events surrounding the creation of *Sláine* must have taken a toll on Mike personally. I would guess he internalised much of the shit that was going down, whereas my approach is always to shove it right back in the faces of the people responsible.

And this is reflected in the less accessible, more extreme art in the prequels; it's almost a punk response to it all. And also the beginning of a new art direction that would take him away from *2000AD*. So it was a *double* tragedy.

It could have been different. His *Zarjaz* cover, even in black and white, could have provided a more suitable role model for all his episodes. But that would have meant Tharg or his art editor talking it through with Mike and saying, 'Look, this *Zarjaz* image is more compatible with Angela's style and more accessible to the readers and it's what they're going to expect. *This* is the right direction to go.'

Clearly, they did nothing of the sort.

There was another solution, too. If you look at Mike's canon of *Sláine* work, and you're really honest with yourself, it's bleeding obvious that, much as we all love Mike's work, something has gone wrong. And when pages come in and they're not right, an editor is meant to *do something* about it. If it's too late to change them, or the artist doesn't agree, then you *have* to pull them.

You've got no choice. It's why you're an editor.

It's not unusual and it doesn't have to be a big deal. I've done it many times. See my *Secret History of 2000AD and Judge Dredd*, where I pulled my *Judge Dredd* that I'd written to be the first episode. I didn't think the story and art were strong enough for a number one, so I made it the second episode. I pulled various *Mach One* episodes and ran them later because I didn't think the art was good enough. I'm known for ditching entire serials and using them later or in an annual. When things don't work out, it's just part of the job.

The prequels could easily have been used later, once Mike's *Sky Chariots* had rightly impressed the readers as the magnum opus it truly was and they had adapted to his style. The pages wouldn't be wasted. So the order of stories would be Belardinelli's *Beast in the Broch*, *Bride of Crom* and *The Creeping Death* followed directly by *Sky Chariots*. The prequels were always extra stories, so it was easy to take them out again.

After all, Titan Books ran Mike's *Sláine* and casually pulled Angela and Belardinelli's pages as if they never existed, because they were only thinking of their elitist fans. Whereas *this* modification would be thinking of the people who really matter: the *ordinary* readers of *2000AD*.

If it had happened, I'd have asked Mike to do a poster image similar to *Zarjaz* to lead us into *Sky Chariots*. I'd have also asked him to make his very first image of Sláine less rugged, more handsome, so the changeover from Belardinelli to Mike was not such a huge shock to the readers.

In mainstream comics, which are aimed at a mass audience, this was not unheard of. Once again, this is what an *editor* is meant to do but which, invariably, I would have to do as writer. It's not even that hard to do. If it had been gently explained to Mike that those early episodes were seriously diminishing the impact of his masterpiece, I know he would have seen the sense of it. That would show *true* support to a colleague and a friend. It would have been in his best interest, and *Sky Chariots* would have been as popular as Belardinelli. In fact, I suspect it would have been *more* popular, and I'd have been thrilled for him!

The decision to do nothing was almost certainly 'emperor's new clothes' syndrome. McManus didn't see anything wrong with the pages. So he was already no longer thinking like a mainstream editor, and was thinking like a fan editor instead, because the readers' thumbs down could have been predicted.

I don't recall seeing the sequel pages in time. If I had, and I did nothing, then it meant I too had succumbed to the 'emperor's new clothes'. Hardly surprising, after all the endless declarations by Mike's fans that this work was truly groundbreaking and amazing. But it would still be my bad. However, if I had intervened, I doubt they'd have paid any attention to me as a freelance writer.

It *is* genuinely sad. It's sad, in particular, because Mike left the series after completing the prequels. He was finished with *Sláine* and with 2000AD. He left a saga that he should really have been an important and ongoing part of. A saga that, as his fans had constantly reminded me, he *was* born to draw.

The readers and myself miss him and we miss what might have been.

So there were no winners in this hitherto never publicly acknowledged battle of wits. I don't even feel any satisfaction that the 2000AD editor and art editor rightly ended up with egg on their faces. Cock-ups happened so regularly on 2000AD, I doubt they barely noticed it.

And I doubt either if Mike's cheerleaders cared that they'd played a key role in the whole fiasco. A failure of that magnitude could have led to this great character being cancelled and all that talent and effort by everyone wasted. That was how I felt after McManus told me just how badly the story had gone down with the readers. To his great credit, he didn't try to minimise the extent of the failure and just how *hostile* the audience were to it. It was the first time that one of my serials had stiffed at the box office. I was not in a good place after that phone call. It was unfortunate timing that one of Mike's cheerleaders chose that moment to ring me up and rave about its brilliance. I finally warped out and responded: 'It's a fucking disaster. It's the fucking anti-Christ!' And more along those lines.

Mike and I met up in 2017 in Paris, where we were both promoting our *Judge Dredd: The Cursed Earth*, and found we still had so much in common, including the same dark sense of humour.

I still feel a real pang that we've never produced anything together, post-*Sláine*, apart from Mike's superb but abortive *Mutomaniac* for *Toxic!* It was not for want of trying. We had both read all the important medieval sagas and we talked, at that time, about producing a comic strip version of Egil's saga together.

Egil, a Viking warlock, was known as 'the ugliest man in Christendom', which I think particularly amused Mike. That worked for me, too. No problems about my insisting on handsome heroes here. Egil wrote his first poem when he was three and killed another boy with an axe when he was seven. After a lifetime of gouging out eyes, tearing out throats with his teeth, vomiting over his enemies, and then writing poems about them, Egil died peacefully in his bed in his 80s, after having killed a slave who helped him bury his treasure.

He sounded perfect. And perhaps that's the moral of the story – that we needed to create something together from the very start. Commercially, developed the right way, Egil was a good possibility. Consider the success of *Peaky Blinders*, about a gang of modern day Egils.

Disappointingly, we never got the project off the ground. I don't recall Mike doing any character sketches for it; in fact, I don't remember much about it, but I understand from other sources that we definitely approached Dick Giordano at DC Comics with our suggestion that we produce such a barbarian hero strip. Apparently we were turned down flat.

I think that tells you just how out of touch so many comic editors are with what modern audiences look for. And how little innovation and invention is encouraged. Stories need to be daring, not safe.

Imagine trying to get the comic equivalent of *Peaky Blinders* or *Killing Eve* past editors like that. No, stick to tried and tested tycoons and merchants of death dressed in weird costumes beating up the poor, it's so much safer.

11

DRAGONHEIST

In the tradition of *Stagecoach,* Sláine and Ukko literally continue their journey in a stagecoach. They're entering the Glamour Land of the Gower in Glamorgan, which was drawn by Massimo, his final *Sláine* strip. They're in a *thatched roof* stagecoach, no less. I love it! It's one of many photo references I sent Massimo and which he beautifully reproduced. Their fellow passengers include the freckle-faced Nest, who is a student from the Druid college at Durringon. She is returning to Worm's Head Farm to take over the family dragon-breeding business. There is also Kicva, a village wise woman, and Cador, a benign Druid engineer.

One of Kicva's son's, Gwawl, is killed by a wild dragon, the Mata, and the stagecoach is held up by Kicva's family. Nest is blamed and is going to be killed by the villagers. Sláine is indifferent to her fate, but then decides that if he stole a dragon, he would be able to get back to his tribe faster, so he saves her life. He and Ukko get jobs as labourers on her dragon farm, a massive 'tent complex', stunningly rendered from another reference I provided. It looks like a scrap-metal dealer's scrapyard and really brings the Neolithic era alive! Various clashes occur between the main characters: Kicva's family are killed by the Mata, which Sláine destroys with the help of an anchor (another idea inspired by *Orlando Furioso*). Kicva laments, 'From now on, life for me will be one big *och*.' Then Sláine, Ukko and Nest fly north on the Knucker, Nest's stud dragon.

The story was inspired by regular visits Angela and I made to the Gower peninsula to visit her family. Worm's Head is one of many real life locations in the Gower that suggested the story and just by looking at that wild and stunning landscape, the whole story almost wrote itself. Nest, the landscape, and above all, the monsters, are superbly realized by Massimo.

However, there were censorship issues as well, where Massimo had clearly been told to tone down his artwork.

Simon Simmons:

'I do wonder if the episode in Part 2, where Sláine attacks Kicva's sons, was censored in some way? Compared to the blood-fest in the colour annual strip it seems rather tame. Or maybe he was self-censoring after the fuss caused by his *'Inferno'* episodes ...'

Simon is right. It was the same problem with the axe that Angela had encountered back in episode one. Never mind what Gerald of Wales has to say about the Irish and their axes, an axe needs to be *in* someone. It needs *embedding*. And it wasn't.

Instead, the axe stops just short of beheading Kicva's son. It's aligned with the man's throat but doesn't actually cut it, and so looks really stupid. Not Massimo's fault: he'd clearly been ordered to draw it that way. I feel for him because Massimo was originally the Sam Peckinpah of comics. Back on *Action*, on *Death Game 1999*, I remember seeing his astonishing (and banned) scene where a player's intestines pour out of him. They're inked in a truly beautiful way as they cascade across the stadium floor.

I'll come back to this censorship problem in Part II, because it was to dramatically affect Sláine's future. And not in a good way.

Sláine himself was not working so well. Visually, Massimo was moving him further away from Angela's original template. I think I could have lived with this, but there was that same old negativity towards his work from professionals and from Titan Books, who were reprinting *2000AD* stories in collections.

Looking back, I really shouldn't have paid attention to them and instead persevered, because the readers' loyalty to Massimo was never in any doubt; he was as popular then as he is today. It was on me that I listened to his critics, the fan-boys, and not to the majority of readers, and I apologise for this.

You, the readers should be the ultimate judges, not a vocal, elite minority who were being allowed to control *2000AD*'s destiny.

I had large photocopies of Massimo's beautiful *Bride of Crom* pages all over my office walls when Nick Landau, publisher of Titan Books, came down to see me. I proudly and enthusiastically showed him those fantastic Wickerman pages that still wow me to this day. But Nick was not convinced and told me categorically that he would never publish any of Massimo's work, and he never did. I remember feeling totally crushed by his rejection of Massimo.

In fact, Nick would later state that he didn't think *Sláine* fitted into *2000AD*. I believe it was actually because it didn't fit in with how *he* wanted to see *Sláine* depicted, by Mike or a similar fan-approved artist, rather than because it was sword and sorcery.

Eventually, as I relate in Part II, I would feel I had no choice but to reluctantly take note of the Titan tail wagging the *2000AD* dog and make further changes to *Sláine's* future.

Also, I was just about to write my most ambitious saga yet: Sláine against the Gods in *Time Killer*. Massimo had already sent me some design sketches that were just not working for me. With one noticeable exception: his drawing of the Dark God known as the Guledig.

But after all that negativity, let's end this chapter on a positive note and the knowledge that today, the readers continue to look back on his work with great affection. As do I.

Pete Stewart:

'"From now, on life will be one big *och*!" Been 30 odd years but I still remember that line. As for the artwork, no one has since recreated a warp spasm in all its skull busting oil spurting glory!'

Simon Simmons:

'If Kincaid set the scene and McMahon re-invented himself for the strip, what did Belardinelli do? The standout feature of his artwork for me is the natural world that he set his characters in. From wildlife, staring out at the reader, to the mountains and forests, to the hide-covered tents, Belardinelli crafted a real-world setting for these fantastic characters. His 'dragon's eye view' of human beings is outstanding; a hideous interpretation of the 'Visible Man'. Compare it to Ian Gibson's skilfully posed but cartoonish cover to Prog 361 and you can see the horror that Belardinelli brought. His dragons are real creatures - you can imagine them walking around the world.'

Mike Gloady:

'Whisper it - I preferred Belardinelli to McMahon (although obviously loved both). Take THAT, Titan!'

And no tribute to Belardinelli would be complete without talking about the reproduction of his work. Whilst we all of us admire Rebellion for reprinting Belardinelli's work, we also recognise that their reproduction is poor and there's a strong case for a better edition. Simon Simmons puts it well:

'Most interesting for me was your comments on 'complacency' (for want of a better word) at Rebellion. As a customer, I've had similar feelings about their reprinting of some of the black & white strips (including most of the *Warrior's Dawn* GN). It's a massive frustration that the files they are using are so poor. So much of Belardinelli's detail is lost. New scans would really get across the vibrancy of Belardinelli's work (as proven by the releases of *Ace Trucking* etc. Not a popular subject on the forum, however, and there was even a snark in the small print comment in the latest Prog, so I'm not sure we'll ever see a decent reprint of those strips...'

I think we might. From recent correspondence, I have the feeling that Rebellion will do something about producing a better version of Massimo's work in the fullness of time. They're certainly aware of the faults of their early collections, so I'm sure they'll try to rectify them.

And even if the forum doesn't love you, Massimo, the rest of us do.

12

'HE DIDN'T THINK IT TOO MANY'

No tribute to Belardinelli would be complete without reference to his rendering of the Battle of Clontarf, 1014AD, in the *2000AD* 1985 annual – in colour! Today, most ancient chronicles are to be found free on the web, but in those pre-internet days I had to buy *The War of the Gaedhil with the Gaill, or the Invasions of Ireland by the Danes and other Norsemen*. It was a reprint of an 1867 academic edition and was hideously expensive, but well worth it. It described in savage and lurid detail how a Celtic warrior, Brian Boru's son, Murchadh, whom I called Murdach, 'warped out' during the battle and mowed down limitless numbers of the Norsemen, ending in a furious fight with a Norse warrior Elbric, whom I call Elfric.

Nothing Robert E. Howard or George R. R. Martin could write quite matches the fury of the original text. I was so enamoured of it, I spent a small fortune trying to buy similar accounts of Irish legends. So if you're an aficionado of original battles, check out *The Triumphs of Turlough* (Irish Texts Society), now online *for free*. It is full of similar descriptions that I would also draw on for *Sláine*.

Like *The Tain*, *The War of the Gaedhil* may have been written down by a monk, perhaps centuries after Irish bards had related it to a fireside audience. The endless adjectives and alliteration give pace and colour to the story and suggest its origins may be in oral story-telling.

In this ancient account, it specifically says that Murdach had been secretly offered, in megalithic mounds, 'all worldly advantages' by the people of the Otherworld, the Tribes of the Earth Goddess Danu. They offered to let him leave Ireland and join them in their magical world, the world of *Sláine*. Murdach's connection to the Otherworld inspired my plot where Sláine takes his place at the Battle of Clontarf.

Here are my adapted excerpts from the original account of this truly supernatural conflagration; scenes worthy of *Lord of the Rings* or a fantasy *Braveheart* film; scenes so intense, so unrelenting, so uniquely *Celtic,* that perhaps they would be almost too much for Hollywood to handle. Only *Excalibur* has such ferocity and power.

'And there arose a wild, impetuous, precipitate, furious, dark, frightful, voracious, merciless, combative, contentious Badb, with vultures screaming and fluttering overhead. And there arose also the satyrs and the mad-men and the maniacs of the valleys and the witches and the goblins and the ancient birds and the destroying demons of the air and of the firma-ment *and* the demoniac phantom host ... And there was fought between the Gaels and the Danes a battle furious, bloody, repulsive, crimson, gory, boisterous, manly, rough, fierce, unmerciful, hostile on both sides and they began to hew and cleave and stab and cut to slaughter, to mutilate each other.

'Murdach was the last man in Erinn who was a match for a hundred warriors. He was the last man in Erinn who killed a hundred in one day. When this very great, very valiant, royal champion and brave, powerful hero saw the crushing and the repulse which the piratical Danes gave to the men of

Erinn, it operated on him like death, or a permanent blemish, to see the conflict of the Foreigners with them; and he
was seized with a boiling terrible anger and an excessive
elevation and greatness of spirit and mind.
'And he made an active, brave, vigorous, sudden rush at their
battalions, like a fierce, tearing, swift, all-powerful lioness
that has been roused and robbed of her whelps. It is testified
by his enemies, that there fell fifty by his right hand and fifty
by his left in that onset; and he never repeated a blow to
anyone, but only the one blow, and neither shield nor mail-
coat was proof to resist any of those blows or prevent its
cutting the body, the skull or the bone of every one of them.'

He didn't think it too many.

Murdach continues in this maniacal vein until he reaches Elfric,
son of the king of Lochlann, and then, an *even more furious combat
begins*!

I'll return to this shortly and quote further from *The War of the
Gaedhil* when we reach artist David Pugh's equally amazing recre-
ation of the Battle of Clontarf later in the *Sláine* saga.

Massimo's full-colour, six-page version does real justice to the
text of the battle; never have we seen Sláine so disturbing and so
warped. *The Incredible Hulk* looks tame by comparison! It's included
at the end of the collected Rebellion *Sláine* volume *Grail War*. It is a
rare masterpiece from Massimo and a final tribute to his visual
genius.

But Massimo's style didn't work for the next saga I had planned,
and Angela and Mike had now both left the series. So after nearly
40 issues, *Sláine* had to exit the comic in order that I could take time
out to find new artists.

Tharg McManus suggested Alan Davis or Cam Kennedy. In
doing so, it's obvious he still didn't understand the *illustrative*
premise on which *Sláine* is based, or felt that it could be disposed of

with Angela. Or perhaps Alan and Cam were the only artists who were available at that time and who had expressed an interest in doing *Sláine*. But, superb artists as they are, it was obvious they would not have been happy with the *Conquering Armies* look, so different to their own, and would have, understandably, replaced it with their own inimitable comic book style. So we would once again have gone down that artistic cul-de-sac.

It's poorly understood by editors, so it bears endless repeating: stories *have* to remain true to their roots. You break this golden rule and ignore it at your peril. So I decided the only solution was for me to go out and find myself two entirely new artists who matched my very precise criteria.

This decision was about as foolhardy and crazy as my earlier decision to write about the Celts, or to have the effrontery to choose a complete unknown to draw it.

My decision meant an unpaid and difficult search for *two* complete unknowns this time. It would mean reviewing endless samples and having long phone conversations with the artists and then preparing their work to run the gauntlet of Tharg McManus and his art editor Robin Smith.

Again!

It would mean, where I was personally concerned, 'From now on, life for me will be one big *och!*' (The nearest I could get to saying 'fuck' in comics.)

But all the aggravation would finally be worth it, because it resulted in the emergence of two great new artists in British comics: Glenn Fabry and David Pugh.

It coincided with Sláine's days as a wanderer coming to an end.

I actually had to stop writing *Kiss My Axe* at this point in 2018, and I've only continued it now, three years later. This was because I was so 'disappointed' by the way Angela, the co-creator of *Sláine*, was treated by *2000AD*. 'Disappointed' is a useful umbrella word to cover a host of other more colourful expressions that I also felt.

I'd put it behind me at the time, but writing my Secret History of Sláine brought all the memories back with a vengeance. I hadn't appreciated just how powerful and painful they were. So if you're planning to write your autobiography, be warned of the dangers of revisiting old wounds!

But do any of these disputes matter now, you may ask? How a character is created and developed is, of course, of huge interest to readers who love *Sláine*. But it's much more than that. Think of the heated disputes about who really created *Spider-man, Batman* and other comic book characters. Therefore it's important to have a clear and provable record of who created *Sláine*, so that we – or our estates – can properly benefit in the future. So, yes, it does matter.

Anyway, enough time has now passed for me to comfortably move on to the next stage of Sláine's journey.

Now he would face his greatest enemies: the Dark Gods!

PART II
SLÁINE AND THE DARK GODS

13

TIME KILLER

I'd been avoiding the top villains ever since I started *Sláine*. I'd actually been dreading creating them. Because I knew they had to be really amazing and if I came up with something weak, the readers would rightly give the saga the thumbs down. So there was a lot at stake. These esoteric villains were behind the Drune Lords and the Lord Weird Slough Feg, but I had no clear idea, as yet, who they were. I'm a huge fan of the various alien villains in *Doctor Who* and I so admire how thoroughly they're worked out. I had to find creatures in the Celtic mythos as potent as the Cybermen or the Daleks.

I consulted numerous books, such as Lewis Spence's *The Mysteries of Britain: Secret Rites and Traditions of Ancient Britain*, and I slowly started to see a way forward. But the real breakthrough was *The Dark Gods* by Anthony Roberts and Geoff Gilbertson, which suggested 'malevolent forces from another dimension have long been plotting against humanity.' They had a Lovecraftian yet Celtic quality that inspired me to come up with the Cythrons, from Cythraul, the Celtic name for Hell.

But such villains needed equally awesome opponents, so I decided on druids based at Dinas Emrys, the Eternal Fortress in

Snowdonia. There was Mogrooth, a blue black Rmoahal, one of the Atlantean root races, in charge of the castle's dragon defences. He was inspired by the druid Mogh Roith, who legend says piloted a flying machine called the Roth Ramach, the 'oared wheel'. The druids were led by Myrrdin: a prophet and a madman who is known to us today as Merlin.

The story was hugely ambitious with ascending castes of villains and heroes. It was designed to pull together all the plot threads I'd been referring to over the previous stories. For example, *Bride of Crom*. What exactly was Crom Cruach, the monstrous maggot that was referred to in the Wickerman? In *Conan*, 'By Crom!' is a curse without explanation, but in *Sláine* there needed to be clarification. There was a danger I'd paint myself into a corner story-wise. It was time the readers and I finally had the answers. And what exactly were these magical realms from where all these weird and wonderful monsters appeared? I'm no admirer of vague, wishy-washy sword and sorcery bullshit. I need to know!

And the saga was about to become even more ambitious by finding two new artists who would, in effect, give the story a complete reboot.

Artist Bryan Talbot, who was now drawing *Nemesis*, suggested Glenn Fabry, who he said was 'the British Moebius' but was currently working as a petrol pump attendant. I looked at his samples, including a fanzine for The Stranglers, and was hugely impressed.

The tasks I set him to get the gig were Herculean, if you'll forgive the Greek expression. I should really say 'Cuchulean'. I wanted a handsome hero – back to Angela's original, or even more handsome and more cool, with a new outfit, because the loincloth wasn't really working for me. Why? In retrospect the answer is obvious: it's not Celtic enough. He needed trousers.

Secondly, I wasn't happy at the way violence with axes was toned down, whereas characters blown apart by laser guns in *2000AD* were perfectly acceptable. So the fight scenes in *Dragonheist* some-times seemed stilted and awkward. But there was a solution: heroic fantasy often features Atlantean weaponry, which are the ancient equivalent of guns, so I asked Glenn to design such a hand-held 'fire weapon' that drew on the Earth power of the Goddess. It seemed like the only solution if *Sláine* was to overcome editorial's visual censorship.

And finally, I asked Glenn to design the Cythrons and their similar 'fire swords'. That's a major design job that many artists would struggle endlessly with today. And I was asking him to do it for nothing! Imagine asking a Doctor Who artist to design the Daleks or the Cybermen for nothing!

Glenn achieved all three objectives effortlessly with superb designs for which I, and all *Sláine* readers – and the publishers – are endlessly in his debt. Plus there was a bonus: Glenn had the illustra-tive style I was looking for! Perhaps for that reason editorial tried faulting him; maybe because they were still carrying a torch for the 'comics look' they had tried and failed to impose on me. So there was talk by art editor Robin Smith that he was concerned about the quality of Glenn's anatomy! Whatever their agenda, McManus must have realized I was unyielding, and this was the only way to get an incredibly popular story back in the comic, so, after an initial hesita-tion, Glenn was in.

A further quality Glenn has that was equally important and was often overlooked by other *Sláine* artists: his very British sense of humour. It's there in spades in his *Sláine*. One example just now: a cover he painted where Ukko is hanging lovingly onto Sláine's leg in a piss-take of Frazetta's *Conan*, who invariably has an admiring semi-naked female at his feet. Similar British humour is there in Angela's episode one, but Glenn was the first artist to develop it further. It's why readers, appreciating this original ingredient, sometimes talk about Angela and Glenn's *Sláine* in the same breath.

Now I had to find a second artist because the story was vast and even a fast artist couldn't have coped with it. And Glenn was very slow!

Once again, Bryan Talbot came to the rescue by introducing me to David Pugh, his colleague at the Society of Strip Illustrators. David submitted a drawing of a Celtic warrior that was unlike anything I had seen either in illustrated fantasy or in historical reconstructions of the Celts. It was totally unique and utterly convincing. He clearly had the crazy imagination I was looking for, and he had a large portfolio of comics work. It had a 'comics book' look which was fine, but I agonised over it for some time simply because it was 'non-illustrative'. In the end, I felt that Dave's empathy and his enthusiasm for the subject matter won the day. And comics, ultimately, are about being pragmatic: in the end, some compromises are inevitable.

Returning now to the story: it was so ambitious I'd first written it as a detailed synopsis. This was unheard of in those days. There would be a brief discussion with the editor, maybe, then they just left you to get on with it. Today, a story synopsis is de rigueur; but whether the quality of stories today is better for it or not, I think the jury is still out. In theory, they should be infinitely superior. In practice, I'm not so sure. Why this is, I have no idea. Perhaps some of the creative spontaneity is lost.

To give you an example of how odd it once was to write a synopsis in comics: I wrote a detailed outline for my *Girl in a Bubble* for *Jinty*. The editor, Mavis Miller, looked alarmed when I brought the text document in for her. I explained it was a detailed synopsis because I wanted to get the tone right before starting the story. 'Oh, thank God,' she sighed. 'I thought you'd written it as a prose story.'

So I had my outline for *Time Killer*, which I had now scripted. The plot structure is a pyramid, like a computer game. It builds up through different levels until we reach the really bad guys. That's commonplace in science fiction and it can work in comics. See for example my *Requiem: Vampire Knight*, which features an even more complex world.

But it's not that common in 2000AD, certainly with such a range of characters and locations. However, it lends itself particularly well to weekly comics because on each episode we have a new level and a new monster. Thus, we start with the Cythrons and the Diluvials, then we move onto Crom Cruach, the El Women, Elfric in historic times and in the El Worlds, the Guledig, leader of the Cythrons and so on. There's always something new and exciting to look at and I think that's why the story worked with the readers despite its faults. Faults? A story this ambitious actually needs two, maybe even three, synopses to perfect and hone and polish. But it was now scheduled and, financially, I'd already taken a dive on it. Again. I couldn't give it anymore time. So the *Sláine* reboot was being developed in front of the readers – its plusses and minuses on very public display.

To the readers' credit, they were very positive and supportive of the reboot and that still means a great deal to me. And they valued both artists equally. By comparison, if such a reboot had been undertaken today, some 2000AD fans would definitely have ripped it apart. Why? Because I've noticed some older fans are less open to change and new ideas today than their youthful counterparts. There's a barely admitted conservatism, which I've reluctantly had to factor in, in order to keep those readers on side.

I would have liked to spend more time on the story, but my first priority was the art. It needed hands-on project management and, as editorial hadn't really got a clue what my objectives were, and seemed rather baffled by the whole thing, it was down to me. There were long conversations on the phone with Glenn and David as I encouraged their wildest imaginations. Each and every design was horribly, even insanely ambitious, and needed to be perfected, so let's look at some of them.

Myrddin was probably the toughest. I'm pathologically against Gandalf-style wizards – men with long white beards who are supposedly full of wisdom. Maybe it's because they seem like a visual metaphor for God. Instead, I am a huge fan of Merlin in *Excalibur*. Nicol Williamson plays a great Merlin and his metal skullcap is so much cooler than a beard. So I wanted something equally cool for our Myrddin. Dave Pugh came up with the 'jester' design which I think works well. It's the fault of the writer, rather than the artist, that Myrddin is not better remembered. I should have put more emphasis on him in the story. It's an excellent costume and I don't think my story really does him justice.

Dave also designed Crom-Cruach, who is perfect. An image that lives up to the tales of him being a monstrous worm or maggot, the 'Dark Crooked Lord of the Bloody Mound.' Arguably this early black and white version is even stronger than colour versions that followed. I sent Dave references of microbes that propelled themselves with their whip-like flagella, as Crom is a macrobe, a creature of the macrocosm. But Dave's version goes so far beyond my references. C. S. Lewis came up with the concept of macrobes in *That Hideous Strength* and those creatures are often referred to by occultists.

Glenn's El Women – who are macrobes – are scarily and fashionably beautiful and still held in high regard today. I thought Glenn would actually start a fashion trend with that letterbox lipstick. His new version of Nest is also supremely cool. She's an early comics feminist character in the not-so-feminist *2000AD* of the 1980s (as I've related with their treatment of Angela). His Elfric and his fellow El Lords – all macrobes – are equally awesome.

The Guledig – the Celtic word for Emperor – proved a challenge to both artists. He's based on the Celtic God Manannan – a physical embodiment of the triskele, the symbol of the enemy established in episode one. So it was right that he should be the supreme leader. I like little guys being the top monster and I think readers feel the same way. Hence our affection for the Mekon in Dan Dare. With three legs growing out of his head as his means of propulsion, he surely is the stuff of wildest fantasy? I think I'd worked out right from the beginning that he had decapitated himself to discard his hated body.

I was spoilt by Belardinelli's brilliant sketches of him (alas, I don't have them anymore: I'm afraid I'm notorious for not keeping anything). Somehow the Guledig didn't quite have the wow factor of those original sketches. It's partly an issue of scale: the Mekon had his flying bowl, I visualised the Guledig perched on the top of a pole carried by his Cythron guards. I wanted to inject some humour into him, as I had done with Torquemada in *Nemesis* when he warns us: 'Be Pure! Be Vigilant! Behave!' So the Guledig would end each statement with 'Praise Be To Me!' At which his guards would point at the Guledig and respond, 'Praise Be To Him.' It deliberately had an echo of the Two Ronnies', 'So it's "goodnight" from me. And it's "goodnight" from him.' Somehow we didn't quite get there to turn the Guledig into another Torquemada.

It's the kind of issue designers would have been paid thousands of pounds, and taken weeks, to get right for a movie. I'm sure Glenn or David hold their own by comparison with any such movie designers. But in comics there just isn't the same time or money, so characters had to appear 'warts and all', as we continued developing the epic in full public view.

The strange UFO, a *Vimana*, an Indian mythological 'flying palace', and 'Pluke', the alien creature tormented by the El Women are also worthy of mention. Pluke was inspired by *The Cosmic Pulse of Life* by Trevor Constable, which includes drawings of the ancient *Vimanas* and photos of biological UFOs. About three years later I actually saw these 'sky critters', as they are often called, and they looked a lot clearer than the rather blurry photos in the book. In fact they are real life examples of macrobes. You can also see them on Google images. I was suitably impressed by my experience and featured them in *Finn*, another *2000AD* saga. I come back to these biological UFOs later in this book.

Sláine's costume had become a further issue. I realized Glenn's first take on the character still wasn't quite there. I decided he needed to have more of 'man in black' look. So Glenn and David had the further awesome task of redesigning him. I was pleased with the new look Sláine Mark 2, and so were the readers.

Looking back, I find myself feeling guilty at the incredible amount of development and design work I was expecting from artists, so a brief diversion is necessary here in case you're feeling the same way! I certainly would be guilty if we were talking about artists' payment rates today. And when I've put at least two artists through that process in recent times, they've often pushed back and declined the job or the revisions I've looked for. I have enormous sympathy for their negative responses. It's to be expected in the current comics 'fast food' climate. Because in real terms, artists and writers are paid much less today than they were back in the 1980s. That's why so many develop quick impressionistic styles, or work horrendous hours seven days a week, or only draw part time. It's creative exploitation in action. It's a gorilla in the corner that no one likes to talk about – apart from 'troublemakers' like me.

By comparison, the page rate in the '80s was far better, and artists could pay the mortgage with it and actually have a life, so it was not as unreasonable and as demanding to ask for re-designs as it may seem.

Ultimately, I think most would agree the star story of *Time Killer* was David Pugh's Battle of Clontarf sequence. That's the one that lingers in everyone's mind and with good reason. Firstly, there's his Elfric. I loved it from the get-go, but for years I've wondered what inspired his creation. Just as much as any obsessed fanboy, I need to know these things! I knew it wasn't the Joker, but I recall asking David to tweak it a bit, just in case he came over as the Joker to some readers. This he duly did. But there was still something familiar about Elfric that I couldn't quite put my finger on...

Then someone pointed out to me just the other week that it had a touch of Boy George about it. Of course! Why didn't I see that before? *Duh!*

The War of the Gaedhil was based closely on the original saga, which was a comic book writer's dream. It's utterly frenetic, wildly homicidal and a celebration of everything Celtic and violent. For decades, Irish and fantasy filmgoers have yearned to see a Hollywood epic featuring Cuchulain, or this epic Battle of Clontarf. The rate we're going, it's decades away from ever happening. But the ancient Celts were luckier than us. We might have Netflix and Amazon Prime, but they had a tale that was clearly designed to be told around the fireside. You can tell from the bombastic and repetitive style of *The War of the Gaedhil* that it can hold its own against any modern, racy TV drama. If you've ever listened to a first-rate storyteller, especially late at night with the lights turned low, you'll know exactly what I mean.

It is without a doubt a magnum opus high point in the *Sláine* saga and if it's a little shoehorned into the story, then that's the price we have to pay for taking our seats to enjoy the visual treat of a lifetime, courtesy of David Pugh!

Never mind Sláine being possessed or warping out, David must have been warping out himself when he drew those episodes. I would run out of superlatives to describe the power and enthusiasm of his artwork. He decided that Sláine (who has taken the place of Murdach, son of Brian Boru) wasn't lethal enough with the conventional weaponry in my script. So *he* came up with the idea of using the revolving blades of a chariot like a lawnmower. *Then* he turns them into two huge evil swords. Absolute genius! I could never have matched him for such a gore-fest. And neither could the original storyteller, who described Elfric's death by a conventional sword. But that wasn't good enough for David. He wanted something more spectacular. So, instead, Sláine picks up a massive Celtic stone pillar and rams it through Elfric's guts.

Imagine now the storyteller reciting this battle to an open-mouthed teenaged audience in the Middle Ages:

Murdach killed fifteen foreigners on his right and fifteen on his left until he reached Elfric. And they fought a stout, furious, bloody, crimson combat and a fierce, vehement, rough, boisterous, implacable battle. And the sword of Murdach was inlaid with ornament and the inlaying melted with the excessive heat of the striking and the burning sword cleft his hand, tearing the fork of his fist. He perceived that and cast the sword from him and he laid hold of the top of Elfric's head and pulled his coat of mail over his head forward and they then fought a wrestling combat. Then Murdach put the foreigner down under him by the force of wrestling and then he caught the foreigner's own sword and thrust it into his breast until it reached the ground through him three times. Elfric then drew his knife and with it gave Murdach a cut that the whole of his entrails were cut out. Then did shiverings and faintings descend on Murdach and they fell by each other. But at the same time Murdach cut off Elfric's head... And... And... And...!

'And that is the War of the Gaedhil so far,' the storyteller blandly concludes.

Phew! Time for the popcorn.

14

TOMB OF TERROR

S o after the Battle of Clontarf and the further frenetic events that follow, we still have not yet reached the pinnacle of our dramatic pyramid. This is ascending drama/thrill power par excellence, and is about to go right off the Richter scale.

Next, Sláine and his companions travel to Cythraul, where a monstrous multi-dimensional demon lies sleeping in the Tomb of Grimnismal. Glenn's depiction on the opening page is a work of genius and one that, perhaps, he is not generally known for: his fantasy architectural skills! Because it's a tomb of truly insane Lovecraftian proportions that even Escher might envy. I believe it took him a week to draw, which makes me wince when I think of all that love and dedication he put into *Sláine*.

I worked the Tomb out with a map based on an architect's drawing of the huge basement of my house, which included three vaulted and rather sinister cellars, so I knew exactly where Sláine and his fellow adventurers were located as they roamed through it. And so did the readers, as the map was included in the story. *Dungeons and Dragons, Games Workshop* and roleplaying games were booming at this time: role players were often using *Sláine* stories in their games so this tale, a veritable monsterfest, surely cried out for a game. Accordingly, I featured gaming text at the end of each episode and Gary Leach drew some fabulous beasts to bring the words to life.

Here's what reader Richard Caird had to say on the subject in 2018:

> 'The 1986 *Sláine - 'Tomb Of Terror* game-comic: I just read it fully over the last two days, played it & truly loved it! So much so that I played the other Diceman game-comics also from way back in 86' (but they don't compare to *Sláine's Tomb Of Terror*)
>
> 'I was truly engrossed for the entire journey & almost, ALMOST, won but died at the final hurdle. I truly loved this 'old-skool' method of playing as your favorite *2000AD* character. (I also played the *Judge Dredd* & *Rogue Trooper* characters along with the *Diceman* but, like I said, I absolutely adored the 15-part *Tomb of Terror* story the most) Pat Mills writing was amazing & the artwork by Pugh was also fantastic and so very detailed. I loved the 'Lovecraftian' element to the main space being/god antagonist & the violent element's (especially hitting Ukko) was fantastic. Truly this *Tomb of Terror* is a work of art and I feel that Pat should seriously think of publishing it on its own, not as part of the 'Sláine the King' graphic novel. I feel that this stand-alone adventure would be financially a hit, even in this current day & age.'

Ah, if only I had that kind of publishing power, but I don't. All such decisions are in the hands of Rebellion.

Undoubtedly, *Sláine* was in the right place at the right time where roleplaying games were concerned. Later there would even be a lush *Sláine* roleplaying book with lots of full-colour plates and gaming supplements.

Much of *Tomb of Terror* was drawn by David Pugh and not only did he make it dark and sinister, but he also provided great moments of comedy when the stupid Tomb guards – the Orgots – enjoyed bashing their heads on what looked like a dartboard. If I stress the role of David during this time it's because, like Belardinelli, he was not on Titan Book's list of 'elite' artists whom they would reprint. Glenn was. Even though David's work was well-loved by readers, once again the Titan tail was wagging the *2000AD* dog and deciding the comic's destiny.

Looking back, David said, 'I so wish I had more time to spend on my pages but I had a family to support.'

Wullie Russell and numerous other readers rightly reassured him:

'Pugh's art was fun and visceral, full of the energy and movement necessary to express the nature of the character and the story.'

I'd second that. Two artists on a story is often the norm, even today, and you never know how it's going to work out, and what pressures they are both going to be under. Undoubtedly, David did all the heavy lifting on *Sláine* and made the reboot possible. As Wullie Russell comments, 'Fabry's one of the few genuine superstar artists, but if he'd drawn the strip himself we'd still be eagerly awaiting the concluding chapters of *Time Killer* today.' I'm sure Glenn himself would agree.

The final words on *Tomb of Terror* go to Richard Caird:

'In this day & age of modern tech, it was truly nice to be transported back into a world of magic and sorcery with such great characters as Sláine, Ukko and the other members of the team were also interesting: the orc-abused woman who was eventually eaten by the large rat, the demonic priestess whom could not be trusted and the disfigured woman who hated how she looked... all these supporting characters made the journey that much more satisfying and I truly felt for them as they left the party one by one. Fantastic in-depth writing and amazing art both combined into a beautifully written adventure that was all consuming.'

15

DICEMAN

There were three *Sláine Diceman* roleplaying games: *Cauldron of Blood*, drawn by David Lloyd; *Dragoncorpse* drawn by Nik Williams, and *The Ring of Danu* drawn by Mike Collins. They were all great fun to write and an outlet for the endless *Sláine* ideas I had, now that I had figured out the Dark Gods mythos of his world. It had opened up a creative flood.

The idea for *Diceman* had arisen after a very heated meeting between John Sanders, his managing editor John Purdie, John Wagner, Alan Grant and myself. They had driven down to Essex specially to see the three of us. Sanders acknowledged that British comics were no longer doing well and was looking for solutions: ways that John, Alan and myself might rescue comics as John and I had rescued them in the past. Of course I explained, as I always do, that the key to comics success is to give the creators a better deal. But this is something that publishers do not want to hear. Publishers still believe there is some magical solution whereby they can endlessly exploit the creators and make lots of money – mainly for themselves. I guess they never ask, what happens when they've eventually strip-mined all the comic classics and there's nothing left?

Perhaps they think it will go on forever and they can just keep recycling them – and perhaps they're right.

But at least the publisher back then realised that he needed to *talk* to leading creators, something that doesn't happen anymore, so I should really cut John Sanders some slack, which I'm afraid I didn't at the time.

I think they wanted us to create another *2000AD*, which was pointless and none of us were keen on that idea. Anyway, I still bore the scars from creating the first one. But I said that we should really be trying to do something new, something different, something that young readers were into today – like *Fighting Fantasy*, the hugely popular gamebooks by Steve Jackson and Ian Livingstone. So how about a gamecomic?

The meeting broke up with no agreement and no way forward, not least because John, Alan and myself were all finding better-paid work in the States. Did any of us need the grief?

But subsequently, Sanders greenlit my gamecomic and I felt I should give it a try. After all, I'd previously designed four board games for comics (*Battle, Action, Starlord* and *Valiant*) and a *'Flesh'* card game for *2000AD*. John Wagner and I came up with *Valiant's 'Go For Gold'* – an Olympic game which involved the readers having to do punitive exercises. And I'm still a big fan of the *Diplomacy* game of World War One.

So I devised a gaming system for comic strip that worked, and was at that time unique. Later I discovered the French had also devised a similar gamecomic system, which was reassuring because it confirmed its potential. Simon Geller was editor and Kevin O'Neill the art editor. I called the comic *Diceman* after the novel *The Diceman* by George Cockcroft. It tells the story of a psychiatrist who makes daily decisions based on the roll of a die. I have a noir Indiana Jones-style lead character who uses magical dice to defeat occult threats. Really, the character should have an independent life of his own now *Diceman* is no more, but, once again, I have no control over my creations.

Diceman worked: there were several issues; it made money, but not enough for IPC to continue with it. And I enjoyed the experience. It was a way of developing comic book characters and taking them in a new direction. It provided an outlet for my political views with *You are Ronald Reagan*, which led to a cartoon book – *You are Maggie Thatcher*, the 'doleplaying' game; both drawn by the brilliant Hunt Emerson. If that seems strange in the conservative comics world of the twenty-first century, it should be remembered that politics were once a subject that comics readers were really passionate about. Hence the comic *Crisis*.

It was largely a solo operation, but if there had been more people, energy, and marketing behind *Diceman*, doubtless it could have been developed further. And doubtless there are computer game possibilities as many readers have suggested to me. But in both cases, it would come up against the lassitude of publishing, supported by a minority of fans who seem hostile to anything innovative in comics.

The Cauldron of Blood was beautifully drawn by David Lloyd: the supreme master of noir comics. It was a story I'd been thinking about for several years. Sláine needed the cauldron for the adventures that would lie ahead, culminating with *The Horned God*. There's a mysterious quote from the *Book of Taliesin*, 'Am I not a candidate for fame? A hero to be praised in the Round Hall four times revolving. Before the portals of Hell, the horns of light shall be burning.' Sláine has to go round the tower four times to activate a hidden energy spiral.

If only the Celtic mysteries were always that easy to decipher! W. F. Skene, who translated *The Four Ancient Books of Wales,* felt he'd wasted his life trying and failing to interpret them adequately. These Bardic poems are indeed baffling to our modern eyes and I think that's why we're so fascinated by our ancient ancestors. It's always been a central premise of *Sláine* that Ireland, Britain and the whole Celtic fringe are equally as mysterious as the Egyptian, Greek and Roman mysteries that are more prevalent in Hollywood and traditional heroic fantasy. Stonehenge, Newgrange and Avebury easily compete with the conventional Ancient Seven Wonders of the World, such as the Great Pyramid and the Hanging Gardens of Babylon. Yet we are socially conditioned to see our own native culture as inferior. Deliberately, in my view, because it's an anarchic, freedom-loving, tribal culture that, whatever its faults, is preferable to our increasingly authoritarian, establishment mindset that still models itself on Roman imperialism.

Dragoncorpse was illustrated by Nik Williams, a friend of Glenn's with a passion for heroic fantasy, who eventually went back to his first love: surfing. The story explored the idea that there are four El Worlds at right angles to each other: the world of Devels; Elder Gods; Elementals, and the Dead, and these are the basis of the Celtic Cross. It brought back Sláine's great enemy, Elfric, and they do battle once more.

It is also noteworthy for featuring Lobo, Ukko's brother, and his wife Pona in their old home, which rejoiced in the name Scragfaggot Green. Ukko, as I've related in Part I, was originally half Finnish, half Russian, and this is explored towards the end of *Sláine*, but I see no reason why Scragfaggot Green might not be in that part of his world.

Reader Feargal Gallagher comments on these Diceman stories:

'They are important in fleshing out the period after *Time Killer* where Sláine was working and learning under Myrddin before he rejoined his tribe. That seems to be a very important period in Sláine's life where he starts to become a champion of the good guys/Earth mother rather than just an uncouth wanderer. They are also important in how many ties with the various strands of Celtic scholarship Mills works into the stories, which is part of *Sláine's* uniqueness.'

That is so true. To put it crudely, he can't be a bum all his life, much as we'd probably all have enjoyed that! Besides, middle-aged bums can be embarrassing. The time to be a bum is when you're a teenager or in your early twenties. So the story was writing itself, following a natural path that can't be denied. Sláine having to grow up, to undertake heroic quests and to achieve something in life like these quests in Diceman, in preparation for his future role as Sláine the King.

Ring of Danu, drawn by Mike Collins and inked by Mark Farmer is a case in point. Here he has to find the Ring of the Goddess, which gave me a valuable opportunity to explore the concepts of Celtic matriarchy and the Triple Goddess as Maiden, Woman and Crone, not only in preparation for *Sláine The King* but also for the story that followed: *Sláine The Horned God*. They are profound archetypes entirely missing from Christian mythology.

This is the first time we see the Goddess. Rider Haggard's *She* was a huge influence on me as a boy: a pagan deity to inspire me at a time when I was surrounded by unappealing Christian idols. I like to think that *Sláine's* Goddess was similarly inspiring to readers.

There are interesting challenges on how the Hero should present himself to the Goddess. She says, 'Describe yourself... so I may decide if you are worthy of me.' The Hero/game player has a choice of three answers: a) 'I am a mighty warrior with hair like a raven, cheeks red as blood and a body of bronze; b) 'I am a man whose tongue is in chains at the sight of such beauty; c) Or would you rather keep away from her and carry straight on? Interesting choices, where the right one is more obvious now, perhaps, than when *Diceman* first appeared.

Delightful visual touches are in this story, such as the Disneyesque Celtic fabulous beasts from the Gundestrup Cauldron. I always felt they'd made the most splendid cartoon animation –

there's simply nothing like them in western art until, perhaps, Hieronymous Bosch. There's also the gae-bolga: the mysterious and dreadful bellows spear that enters the body with one wound and then opens up inside the victim with thirty barbs! We tried an umbrella principle here to explain it; I'm not sure our solution is entirely convincing, but every Celtic mystery needs exploring and some we may never know the answer to. In retrospect, I would aim for a magical solution – I'm not comfortable with Bronze Age rational explanations in a fantasy story. I need to retain my sense of wonder and I believe that goes for the readers, too.

Sláine comes across Morgawr Iron Claw, who wears the helmet Angela had originally designed for Sláine. Complete with a hole in the top and the horns knotted crudely on the front, it still looks pretty cool and rather special – a further tribute to her design skills. I wince when I remember that designing the right helmet took Angela a week's work, only to be relegated to a minor character in this story.

Once again, Sláine encounters Elfric who is the leader of the Wild Hunt here, and wants to hunt down Sláine for sport. But the Triple Goddess steals the show in this, the most potent of the three *Sláine Diceman* stories with some fascinating and intricate story ideas. I still felt a chill in the final scene where the game player over-comes the dangers, defeats the monsters, wins the game, and then the Goddess confronts him and prophesies his future.

> Maiden: You will rule for seven years, then go into the Earth and be mine forever.
> Woman: Ours!
> Crone: Ours, Dearie... Heh, Heh!

Final words from reader Figserello on the *Sláine Diceman* games:

'I might have been around 10-12 when it peaked but I bought

every type of "you are the hero" book and publication that I could get me hands on. Some were much more satisfying and well-crafted than others. I have to say, your *Diceman* strips and the Tomb of Grimnismal story were amongst the best of any of them. You certainly completely cracked and owned the illustration-dependent end of that genre. I dug out and replayed the *Sláine* stories a while back. Such fun! Really expanded his world, too.'

There was also a noteworthy book, long out of print: *Sláine The Roleplaying Game of Celtic Heroes* from Mongoose Publishing. It's a deluxe book: 192 pages, selling in 2002 for $34.95 with beautiful full colour images from *Sláine*. They're larger and on glossy, better quality paper than the Rebellion reprints. This is the way *Sláine* *should* appear in colour. So it's worth getting hold of, as long as you don't have to pay some insane price on Ebay. The author drew extensively on the *Sláine* mythos I had developed over many years.

But it was also an excuse for Mongoose to collect together the very best of *Sláine* art, both colour and black and white, and it's valuable for that reason, just to see *Sláine* fantasy art as it should be seen. I'm sure lots of people must have bought it purely as a coffee table book. That's how I refer to it. The cover by Greg Staples is amazing. As indeed is the art inside – they really cherry-picked the very best of *Sláine* art. All I can recall about it is the author of the game didn't include my name on later versions – probably the *Runequest* edition of 2007 – and the numerous modules that were sold to go with the book. The author had decided that I wasn't important to my El Worlds of Fomorians, Shoggey Beasts and Drune Lords, which he now saw as his creation alone. I recall reading his explanation to that effect. This is why I'm not including his name here. He really isn't that important.

And I also recall not being paid any royalties on this sumptuous book because – I was told – Rebellion had not received royalties from Mongoose and their relationship had therefore ended.

At this time of writing, I've learnt that Warlord Games are putting together a new *Sláine* board game with miniatures, due out in 2022. Hopefully this one will work out better financially for creators. The licence deal sounds better. We'll see.

16

THE TEMPLE OF THE STARS

The *Spoils of Annwn* – the Temple of the Stars – was drawn by Mike Collins and inked by Mark Farmer. On the opening picture there is an enigmatic poem:

> *Heavens above, Heavens below,*
> *Stars above, Stars below,*
> *All that is over,*
> *Under shall show,*
> *Happy thou who the riddle readest*

My wife Lisa has flown over the Nazca Lines in Peru in a six-seater plane and she described it to me as an incredible and beautiful experience (apart from when the plane made its descent to land and the turbulence caused a fellow passenger to be sick). As you may know, it consists of astonishing animals carved into the desert, so vast that their shape is often not visible from the ground. It's been suggested by leading authority Maria Reiche that they may have formed a Zodiac: a star map. Even more astonishing are the myriad of geometric lines cut in the Earth which may also relate to the stars, but for which there is no provable explanation. Scientists seem baffled and they remain a genuine mystery.

So it's gratifying to know that we just may have an equally mysterious phenomena right here in Britain: a massive Zodiac carved in the Earth around Glastonbury that is, once again, only visible from the air. It may exist, it may not. It can easily be dismissed as 'New Age bollocks', but it's still your ticket into fantasy in our very own green and pleasant land.

An open air Cathedral to a Goddess, a celebration of the Earth and life itself. Neither of which you will find in sombre, dark and fear-inducing churches with their disturbing celebrations of torture, misery, fear and death.

The Glastonbury Zodiac theory was put forward in 1934 by Katherine Maltwood, who discovered the Zodiac in a vision and held that the 'Temple' was created by Sumerians in 2700BC. Further authors have explored its mysteries such as Mary Caine, who by coincidence was later Glenn Fabry's art teacher. Sceptics have argued the Zodiac is a good example of confirmation bias where you see what you want to see, like figures in a fire, and I take their point. However, if Stonehenge and Avebury were not literally set in stone, I doubt that sceptics would believe those achievements were possible either.

On the subject of Stonehenge, I should mention the recent theory that it was actually an enclosed temple with a thatched roof, of similar proportions to the Globe theatre in London. The idea was put forward by landscape architect Sarah Ewbank, who has made scale models of it. Needless to say, her theory has been ignored by orthodox archeologists. See her book, *Stonehenge – Temple Cipher Roof* at stonehengeroof.uk.

I had a girlfriend who lived at the foot of Glastonbury Tor and I'd regularly climb to the summit and look out over the Somerset Levels and try to imagine our very own British equivalent of the Nazca Lines. There had to be a story in it, but I couldn't solve how it could be viewed from the ground. Perhaps there were giant watch-towers? That was one theory suggested to explain the Nazca lines. Then I read somewhere that perhaps there was an ice cloud canopy and, thanks to Druidic magic, these astonishing Zodiacal figures would be reflected on the ice clouds, which provided a giant screen above the earth. Outrageous? Certainly. But that is surely the very definition of magic – it *should* challenge our view of a rational world. It's one of the purposes of heroic fantasy.

I love it and if it seems a little too outrageous for your taste, I venture to suggest it may be because you're used to a certain magical orthodoxy as laid down by Lord Dunsany. So this is probably the right place to mention his Lordship, because his work has influenced most fantasy writers, but – illiterate that I am – I'd never heard of him until about four years ago.

Dunsany was the founder of modern fantasy who inspired just about every classic fantasy writer such as Tolkien, Lovecraft, Robert E. Howard, Michael Moorcock and Neil Gaiman, all of whom acknowledge his importance to them. So there's a familiar quality and style about their works that you may be more comfortable with. Check out Dunsany's stories on Project Gutenberg and you'll see what I mean. They're really well done and you can see just how far he influenced these excellent writers.

His Lordship was described by his contemporary writers as arrogant and obnoxious. Having read some contemporary anecdotes about him, I would agree. He was also a member of the Anglo-Irish ascendancy and took part in suppressing Ireland's Easter Rising in 1916. Accordingly, I'm not sure how far or how deep his love of Celtic magic goes, despite his family being the local Anglo-Irish landlords. I wasn't even aware of him until I recently researched a story about World War One, and I'm rather glad of that. For I learnt how his Lordship, a serving British officer, had his chauffeur drive him to Dublin so he could personally shoot some freedom fighters, and was wounded in the head by one of them.

One amusing and revealing anecdote about Dunsany was written by a contemporary author – the infamous Captain Pollard, a real life Flashman – who shared an office with him during the Great War, where he and other well known authors wrote government war propaganda.

To set the fantasy scene: Dunsany had one of his plays rejected and 'died of temper'. Dunsany and another writer, the noted humorist J. B. Morton, who died from the shock of having one of his plays accepted, float up together through the Milky Way. Dunsany swears when the stars burn his ghostly body.

His other fellow authors are already dead and are alerted on the psychophone that Dunsany is finally coming to join them in Heaven. These famous authors include the travel writer and clergyman J. A. F. Ozanne, the writer about life in the trenches Patrick McGill, and A. A. Milne, of *Winnie the Pooh* fame. His Lordship has a low opinion of his peers, which becomes clear when he reaches the astral realm and goes through the Golden Gates. He sits down for a nectar in the Sapphire Bar where the literati are all gathered to welcome him.

'So this is Heaven?' asked Morton dubiously, missing his beer already. Dunsany was obviously distraught. At last he came over to me, 'Look here, Pollard,' said he, 'Isn't there some mistake? *You* are here! *Ozanne* is here! Now, no leg-pulling, *is* this Heaven?'

Just then God came in and I introduced Dunsany.

'Glad to meet you,' said God. 'Have a cigar?'

Then, after a moment's thought, 'Who and what were you?' asked God.

Then Dunsany knew for certain that he was in Hell.

I think that gives you the character of the man. This is not a writer I would like to be influenced by, despite his incredible talent.

Sláine's magic and stories are inspired by very different sources to his Lordship's, and it's important to mention this as the sagas increasingly draw on this *real life* magic. It's pagan and heathen: literally 'from the country', meaning it's from the common people; it's non-elitist, just like *Sláine*. And so it has always come from other sources: the original myths and legends and the magic that may be all around us, just waiting to be rediscovered. Perhaps including the Temple of the Stars.

In the opening episode there is a magnificent double page spread that shows the giant figures in the landscape. Mike and Mark have done a terrific job on it. We all love seeing strange fantasy temples in films and comics, and this is surely the strangest.

As the story progresses, Sláine and his companions, Nest and Ukko, encounter various threats based on the Zodiac. Strange animals are mutated by the energy of the Temple and Sláine, inevitably, has to fight them. The stories had to be episodic and I think they work well enough. But, looking back, I think possibly I should have written something less predictable: a little less comic book and frenetic, and a little more magical. I'd read every imaginable book on the Glastonbury Zodiac, yet somehow I feel I didn't quite crack it. I believe the story was designed to fill the gap while Glenn was drawing the next story. Perhaps that 'filler' element influenced the writing.

Mike and Mark were true professionals, you can see they put a lot of love into this story, and there are some beautiful images, but it doesn't fully engage us, despite their best efforts. It's not their fault, it's mine – I feel I should have somehow been more involved in the visual execution, maybe re-scripting some scenes to suit them better. But, as always, there are economic criteria at stake, and as often happens in comics, you just have to let some things go. I'm not aware that the story was unpopular, it's just a feeling I have holding a post-mortem on it today. And my critical opinion of my story may be unfair, too. After all, I've just read that Douglas Adams had a low opinion of his great characters in *Hitchhiker's Guide to the Galaxy*!

One scene I am still enamoured of is the image of the Triple Goddess carved in the landscape. It's a truly romantic image, followed by a magnificent Centaur Archer (an 'obby oss) and finally Glastonbury Tor, the Castle of the Stars. There is a sequence there that is straight out of the Wickerman.

The story concludes with the fanfare that Sláine is destined for great things in the future. His days of being a bum are now definitely behind him. The challenge is to ensure that he isn't boring as so many heroes can be when they 'reform'. It's why we all love villains, the more loathsome the better, and we barely tolerate heroes if they're too goody-good, like Superman. Thankfully, there's no danger of Sláine ever being that kind of hero.

17

THE PUNK KING

The Fomorian sea demons, servants of the Dark Gods, were the 'Orcs' of the *Sláine* saga. The description of them on page one of *Sláine the King*, taken from Irish legends, deserves repeating:

'From Tory Island, their outpost on Earth, a race of mystery and horror – the Fomorian Sea Demons – had written sorrow on the Land of the Young. The offspring of chaos and old night, they had swept down through Lochlann, the region of ice and gloom, led by their King ... Balor of the Evil Eye, whose death-dealing eye withered all who stood before it! Ugly and deformed, some Fomorians had the heads of goats and bulls, others three rows of teeth.'

Tory Island means Outlaw or Robber Island and this was how our modern day Tories got their name. The connection with modern Tories was just too good to miss and so I feature Quagslime the Collector of Taxes who cuts off the noses of those who don't pay their dues. The Fomorians really deserved a story all of their own to fully explore those mythical descriptions of these monstrous demonic pirates.

But Sláine had to get back to his tribe so I had to focus on this world alone. It was clear that Glenn attracted the stronger fan following and it was necessary to respond to that feedback, as I'll explain.

I think it was the right thing to do, not least because it resulted in *Sláine The King* being collected as a rather beautiful Titan book, although the earlier Dark Gods tales were pointedly missing. It would have been good if I could have written a separate *Sláine* story for David Pugh, but there was none that came to mind. By now, the saga had a momentum and a direction of its own and the days when there could be an extra comic serial – as there might be with other *2000AD* characters – were gone. Each story seemed to be a step up from the last and there was no room for a landing story before Sláine reached his pinnacle in *The Horned God*. It was ascending drama and it would brook no slowing down.

Meanwhile, there was a reluctant recognition on my part that the readership was changing and I would have to change with them. How true is this, in retrospect? I think the jury is still out! But it did coincide with Sláine's own personal development, so it was fortuitous from that perspective. And it also coincided with the rise of fan writers with a more sophisticated style, who I'd previously ignored, knowing full well that mainstream readers tastes were often happier with the 'traditional' style of *2000AD*. Other key writers – like Gerry Finley-Day – didn't evolve and paid the price: his stories, such as *Rogue Trooper,* were divided up amongst subsequent writers who never succeeded in giving it his original appeal.

Whatever the truth, I knew I would have to evolve in order not to meet a similar fate.

I can actually remember the milestone moment when it happened on episode three, where Niamh confronts Megrim – in reality Medb who had been sent by Slough Feg to put a glamour on

King Ragall, Sláine's best friend. I can't point to anything specific, but there's a general sophistication to the scene that might have not been there otherwise. The story slows down – which always appeals to *older* readers – and there's no frenetic pacing as in the previous Temple of the Stars.

This slower pacing was helped by Glenn's superb facial expressions, which are so mobile, it's like watching actors performing on stage. Ukko – as depicted by Glenn – still makes me laugh when I read this story today. And see, for example, the scene where Sláine is reunited with Niamh and she groins him. These are superb expressions that engage us and draw us into the story. That's a gift *not* given to every comic strip artist.

Sláine The King has aged well. Never had Sláine – or indeed any *2000AD* character – ever been this handsome before. I strongly suspect we take it for granted today and have got a bit blasé now we've seen Glenn's subsequent work on *Preacher* and so on, but just remember: at the time, this was revolutionary! Unheard of! And never had the women been so beautiful. Both are surely paramount in a fantasy story, especially a Celtic fantasy story where the sagas praise their characters' stunning good looks. I've heard it said that it's 'all a bit too rich, too chocolate box'. A view I disagree with. My response? 'Jeez! Aren't fans *ever* happy? Bring on the chocs!'

The reader, artist and writer identifying with the hero is particularly obvious from this point onwards. I can see my own identification with the character creeping in, in ways I barely paid attention to at the time. Thus Niamh is determined to send her son Kai to a druidic seminary. It's reminiscent of my own boyhood, where I was signed up for a junior Catholic seminary, a kind of Catholic boot camp for bringing 'troublemakers' to heel. I had the medical etc., and then stubbornly refused to go. Looking at those pages, where Kai is passed into the hands of the sinister Druid Cathbad, they are full of Catholic references and remind me of what a lucky escape I had.

As Sláine looks longingly after his son Kai, once again, we come
back to the father/son dynamic – first introduced in *Bride of Crom* –
that will actually go on to underpin the whole saga. This recurring
visual image of the father looking longingly after his son shows just
how important it was to me.

The story then moves to Sláine's coronation, but it is very
different to any real or stereotypical heroic fantasy coronation and
I'm so delighted by this. The idea of *Sláine* was always to take the
reader to somewhere new, not to rekindle old clichés. Especially the
clichés of the elite. We see here how extraordinary our Celtic ancestors really were. As an ancient text describes it:

> 'They appoint their King with a rite altogether barbarous
> and abominable. A white mare is brought into the assembly
> and killed, cut up into pieces and boiled in water. Then he
> who is to be inaugurated, not as a prince but a beast, comes
> before the people on all fours, confessing himself a beast
> also. He sits in the cauldron surrounded by his people and he
> and they eat of the meat which he gives to them. He is then
> required to drink of the broth *in which he bathes*, not in any
> cup, not even in his hand, but lapping it with his mouth.'

A punk coronation for a punk King! With Ukko appointed as the
royal parasite, an actual title that existed and a role he was
supremely qualified for. 'Barbarous and abominable' – I love it!

By now, time was really proving against Glenn, and I searched
for viable solutions that would showcase his talent and yet not take
him too long to draw. There was *Scatha*, the magical female Celtic
warrior newspaper strip we produced together for the *News on
Sunday* which, unfortunately, was short-lived. *Scatha* was based on
Scathach, the Scottish warrior woman and martial arts teacher who
trains Cuchulain. If the newspaper had succeeded, Glenn and I
might still be producing the story today because it had huge poten-

tial. Scathach is pronounced skah-hahk. My pagan friends tell me Scatha is pronounced Scawtha.

And there was the *Sláine* mini-series, with shorter episodes that explored his role as King and provided a valuable lead-up to the vast saga that would follow. It was a way of keeping *Sláine* in the comic, but it became obvious I would need another artist and one was already volunteering for the job.

I could never run out of compliments to describe Glenn's art and the colossal impact it had on readers. Sláine was now at the very pinnacle of his success and he was just about to go even higher.

PART III
SLÁINE THE HORNED GOD

18

THE HORNED GOD

Part III of this book has the same title as this chapter. This is because Sláine, following his punk coronation, is now *The Horned God*, Consort of the Goddess, carrying out her will across the aeons of time in a series of adventures before returning to his tribe. It features all the painted full-colour adventures from Simon Bisley right through to Steve Tappin. As always, there are plusses and minuses, highs and lows, achievements and disappointments.

We'll focus on Simon's art a little later, but let's start with the words. I began by writing up a long synopsis, an episode breakdown of *The Horned God*. Because it was a complex story involving the four treasures held by her tribes: The Spear of Lugh; the Cauldron of Plenty; the Stone of Destiny, and the Sword of Danu. Sláine would need to unite them and become High King in order to face the long-threatened Apocalypse, forecast since the days of *Sky Chariots*. It was now imminent, with the Fomorians and the Skull Swords – led by the Old Horned God, the Lord Weird Slough Feg – about to destroy the Land of the Young.

As an action story, that had great possibilities, and perhaps for some readers that would have been enough, but I needed something more: a subtext; a theme, so this was an intellectual, spiritual conclusion to the first phase of Sláine's life, making it so much more than a hack and slay tale of sword and sorcery.

I wanted to explore matriarchy and the role of male heroes in it. Firstly, because it's central to an exploration of the Celts so it couldn't be avoided forever. Secondly, for myself. And thirdly, because it was surely time readers saw characters and themes that could break or challenge the stereotypes.

If you're unsure what those stereotypes are, I'd refer you to the popular *Gor* novels by John Norman. According to Wikipedia, the *Gor* series repeatedly depicts men abducting and physically and sexually brutalising women, who grow to enjoy their submissive state. Although it's extreme, traditional sword and sorcery tales have echoes of *Gor*, and this is also true for fantasy art.

It was time to say something different that was closer to the truth in Celtic legends and in the archaeological records.

It was a risk because there was a danger of pushback from the readers, but as I said in the last chapter, comics were changing, so if ever there was a good time, it was now. Plus, I had Ukko there as the storyteller to provide some humour, which would keep things light and appealing to a wider audience who might shy away from anything seen as preachy or polemic.

On balance, I think it worked. Thus I recall one of my daughters (who usually took no interest in my stories) read the first collected edition. I rather suspect she felt she had to because her male friends were fans and she needed to keep up to speed with them. I recall her saying with a look of surprise, 'I actually enjoyed it. I wasn't expecting it to be so funny.' Praise indeed!

Without being worthy, or all the usual criticisms chucked at stories that try to effect change, feminism was already starting to seep into *2000AD* and not before time. For example, there was *Halo Jones*, which certainly challenged many readers. There were the odd digs I'd present in *Sláine The King*, such as the sequence where

Niamh's bearded charioteer has twisted his ankle and has to lean on Niamh as they escape the wolves. And the Celtic sagas are full of strong Celtic women. Megrim – in reality Medb – is undoubtedly the strongest. Check out *The Tain*, translated by Thomas Kinsella, and you'll see what I mean. She is lethal – the Bronze Age equivalent of Milady from *Three Musketeers*. Significantly, I had Glenn draw her with blonde hair because I wanted to break the stereotypical mould in comics and films that villainous women have black hair and heroines have blonde hair.

Most of us have been raised in a patriarchal society of male Gods and male achievements, yet the Neolithic archeological record and early Celtic sagas indicate the supreme role of the Goddess, not a God. At some point, long before Christianity, there had been a switch, a usurping of power, as I'm sure any expert on the pre-Christian Irish Brehon Laws would tell me. Yet there were still vestiges of a proto-feminist earlier era, even in those Laws: a trial marriage for a year and a day, for example.

There were three primary sources I used. Monica Sjoo's superb and passionate: *The Great Cosmic Mother,* 'This classic exploration of the Goddess through time and throughout the world draws on religious, cultural, and archaeological sources to recreate the Goddess religion that is humanity's heritage.'

Robert Graves: *The White Goddess*, 'An historical grammar of poetic myth.' It sounds formidable and it is. A book that needs dipping into and absorbing, unless you can afford two weeks in a retreat meditating on its mysteries. What I would take away from it just now, and it is open to challenge, as well as being simplistic, is that language was originally feminine, poetic, a language of feelings and emotions, and this has been usurped by the male language of prose. Deep waters!

Graves cites *The Rime of the Ancient Mariner* by Coleridge, which sums up the White Goddess:

Her lips were red, her looks were free,
Her locks were yellow as gold,
Her skin was white as leprosy,
The Nightmare Life-In-Death was she
Who thicks man's blood with cold.

Those terrifying aspects of the Goddess come through in *The Horned God* when she warns Sláine she may stab him in the back.

And we go deeper yet with the third source. John Rowan's *The Horned God, Feminism and Men as Wounding and Healing.* 'His original and pioneering study of how men relate to feminism will appeal to all men who are concerned about their response to the women's movement and to the women in their lives.'

Wouldn't it have been so much easier to stick to a simple hack and slay saga? Possibly. But I truly believe writers stagnate if they just produce the same stories, decade after decade. *Conan* started off powerfully written by its creator, yet I was quickly bored by the writers who followed Howard. To stay fresh, most of us need to evolve and explore new ideas and new directions.

So now let's move onto the art.

My recollection is the early episodes were actually written to be drawn in black and white art. They would be drawn by Simon Bisley, who had volunteered for the task. He had already established himself as a premier artist with his stunning black and white work on *ABC Warriors.*

In that sense it would be a continuum with the past and I was already thinking ahead to Glenn producing the subsequent *Sláine* saga, when he would become a time traveller and fight alongside Boudicca. It's a story that I'd been itching to write for years, as it's central to an understanding of the Celts.

Everything was mapped out for these black and white pages. I felt I needed to reintroduce the story, such as a depiction of the Wickerman story. Not least because Titan Books had blocked collected editions of Belardinelli and I wanted this scene to be remembered in a collected edition.

Then Simon threw a wild card onto the table! He produced a double page, *colour* spread of Sláine in a stunning new tartan outfit, sporting an incredible 'hero harness' consisting of a wild boar's horns. There was no doubt: it trumped Sláine's existing outfit and it showed the story's potential for full-colour artwork, which barely featured at that time in *2000AD*.

It was clearly the way ahead and *2000AD* editorial and myself were on the same page for once. His subsequent strip pages were amazing. It was like they had been painted by Frank Frazetta! They were world class. We talked over many of the subsequent episodes and I expanded on many of the concepts in my synopsis.

This expansion was possible because Simon was ablaze with ideas. The muse was driving him, too. Doubtless that's why Sláine increasingly looks like Simon. And because Simon was fast, even as a painted artist. It meant that ideas that I'd reluctantly had to put on hold could now be explored. Such as Ukko relating the saga in the Eternal Fortress where his work would be scrutinised and edited by a rather prissy Nest. Great fun to do, but it eats up the pages.

I recall Simon suggesting a pre-Raphaelite sequence where Medb could travel into the magical Otherworld to meet her mentor Slough Feg. Other visual possibilities were also opening up, such as the Cauldron, which became a kind of Tardis that Sláine uses to descend into the Land of the Goddess.

In all this, there were some interesting differences between Simon and me. He saw Medb with the classic black hair of an evil witch and his Goddess was hardly a typical feminist, right-on representation in the 1980s, as some readers commented at the time. But so what? It was how Simon saw her. His Slough Feg was superb but classically evil, not really the shaman on the Neolithic cave wall that was impossible for any artist to recreate – with the probable exception of Angela. But it was all to the good, because Simon had to portray things with conviction, he had to believe in them, and it was not for me to interrupt that process when he was producing a world-class saga. A certain tension, a certain difference of view between script and art is arguably a good thing. It was the same with Joe Colquhoun on *Charley's War*: the fact that he was from an older and more traditional generation than me, actually *adds* to the story's conviction and anti-war message.

For the most part, though, we were firmly on the same page. But *2000AD* editorial were rattled when there was a noticeable change of his painting style, notably at the start of Book Three, which continues all the way through to his present work. It was a much heavier, rather stylised look, and they asked me to talk to Simon about it. I decided not to get involved – firstly because it wasn't my job and secondly because it was a creative phase Simon was going through as he explored his full-colour potential and it was best to let him work it through. When an artist is this gifted, it's best to leave well alone. Whatever you may have read to the contrary, I only inter-vene on art when the artist clearly needs some guidelines or it's going badly wrong. Interventions do not make you popular, and are all too often ignored, so they are very much a last resort.

Simon's sense of comedy really came through on *The Horned God*. One of my favourite comedy moments is when Sláine is made King of Kings and Conan is seen looking on jealously! Simon's intention may well have been different, but I see this as symbolising British sword and sorcery moving away from the influence of American sword and sorcery orthodoxy.

As the epic approaches its conclusion, Simon's style becomes worryingly faster as – inevitably – DC Comics had come a-poaching and were knocking on his door with *Lobo*. I say 'inevitable' because that's the price to be paid when publishers don't offer a proper deal. We were lucky we held onto Simon as long as we did. But there was still time to include a Green Man sequence. This was specially written and painted to tie in with a *BBC Omnibus* documentary on the myths about the Green Man and its impact on culture today. Simon and I were filmed walking around Rollright Stones and talking about the character.

In the same arts programme, my pagan friend Tony Skinner is filmed at a ritual of the Green Man. Later, Tony and I would write *Finn* and other stories drawing on and heavily fictionalising, of course, his life. The producers had asked me if I knew any real-life practising pagans and I had introduced them to Tony. With some reluctance he courageously agreed to take part because as he rightly said, 'It's not really a spectator sport'. He was leaving himself open to couch potatoes who sneer and denigrate real-life magic. A brave thing to do.

In recent years Lisa and I have been to his annual celebration of the Green Man and, as with his previous Beltane events it was a rewarding, spiritual and bawdily humorous experience with more than a dash of real magic thrown in. On the far horizon, miles from his home, an unlikely forest fire began at a key moment in the ceremony just as everyone was jumping over the Beltane fire. Lisa and I were suitably impressed, but Tony shrugged it off with indifference: when you live in a magical world, you take these 'coincidences' for granted.

Tony had been my unofficial consultant on *The Horned God*, explaining the role of the consort to the Goddess. Some of the most memorable lines in the story are Tony's such as when Danu tells Sláine:

'You will never know in which guise you will meet me again... Sometimes I am your mother and hold you ... Sometimes I am your sister and befriend you ... And other times your lover who will stick one in your back.'

It was powerful material and so, in retrospect, it was not surprising that these themes did not go down well with all the readers. Even so, as the story started to appear in print, I was taken aback by the ferocity of one reader, at least. He 'ambushed' me at a signing and launched into a long and angry tirade against the story that bordered on the physical. He claimed to be Simon's official spokesperson and insisted he was reflecting Simon's opinions, so I couldn't ignore him. He wanted a *Conan* approach to the story and was dismissive of the saga's subtext. I was ruining Simon's artistic potential, he told me. It was no good pointing out that *Sláine* is not *Conan*, or that there was non-stop action coming *later* in *The Horned God*; he was passionate and unyielding in his perspective, which he angrily claimed was Simon's, too.

Of course if he – and Simon – were *Conan* fans, they were unlikely to appreciate my point of view. Namely, that I admire Howard's original stories greatly, but I see *Conan* the comic, alongside *Batman*, *Superman*, *Spider-man*, *Vertigo* et al., as part of the American comics establishment adored by some comics fans, but not by ordinary British readers and certainly having no place in *2000AD* or *Sláine*. Such devotees of comics orthodoxy choose not to understand that I, alongside some other *2000AD* creators, are – or were – trying to do something different: something British; something punk; something fresh, rather than endlessly recycling safe corporate comics from yesteryear combined with corporate cool. Fans of *Marshal Law* will know that I despise these American heroes for their phoney morality and this sentiment could be easily extended to include the comic book version of *Conan*. In fact if *Law* had continued, the Marshal might well have satirised *Conan* at least as fiercely as our satire of *Batman*, which fan Simon described as 'mean-spirited'. *Absolutely*, I'm proud to say.

I later reflected on the fan's tirade and realised that the esoteric discussions he hated were originally planned for Glenn Fabry to illustrate. You only have to look at *Sláine The King* to see how well he brought similar scenes to life. But the saga had been planned to reach a crescendo in *The Horned God* and it was too late to change direction. After Angela, *Sláine* was always writer driven, not artist driven, and attempts to change direction had been a disaster – namely the McMahon era stories. I sensed another possible coup in the making and this time I intended to nip it in the bud.

I wondered if Simon might have been better off with something else, like the subsequent Roman story, which was a more straightforward action 'hack and slay', Conanesque tale. Perhaps we were not on the same page after all. So I rang Simon to discuss his spokesman's concerns. Was he happy to continue? If not, maybe we had to find a way for him to 'jump ship'. It was still early enough to do so and then he could rejoin *Sláine* later with some kick-ass action against the Romans. Whatever the reality, Simon told me he had absolutely no problem with my story and this *Conan* fan was nothing to do with him and to just ignore him, which I duly did.

Well, not entirely. I immortalised Simon's 'spokesman' as Mor Ronne the Dung Collector later in the story who memorably says of Sláine,

'Yurrr! I don't like the comp … comp … complicated bits. I only like it when he's killing people.'

Looking back, Mor Ronne's criticism raises some interesting points. It highlights how *2000AD* was changing, with talking head scenes in *The Horned God* that would have been unacceptable in earlier times. They worked: in fact they're beautifully painted and amongst the best scenes in the comic – but there's a 'but'.

It was encouraging changes of direction on other stories that would also not find favour with some readers. The same would apply to the art: it too, was boldly going where comic art had never gone before, and there would be some negative repercussions as other artists tried and often failed to imitate Simon, playing Salieri to his Mozart.

In a text novel, large sections devoted to talking head debates and exposition are commonplace and readers simply don't care. They expect it and accept it. The action-packed novels of Rider Haggard, which I adored as a kid, are a case in point. In a graphic novel, talking heads are riskier and need to be handled more gingerly. If exposition puts some readers off, that needs acknowledging. Today, I would approach it more like a movie script and feed exposition into the action rather more subtly, although there's no guarantee that is necessarily better, as the readers could miss the point being made.

So I have a certain sympathy for Mor Ronne. Many people read popular culture and comics, expecting a quick hit and want nothing more. A female friend told me when she was depressed she would read two Barbara Cartland or Mills & Boon novels in a day. And she would continue with her prescription of two romantic novels every day, until she had overcome her depression. Yes, I know – reading Barbara Cartland every day would make many of us suicidal, but each to their own...

Sláine – being in the sword and sorcery genre – must have often seemed like that to readers who just wanted a quick fix of muscle-bound men, 'naked but for a loin-cloth', bashing each other with axes and swords as semi-naked females look on adoringly. So I can imagine their shock and disappointment when they're taken way out of their comfort zone with *The Horned God*.

And whilst retaining subtext, it's always been my intention to appeal to *this* audience – the 'downmarket' audience of popular culture – rather than the Lord Snooties of the Literati. Why would I choose 'pulp fiction' readers over *Guardian* readers? For a host of reasons, not to do with my background as you might assume, but all relating to subversion. The muse that motivates me requires subversion in my stories and always has from my very first stories as a boy. If it's missing, she's not happy. So that means finding an audience that can be subverted. Subverting *Guardian* readers would be far beyond my abilities.

It's something I think about carefully when I use subversion in popular culture. How best to reach an audience. How to try and affect them. How best to disguise my polemics to make them more acceptable to that audience and to an editor. And I even wonder – in recent years – if there is any point anymore, now my audience is so much older. So, although though Mor Ronne annoyed me at the time, I think there was some truth in his complaints.

I may well have neglected the very audience that I am most committed to writing for.

Whatever its faults, *The Horned God* was an astonishing success. *2000AD*'s circulation actually went up, although there were no bonuses for Simon and me. It sold across the continent: the first time that British comics had successfully broken into the European market. It sold equally well in the United States. It led to top French artist Olivier Ledroit (*Chronicles of the Black Moon*) wanting to work with me on French comic books – so our series *Sha* and later *Requiem: Vampire Knight*, would follow.

Many readers have told me how its spiritual subtext deeply affected them. Some became pagans on the strength of it. It undoubtedly put British comics on the map with an adult audience. Simon was rightly fêted as an artist super-star.

Today, *The Horned God* is still as successful as ever. It was the first volume in the *2000AD Ultimate Collection* and then in May 2020 there was a larger separate edition. Of the two, I would recommend the *Ultimate* edition because it has a gloss finish, even though it is too small. In fact, both versions need to be larger and glossier to truly appreciate Simon's lush artwork. Why cut corners on a classic? Sigh!

For a fascinating and detailed analysis of *The Horned God*, and how much it meant to readers, I recommend the podcast: *Never Iron Anything The Comics Review Show* episode 85. 'Chatting about Sláine *The Horned God*' with *Spacewarp* artist Ian Ashcroft and comics writer Tony Esmond.

Then there is the Penguin Books full-cast audioplay out this year. 'Colin Morgan is brilliant as the brutal yet cunning Sláine, but it's Gerry O'Brien who steals the show as Ukko the Dwarf,' (*Starburst Magazine*). It's unabridged, 167 minutes long and, as an audio play, is not dependant on Simon's art, but relies on the words and the talents of the actors alone.

Here's what one reader, @Sweetnightmaresmedia, had to say about it on Twitter:

> Listened to this yesterday. I haven't read *The Horned God* since it's initial run in the weekly @insta2000AD. It's a great story and the trademark loquacious style of @patmillswriter translates exceptionally well to this audio format.
>
> Definitely some themes in this epic tale that resonate today. Right down to the Goddess's own take on what is now known as sex-positive feminism. Gonna have to get my hands on the graphic novel now so that I can experience @theofficialsimonbisley's mind blowing artwork all over again.'

19
DEMON KILLER

To say that *The Horned God* was a hard act to follow would be something of an understatement.

The reasons are self-evident but bear repeating. *Sláine* would have to continue in full colour, with art that would need to be of a comparable standard to Simon Bisley. No pressure there! Where could we possibly find such an artist? Equally, *The Horned God* appeared to many to be a finale story built up over the years. Where could it possibly go from there? Plus, there is always a crunch of gears when a James Bond film or a *Doctor Who* series replaces a well-loved star with a new actor.

Fortunately, Glenn was returning, his art now in full colour. And there was a time travel element, established since episode one, actually anticipating this day. So it seemed legitimate that Sláine, as The Horned God, would now fight for his Goddess in other eras, beginning in *Demon Killer* with the Boudicca rebellion against the Romans. I focused on the Boudicca rebellion against the Roman imperialists because it is essential to our understanding of the true nature of the Celts, rather than the carefully prepared establishment narrative, which is firmly in the camp of the Empire.

Plus the saga needed the wider canvas of history. It was the only way I could find new epic worlds and challenges to equal what had gone before.

Yes, there was a crunch of gears, that was inevitable, but it's worth noting that *Sláine* maintained its popularity during this period. Some comics observers have suggested otherwise, which was wishful thinking on their part. The danger from these 'enemies of *Sláine*' – I can't find another polite way to describe them – was that if they kept repeating this lie often enough, readers or fans could believe it, which is why I need to challenge it here. In fact, *Demon Killer* and some of the other *Sláine* historical sagas continue to sell well in foreign language editions across Europe. And there was huge pressure to get *Sláine* back into the comic as quickly as possible. After all, it had increased *2000AD's* circulation.

To set the scene, I had established that Sláine was bored with being *The High King* in a one-off story in the *2000AD* 1992 Yearbook. This would be relevant much later in the series when editorial insisted he return to his tribe and continue being High King, despite what I am about to relate. Illustrated in black and white half tone by Glenn Fabry, it's a very funny tale where Sláine is jealous of one of his warriors being sacrificed to the triple death. He has grown weary of the pleasures of life and yearns for death himself. He tries to pick a fight with his knights, but they cannot allow the High King to have a blemish on him.

Finally, he confronts Conall the Handsome, says 'Your face offends me' and smashes him in the face. Conall, whose looks are now ruined forever, is concerned that Sláine might have damaged his hand!

Sláine eventually cheers up when he is told that he will soon be a wanderer in time, engaged in even bloodier battles than ever before.

It's a great little story that I still laugh at today.

The satirical tone continues in *Demon Killer*. Ukko introduces the story with a single page where he announces that nothing very interesting happened during Sláine's *seven years* as High King, at the end of which he announces that he was put to death, 'As was the custom in those days.'

'And so ends the story of Sláine Mac Roth. Yes, this has been – the final saga.'

THE END

Ukko, of course, is lying. He's just too lazy to write up the story. But the magical *torc of truth* around his neck has other ideas and forces him to continue.

Unlike Ukko, I really wanted to write the Boudicca story. Colchester was my hometown, which the rebel Queen had once razed to the ground, massacring the Roman population. We have been conditioned in our education system to see the Conquest as a necessary step to 'civilising' the barbaric Celts. Necessary because it legitimises colonization. And legitimises the crimes of the British Empire. Colchester was the first colony in Britain, and the Celts described the Romans as Caesareans, literally 'Imperialists'.

Establishment censorship is fiercer than you may have been led to believe, as I discovered following up *Charley's War,* my best-selling anti-war series, during the centenary years of the Great War. There were no takers for any story that was anti-war. We provably have the tightest censorship in Western Europe, with ingenious excuses and gaslighting ready to deter critics with plausible deniability.

Historical stories in comics can be po-faced, worthy, and rather like a history lesson, but there was no danger of that happening with the anarchic Celts, particularly with Ukko by Sláine's side. Plus the demon Elfric on the Roman side, who often steals the show, as all good villains should. All memorably, humorously and beautifully depicted by Glenn.

Boudicca destroys Colchester, 'the home of collaborators and ex-soldiers who settled on our land' with Sláine by her side. The Celts' massacre of men, women and children, is a matter of record and I felt it would be a cop-out if Sláine wasn't a savage and integral part of it. We don't see anything graphic, but it is stated nevertheless. Usually in comics, the protagonist would never do anything so unheroic. He might even try and stop the bloodshed, or at least spare the women and children. But I knew the Celts and their Goddess were not that merciful, and I wanted to be authentic.

Even so, it's a difficult sequence that I don't think works well in words or art. Both feel a little uneven and perhaps lacking in conviction. If I were writing it today, I would try and find a solution that wasn't a cop-out nor bestowed on Sláine a modern-day hero's moral compass. There is always a solution and it's on me that I didn't think of it at the time.

Thus, the Goddess might explain to Sláine that Boudicca and her army of freedom fighters are enraged by the Roman oppressors and their vengeance is therefore restoring balance. But the Goddess could say that Sláine is different, he is an outsider, her champion from another time, who has lost no loved ones in the Roman conquest. Therefore he can feel and behave different to the other Celts and even legitimately prevent the deaths of the children. They might, for instance, remind him of his son Kai.

So, at the time, Glenn was right to pick up on Sláine's questionable participation in the massacre. Recently he said:

'The reason why we fell out on *Demon Killer* was this, there were things you wrote, Sláine (your child of course) killing women and children. At the time I was a new father, couldn't take it. Now I understand.'

Whatever is going on in our personal lives always affects our stories and art and I don't think we should apologise for it. It seems particularly the case with *Sláine*.

Thus, on a lighter note, I'm reminded of a French comic series where the artist writer produced a very successful series dripping with blood and gore. Then he became a dad and the next volume was full of happiness and the joys of fatherhood that he was keen to share with his readers. In response, sales plummeted overnight so his publisher told him in no uncertain terms to get back to the blood and gore.

By now, Glenn was taking longer and longer over the pages in a search for perfectionism, and it's apparent in some style variations. That again seems to be one of the demands of fully painted art, making it a sometimes thankless task which doesn't always endear it to the audience. Then if I recall correctly, editorial – as always obsessed with breaking into American comics and rarely succeeding – lured Glenn away from *Sláine* with the prospect of doing a *Batman Judge Dredd* crossover.

But he left behind a wonderful visual legacy – in particular his characterisation of the decadent Elfric. I recall a scene where he's reclining in the Roman baths and saying,

'Flamingoes' tongues… Badgers noses… Parrots boiled in their feathers… Mmm! Delicious as the company I keep.'

The true face of Roman 'civilisation.'

20

QUEEN OF WITCHES

D ermot Power finished off *Demon Killer* and then the saga continued under the new title *Queen of Witches*. Dermot did a superb job maintaining continuity with Glenn's work, including some great comical moments such as where Sláine has sentenced Ukko to the Wickerman for selling drugs to the Romans. He is spared the bonefire at the last moment, when he comes up with a fiendish plan to break up the formidable Roman testudo, or tortoise shield formation, by throwing wasp and hornet nests into it. It worked with devastating consequences for the Legion.

The idea had been suggested to me by a fight instructor who worked on movies, and I became increasingly interested in the practicalities of sword fighting. Equipped with chain mail gloves, sword and shield, we'd practice on Colchester Common and I'd get some idea of what it was really all about. The Celts left no written record of their martial arts, but it was obvious from odd references in their sagas that they had a complex and fantastic system that may well have surpassed the ubiquitous Oriental martial arts. The subject fascinated me, so much so that I later researched Irish stick fighting. Amongst the books I read on the subject were *Shillelagh the Irish*

Fighting Stick and *Irish Gangs and Stick-Fighting,* both by John W. Hurley. It explored accounts written in the nineteenth century and enabled me to see, through a glass darkly, how the ancient tribal battles might have been conducted.

Queen of Witches featured the astonishing 'Shield of Alarms', ornamented with seven bosses. 'They were the Seven Voices of the Queen ... Each one emitting a different tone ... allowing her to direct her troops in combat.' Military experts dismiss this as a 'poetical embellishment' not having any practical purpose in a melee with everyone shouting, swearing, cursing and screaming. And why not use the dreadful wail of the carnyx, the Celtic trumpet, instead? But, as always in *Sláine*, I follow the poetical embellishments, if that is what they are, in praise of the fantastic, remembering the Celts as they saw themselves, not as modern day experts believe they were.

Thus it's followed by The Bone Prison of Oeth, a magnificent fantasy edifice built from the bones of slaughtered Roman legionnaires.

'This gruesome if impractical prison was destroyed and rebuilt several times during the wars between the Romans and the Britons. In the end, the bones decayed to dust whereupon the industrious locals used them as fertilizers for their wheat and barley, resulting in astonishing crops for many years.' *Singing in Chains, Medieval Welsh Tales of the Past* by Sam Lasman.

Only the Celts could come up with something so extraordinary and even comedic with the Romans' bones used for fertilizer. These were the weird details I would be endlessly looking for when I wrote *Sláine*. They are unlikely to be found in any other sword and sorcery saga.

Elfric uses the bone prison's dark horrors to recreate himself and direct the Romans to commit new atrocities against the Goddess. Sláine warps out with rage and finally beheads Elfric. But all is lost and Boudicca and Sláine take poison. Although not quite everything is lost. Because the Boudicca rebellion stops the Roman plans to invade Ireland.

So that 'Sláine's death was a noble sacrifice by the First High King of Ireland to save his country.'

The Goddess reanimates Sláine and grants him his deep desire to return to Ireland.

Looking back, I feel the story and art of both Glenn and Dermot's stories are powerful and yet, although they were successful, there is something missing. It might be the colour, which perhaps is too bright, too 'technicolour' in places, and not always thematically consistent. It might be the Romans who, despite abundant references being available, are still somewhat visually lacking in conviction compared to other armies that have appeared in *Sláine*. And they just don't have the splendour of their fantasy cousins in Conquering Armies.

Certainly Elfric, as a fantasy villain, works well for the most part. It could be the script is too fast paced. This befits an action story, rather different to its predecessor *The Horned God*. But it needed slowing down to ensure the stronger emotional beats are there – as I've exampled with the scene where Sláine massacred the citizens of Colchester.

Probably the problem was communication between artist and writer. Because the underlying quality from Glenn, Dermot and myself is already there. It just needs augmenting. Thus Glenn might voice his story reservations about Sláine at the massacre. He could tell me the things he liked painting and the things he hated or had difficulty with, so I could try and avoid them. In return, I might raise the colour issues and deluge him with Roman references or discuss other, better ways to depict them. A few pints down the line we'd doubtless both have had brainwaves. We would also be united in our love of *Sláine* and the central anti-Roman theme and how best to bring it out. Then we would both go away and think about the issues raised.

With regular communication, those difficulties I've described can be ironed out. That's how it worked on *Nemesis The Warlock* with Kevin O'Neill, and on later *Sláine* stories with Clint Langley.

On my French series, *Requiem: Vampire Knight*, with Olivier Ledroit, we would meet up maybe twice a year to discuss the story and art. But it was worth my while financially to fly over to Paris or drive to Brittany to meet up with Olivier and discuss our differing views. Our publisher Jacques Collin would act as interpreter and umpire, for which he should have received a medal for his diplomacy. Sometimes Olivier and Jacques would also come over to Colchester to talk about the story. Because *Requiem* required numerous changes to make it into the bestseller that it is. Every page of story and art are of the very highest quality as a result.

But for *2000AD*, any such serious meetings and two-day creative jam sessions are simply not economic. You can see in both *Demon Killer* and *Queen of the Witches* there are several art pages where the meter is running, because the artist's mortgage has to be paid and he has his family to feed. The same is true in the text – my use of curses I've used before, for example. That the British comics industry, and especially its publishers, should be perfectly content that we are second-class comics citizens compared to the French, appals me. The lousy rights deal is the reason why, not because the French are artistically superior to us. But their contracts are.

A six-page story, *The Return of the High King,* followed directly after Sláine's adventures with Queen Boudicca. It was part of an incredibly exciting, giant poster by Dermot Power, which was number one in the *2000AD* poster series, a sign of just how popular *Sláine* had become.

It was based on a tale of how Cuchulain travels through time to the Christian era and rejects the new religion. Sláine's story follows a similar direction. A Christian monk warns him to renounce his pagan Goddess or burn forever in Hell. Sláine's response is predictable: 'I shall join my tribe whether they sit at the feast or in the fire.'

Sláine now realises that the Goddess wants him to be a wanderer in time and he can never go home again. It's a poignant tale that I felt a pang reading again today.

It's also beautifully illustrated by Dermot Power, and a sign of his breathtaking art yet to come.

21

SOMEWHERE IN TIME

Behind *The Name of the Sword* by Greg Staples and the main saga that follows *Lord of Misrule* by Clint Langley is an exploration of the magical theme of reincarnation, which is a mainstay of Celtic, ancient and, indeed, modern worldwide beliefs.

Around this time I had some experience of past lives myself, which feed into both these stories. Not the 'I was Napoleon' or 'a priest king of Atlantis', beloved of cynics, but rather more lowly, emotional and insightful experiences into how reincarnation may work. Not only did it inspire these stories, but also a three-volume series *Sha* published by Editions Soleil in France, illustrated by Olivier Ledroit. And *Requiem: Vampire Knight*, too. So if it was an illusion, it was a very profitable one.

What made the experience interesting was that it included external evidence from other people, which made it relatively objective. Plus there were elements of the past that I could not have known and I have yet to discover in history books of the relevant period. Yet they seem authentic to me, rather than the product of a vivid imagination. Today, a sceptic, a scientist or a psychologist would have trouble explaining it as an illusion. Although they would, of course, attempt to do so, because it threatens their own belief systems and they need the ground to feel firm beneath their feet. But the esoteric is simply outside their experience, just as science is outside mine.

These events bear out the premise in my introduction: if you take an interest in magic, it will take an interest in *you*.

My experiences provided the basis for a presentation and talk I gave at the Psychic Questing Conference at London's Conway Hall. Past speakers have included Graham Hancock and Andrew Collins, its founder. It went down so well, I was invited back to give the same talk the following year. This I duly did and I have it a videotape of it somewhere that I must convert into a digital format.

I could have polished and perfected my 'show' and gone on magical lecture tours talking about it for years to come, but I chose to end it there, out of respect for those past lives. I could not allow these events to be turned into 'party pieces'. They were real people who had lived and died and I needed to honour them.

With that knowledge, it was with great conviction that I had Niamh reincarnate as a nun and then later become a victim of the medieval Burning Times.

So Sláine and Niamh meet again – somewhere in time.

She as a nun, and he as the King of the Greenwood and Leader of the Wildhunt. Otherwise known as Robin Goodfellow.

Greg Staples' opening image of Sláine sums the theme up so well. We've seen elements of the similar Herne the Hunter in the brilliant and absorbing TV series *Robin of Sherwood* (1984) and this painting evokes that same sense of Celtic magic.

So Niamh is now a nun, Sister Marian, and comes across a pagan girl who worships Robin Goodfellow, *The Horned God* whom Niamh regards as the devil himself. She has no knowledge of her past life as a pagan warrior. The girl is taken away to be put to death by a sinister cult.

The style and sense of design Greg brings to these pages is

extraordinary. In particular, it sets a dark and atmospheric theme to the story, which is a welcome change from the bright colours of the Roman saga or, indeed, *The Horned God*.

With that darkness, though, come problems with fully painted art, which I would argue 2000AD was simply not equipped to deal with. I don't think any of us had the necessary skills and experience to properly assess an entirely new style of British comic. Firstly, there's the issue of reproduction. The Rebellion reprint I'm looking at is too murky in places, so I found myself struggling to see exactly what was going on. I think it would have benefited from a larger edition. I don't think the original was much better.

Secondly, painted art often doesn't have the detail, clarity, facial expression and movement that black and white artwork should have. Readers miss the 'immediacy' of black and white art. It must have been a factor in why older readers loved painted art for the most part, but younger readers moved away from 2000AD.

But all this is offset in *Name of the Sword* by Greg's passion for the subject and individual scenes that are glorious, such as Sláine and Ukko walking through a winter forest; a sequence where Marian consults an ancient tome relating the history of Sláine; our hero as the Green Man, and Ukko as a church gargoyle!

Name of the Sword is a deeper story than the Roman saga, dramatising esoteric truths not usually covered in heroic fantasy. It's actually a classic mystery thriller that obeys all the tropes of that genre, especially the dark mystery at its heart:

'What is the secret unspeakable name of God?'

The idea that we reincarnate and meet enemies or loved ones over and over again in new guises in other lives, somewhere in time, is a chilling one. Personally, I can't think of anything worse and would far prefer it to be the product of imagination. But I fear it is true. Perhaps this is why evidence that confirms reincarnation is generally overlooked or rejected. If it were ever proven, it would change our society beyond recognition. But it's delightful to see these issues played out here between Sister Marian and Robin Goodfellow; Sláine and Niamh. And Marian's slow recognition that she was married to Sláine in a former life: 'Could I really have been married to such a brute?'

A key source for this tale was Robert Graves's *The White Goddess*. It inspired the revelation that the sword of the Blood God Sláine must seek is inscribed with the secret, unspeakable name of God. More on *The White Goddess* in the next chapter.

The title *The Name of the Sword* is clearly inspired by *The Name of the Rose*. But there's an underlying truth here that also motivated me to choose this title and write this story. It doesn't matter what we call ourselves, which side we are on, what religion we adhere to, it's *not* who we really are.

It's just the Name of your Sword.

22

THE ETERNAL WAR

Time problems were once again bedevilling the series. Greg was unable to continue and so the saga was split, with a new title *Lord of Misrule*, and a new artist, Clint Langley, for the second half. Clint and I met Tharg MacManus in the *2000AD* office. It was obvious Steve was becoming exasperated by the endless time problems on the series.

However, he seemed desperate to keep *Sláine* in the comic, which is confirmation of its success. Hence there was only a two-week gap between Greg's section concluding and Clint's beginning. In order to have a fast turnaround on the art, MacManus wanted to drop painted artwork and have it coloured by Dondie Cox. Clint and I were dismayed. It would be another crunch of gears for the readers, particularly in mid-saga, adjusting from lush painted art to black and white coloured art. And we weren't sure that Dondie would be able to carry out Clint's very precise requirements. But MacManus was insistent that this was the way it was going to be. He was surprisingly bullish. I'd already written and been paid for some of the episodes, so there was nothing I could do – otherwise I'd have refused to continue. Instead, I had to make the best of it.

Whenever I look at the book, I'm always confronted by Clint's opening page and I find myself smiling ... so let me explain why.

In this opening scene, Sláine and his men look directly into the readers' eyes and raise their two bow fingers in a gesture of defiance. It was at the battle of Crecy against the French that the English bowmen all waved their two fingers at the enemy. This was because bowmen who had previously been captured by the French had their two fingers amputated.

I was told that after the boss of the French publishers Glénat saw *Lord of Misrule*, he stopped publishing *Sláine*. I believe it went to Soleil next. The publisher took particular exception to this scene, which he found 'very vulgar'.

Sadly, I know that sharing this information with you, which should shame us Brits, will only make us worse. That eternal war between French and British clearly didn't end with Crécy, as a glance at any newspaper headlines about Brexit will confirm.

But let's go back to Clint's art. It was a particularly tough challenge for Clint. Working in black line, he would not only be in the shadow of Simon Bisley and Greg Staples, but also in the shadow of Glenn Fabry. Faced with these comparisons, I think both art and story came out very well. It certainly had the virtue of clarity. We can really see what's going on, so it's great for storytelling, even if we are deprived of the mystique and the atmosphere of painted art. Following Clint's direction, Dondie did a good job and Clint also coloured many of the pages himself. Clint and I stayed in regular contact, talking through various episodes, and that's a key reason they work so well.

Notably, on the famous Celtic Battle of the Trees. This was inspired by *The White Goddess*, where Graves interprets the meaning of a titanic battle between the trees. Perfect for heroic fantasy. Animated trees, the Ents, work in *Lord of the Rings*, but to feature them in a comic is taking writer, artist and readers into dangerous territory. They could easily look awful. But that's always been the nature of *Sláine*: to risk everything in an exploration of all the aspects of Celtic magic. It would be a cop-out to ignore it, especially on a story set in a forest. But I'll admit I was nervous!

If we were back in the Belardinelli era, I would have gone for it like a shot because Massimo had an obvious love of nature and the enchantment of the magical, deep dark forest, which made him such a premier *Sláine* artist. If you consider his warp spasm, imagine what he would have done with violent tree warriors! Clint, by comparison, was more of an urban artist, so I wasn't sure. We had several long phone conversations about them. Was it fair to give him this challenge? Could he make them work? Clint was confident he could.

And he easily rose to the occasion. His tree warriors have the same fantastic quality as the Ents. His love of *Sláine* and his enthusiasm for the project easily carries the day. They're superb! Using the words of the ancient poem, the tree warriors come alive and are seen to impressive effect in a double page spread finale.

But setting stories in a historical era always presents challenges to fantasy artists. So the Normans, like the Romans before them, don't seem to have the heightened reality necessary. If you're unsure what I mean by that, take a look at the TV series 'Peaky Blinders', where Birmingham and its gangs have been given heightened visual reality. It's not just down to the music of Nick Cave. Never has Birmingham looked so cool! It surely has to be a fantasy version of Brum? Unfortunately, the Normans in this story don't have a similar heightened reality. They therefore look like something out of a history comic.

Aware of the danger, I had considered Robin Goodfellow's merry men and I knew I had to avoid them being drawn straight, because they could also make the series look like a history comic – a genre they're very fond of in Europe, alongside cowboy comics. But in Britain, readers usually loathe them and creators are well advised to stay away from both! If you're a creator, for your own sake, please don't try to prove me wrong and do a 'straight' history comic! War comics, on the other hand, we love – hence the ongoing success of *Commando Comics* and *Charley's War*. Yes, we Brits are damn fussy. But if we don't always know what we like, we certainly know what we don't like.

So I gave the merry men animal masks, which are a strong tradition in British mythology. Consider, for instance, the masks in the film *The Wickerman*, beloved of fantasy fans. Or imagine them being used in a similar way in the TV series *Robin of Sherwood*, with these scary beasts watching from the undergrowth. So I felt I was safe there. No chance of falling into the 'history comic' trap.

In this, at least, I succeeded. There were no Little Johns or Friar Tucks. But somehow, they don't have enough visual presence to really register in either of the Robin Goodfellow stories. In Greg's section, they seem more like real animals than outlaws and one even appears to be a polar bear! Maybe I didn't give them enough emphasis in the script or supply enough references to show how they could work as masks. Hopefully the readers were distracted by the enthralling Goddess and Inquisition scenes, and the final battle, so as not to care.

I love the way the secret name of God is exposed. It's inspired by the premise of *The White Goddess*. In broad brushstrokes, that the original matriarch language of poetry, emotion and feelings, was replaced by the Blood God with the new patriarchal prison language of prose. Of course prose can be emotional, too, but that's the core idea.

The superb *Snowcrash* by Neil Stephenson also explores the idea of language as a virus, the product of the Sumerians or their Gods.

In fact, the *other* remarkable source of inspiration for me was an unpublished author who, in 1990, was sending me typewritten pages of his *meisterwerk* that – if I'd collected them into one pile – would have towered four feet high. I asked him why he was passing his work to me and he replied, 'I just know you are meant to have it.' His style of writing was circular rather than linear, which made it an impossible proposition to ever get published, even by the most esoteric of publishers.

It was clear to me he was possessed by the muse.

Every one of us has a muse – an inner voice that guides us – but few like to acknowledge it for fear of being locked up ('It was my voices that told me to do it, your honour'). His muse had been making him work overtime to produce this astonishing tome. Entirely independent of Graves and Stephenson, he had reached a similar conclusion. To bear it out, he had a remarkable gift of being able to trace the etymology of any word I cared to give him back to its matriarchal roots, from Pater back to Mater, from the present day to Ancient Sumeria, usually in about four words. He was a 'blue collar', self-taught writer and I've noted they are often despised by academics, so I'm not going to give examples here which would give them the opportunity to get into the academic equivalent of trolling, rejecting his talent with their intellectual superiority. I'm a writer of fiction, so I don't care. It certainly seemed impressive to my untutored eyes.

And it helped to give me the basis of an Eternal War in which this story is set.

It was rather spooky. And it actually got spookier, because he was the same gentleman who introduced me to the biological UFOs, the 'sky critters'. The macrobes. They were also described in detail in his tome. My first reaction was, 'Oh, God! He's a UFO nut!' But when he invited me up to his hometown see them, I couldn't resist. And they turned up, sure enough, sadly in the pre-mobile phone era (so I have no photos). Although they were fairly boring compared to 'Close Encounters', so you haven't missed much. When I got home, my daughters' contrasting reactions were interesting. One pleaded, 'Can I come with you next time?' The other asked sternly, 'Have the police been informed?'

But there wasn't going to be a next time, because I felt it was too weird and even dangerous. How these 'sky critters' fit into the mythos of a Blood God and an Eternal War is outside the scope of this chapter. But they are certainly not benign. As I've said earlier, I feature them in *Finn*. Even so, I can't resist adding an even weirder footnote to the story. This really happened, even though it seems like a scene out of *I'm Alan Partridge*.

The host of a Birmingham-based, esoteric, *very* late night satellite TV show invited me on his programme to talk about my UFO experience. It was rather a bizarre set-up because it was funded by a porn show in the adjoining studio. I remember being rather distracted by it on my way to the Green Room. The show had guests like David Icke in earlier episodes, but I think they were getting down to the bottom of the barrel now, with my fellow guest and me. The tone was a tad cynical and light-hearted, with street scene intercuts of teenagers being interviewed: 'UFOs? It's all bollocks, innit?' which had me chuckling away. But my fellow guest, a magical quester of some repute (wearing an immaculate, vintage suit the colour of crème brûlée), was on the show to promote his book about meeting South American shamans and the esoteric experiences that ensued. He took it all rather more seriously than I did. He was already annoyed, because he felt the lowly comic books I was promoting were given more prominence than his on the glass coffee table in the studio. The piss-taking teenagers were the final straw for him. He took huge exception to their sneering at magical phenomena and became very threatening and abusive. The host and I sat in open-mouthed horror as he suddenly exploded and smashed the coffee table and then started to trash the rest of the studio. He had to be removed by security guards. The debris was swept up and – now short of a guest – I then took up the whole 50 minutes on the show, rather than my original 25 minutes time slot. I'm told it's out there on YouTube somewhere, sadly without the footage of my fellow guest warping out. I think the cameramen were probably running for their lives at the time.

Sorry about that digression. Let's get back to the nature of language.

To demonstrate the power of poetry over prose, Nest recites a poem. I wrote the original when I was fifteen, after a spooky dream. Remarkably for me, I actually held onto a copy until the 1990s. So I took the verse and added to it considerably to fit the storyline, but the tone, the beat and some of the original lines remain.

Niamh is tried before the Inquisition as a witch. The poem concludes:

> *A blessing given,*
> *Her crime forgiven,*
> *The prisoner shriven,*
> *She is free to go.*
> *But no!*
> *Absolution is for the men-at-arms,*
> *Given the right to steal her charms,*
> *For a maiden they cannot take,*
> *To burn as a witch at the stake.*

It's one of the chilling high points of the story, almost certainly because it's written as verse.

The subsequent scenes of Niamh facing this terrible death are powerful, distressing and truly epic. Clint did a magnificent job of building the story up to its grand finale. I drew on similar material for my French series *Sha*, which begins with a girl being burnt at the stake as a witch. She is later reincarnated as a police detective in the fantasy city of New Eden to hunt down her persecutors, who have also reincarnated. Originally, Olivier and I had sold the series to Dargaud, the *Asterix* publishers, but they pulled out over a technical point on the contract at an advanced stage. I'm told, rightly or wrongly, that it was really because Dargaud were backed by a Christian organisation that didn't care for the opening scenes of the Church killing a witch. So we were published by Soleil, instead.

This demonstrates that these issues and the nature of the Eternal War are still very real for many people.

As Nest says to Ukko in the story, 'Why are you so enslaved by time? Everything is "now". So what they did to Marian in "the past" is relevant to "today" and in "the future" ...'

The Church has apologised for the Burning Times, the medieval holocaust in which countless women were burnt at the stake.

'During his long reign as Pope, John Paul II apologised to Jews, women, people convicted by the Inquisition, Muslims killed by the Crusaders and almost everyone who had suffered at the hands of the Catholic Church over the years.'

To me, this is just cold, calculated public relations. The Church only apologises when it's caught, although optimists may believe otherwise.

However, the Pope should have added gays, who were also burnt at the stake. There is a gay man depicted, burning at the stake, in *Lord of Misrule*. It's where the insulting word 'faggot' comes from. In the 1950s, the Catholic Church *castrated* twelve Dutch gay teenagers. In the 1970s, they subjected gay Catholic teenagers to electric shock aversion therapy, destroying their lives. Endless other unspeakable methods have been used, through to the present day where conversion therapy (psychological torture) is *still* being practised on the gay community, with the encouragement of the Church.

The Eternal War is forever and I'm afraid, for the most part, the Blood God wins.

The ending of the story is particularly emotional and powerful. Clint surpasses himself. You can see he's with me every single step of the way. It's certainly one of the *Sláine* sagas I'm particularly proud of, and I most definitely recommend it to you to read again or check

out for the first time. It really deserves a new, larger edition to do it justice. You're in for a treat. It confirms that subtext is everything in *Sláine* and without it, you've just got a hack and slay story.

I'll leave you with Nest's final words. She asks that we see the Blood God as the false deity it really is, and come under the spell of the Goddess again:

> *So the world will once again become an enchanted place.*
> *That is my chant.*
> *That is my spell.*
> *That is my prayer.*
> *Let it be.*

THE TREASURES OF BRITAIN

Dermot Power's work on this story about the Thirteen Treasures of Britain is outstanding. Sláine must find the Treasures to free King Arthur from the curse of the Guledig. It's perfect in every way. The style is actually more consistent than *The Horned God*: it's clear and easy to follow as Dermot effortlessly handles even the most complex and demanding sequences.

For example, consider Dermot's depiction of the classic Arthurian sequence, where Uther Pendragon lusts after Igraine. He uses a cloak of invisibility, one of the Treasures of Britain, to enter Tintagel Castle where she is sleeping. It is *so* beautiful! I loved a similar scene in the film *Excalibur,* but this comic book gem easily surpasses it. It takes us to an enchanted world, which is the purpose of heroic fantasy like *Sláine.*

Equally beautiful is his portrayal of the Pavilion of Peredur. This is a silken tent 'used by the dragon priestesses to bless the knights before battle and to console them after.' It's a kind of mythical Tardis, as we see it's a vast emporium within. Sláine is defeated by the Guledig and rolled up inside the tent, but thanks to Ukko's greed, he escapes and triumphs.

All the Treasures were fascinating, and could have been the subject of stories of their own. They show the richness of the Celtic mythos, often barely known to the general reader, and this is why it was *essential* for Sláine to travel in time to explore these magical mysteries.

But my favourite Treasure comes later in the book. At the Feast of Fools on All Fools Day, where gleemen have to make White Tusk, King of the Orcs, laugh … or die! It's a tough life being a comedian. Ukko is the next jester, only he also has a secret agenda: to steal the Orc's tusk – one of the Treasures of Britain – from his mouth!

Dermot loved illustrating *Sláine* and wanted to continue, but – as always with any of us working on *2000AD* – economics were a factor and he understandably felt he had to move on to better paid work. He's now a leading film concept designer working on movies like *Harry Potter, Star Wars* and *Batman*.

Thanks to his contacts, I later got the gig of being the first researcher on the 2004 film *King Arthur*. My job was to find and purchase illustrated books that would bear out the premise of the movie that Arthur was actually a Roman officer and his Knights were horsemen from the Russian steppes. It was a fun job because down the road from me in Colchester was Barbarossa Books in Tiptree. It is the ultimate in militaria, with the most fascinating, obscure and highly illustrated historical and World War Two books, notably on the Russian Front – hence the shop's name. I thoroughly recommend a visit. You'll spend a fortune. I did. Fortunately, it was the film company's money.

I don't recall if Dave Bishop was the commissioning editor of *Treasures of Britain*. My feeling is he had taken it over from his predecessor, Alan McKenzie, sometime in the course of Part One. Thankfully, Bishop seemed surprised and enthralled by *Treasures*. Then he said I'd have to cut down my planned episodes for Part Two because *2000AD* was changing its proportions to a more American size and *Treasures* would have to conclude before this happened. The discerning reader may notice some speeding up in the storyline in order to make this possible.

The story explores the complex family dynamics around King Arthur. Usually this kind of story would be told in a text novel due to its in-depth exploration of a dysfunctional family. Looking back, I doubt I would risk writing a comic strip this ambitious today. It's far too risky – even pointless. For example, in this story Morgaine and Merlin have conducted a spell of merging and become one flesh, leading to amusing altercations between them. That's just one of endless novel ideas in the saga for the reader to enjoy. Novel, because every retelling of the Arthur legend *must* find a new angle and provide new insights for an adult audience that is already familiar with the tale from movies and books.

It may just be my perception, but I feel that the pendulum has swung back to a requirement for *simpler* stories and that may be a good thing for today's audience. Certainly for creators. Because they're faster to write, and it thus makes the whole process of in-depth research on Arthur seem rather pointless today.

But there was once a fascination for paganism and Arthurian legends in 2000AD's audience which, at the time, included travellers, road protestors, pagans, punks, hippies, students and other counter-culture members who regularly read 2000AD not just for *Sláine*, but also for other stories that challenged the establishment such as *Finn*, the fantasy eco-warrior.

Their interest in King Arthur was very real.

Whatever the historical reality, he inspired many of their lives as a symbol of freedom and courage. I gave my first talk at the pagan venue Talking Stick, when their original speaker, the famous road protester 'King Arthur', was arrested. Later, I stayed overnight at a road demonstration and talked this story over with protesters, some of whom had grown up reading *Sláine*.

These modern Sláines continue fighting for the Earth Goddess today. Amongst their key targets is the HS2 high-speed rail development, which has already destroyed countless ancient woodlands and the habitats of protected species such as bats, hedgehogs and badgers. The authorities say they mitigate by planting new trees, but ancient woodlands are priceless and irreplaceable. Once gone, they're lost forever. The authorities pay private security companies to use violent intimidation, and cut off food and water supplies to peaceful and legal demonstrators.

It's hard to convey just how important 2000AD once was to the counterculture, because that time is largely over. Perhaps one example will demonstrate: the London nightclub Megatripolis, where they regularly had guest speakers on esoteric and Celtic subjects. The huge venue under Charing Cross railway station was also used for Heaven, the gay nightclub. I believe they had John Sharkey giving a talk about his excellent book *Celtic Mysteries – The Ancient Religion,* one of my visual bibles for *Sláine.* Then I was invited to talk about *Sláine.* A couple of female art students made a massive bas-relief sculpture, painted in green and gold, of a Celtic Sheela-na-gig, a female exhibitionist and symbol of fertility. This was used as a backdrop to my talk, which went down well. I was so impressed by the sculpture that I bought it off the students. It had pride of place on my lounge wall to the horror of a conservative female friend, who thought it was obscene.

Perhaps Bishop had similar negative feelings about the pagan Celts. It's a matter of record that he eventually drove such counterculture readers out of the comic. He presumably didn't want them 'dominating' 2000AD with their 'pagan power' (cover lines on a pre-Bishop 2000AD cover). He strongly disapproved of subtext in *Sláine* and axed *Finn,* even though it was actually more popular. He has given as his reason that it was too similar to *Sláine.* Of course *Finn* is radically different, but I imagine what he meant was it had a similar subversive, counterculture and pagan tone to *Sláine.* In this he would be quite correct.

In any event, many counterculture readers got the message and stopped buying *2000AD*. I guess Bishop felt more comfortable after he had 'cleansed' the comic of these disparate elements, including Megatripolis rave culture party-goers and the latter day Sláines.

I suspect today some hard-core comics fans would find Arthurian myths or indeed any of the other subtexts in Sláine not to their liking. The fact that Arthur is our country's greatest legend, loved by millions, would not impress them in the slightest. So no, I wouldn't risk writing *Treasures of Britain* today. It has to be viewed from the perspective of those halcyon days when *2000AD* had a wider and more diverse audience that was often looking for something more from comics.

Some verses from Caitlin Johnstone's song *Alien* tell me that audience is still out there today.

> *I can name more stars in the Marvel universe*
> *Than I know in the sky*
> *There are more pokemon I can tell apart*
> *Than plants I can identify*
> *My culture was strategized*
> *My culture was bastardized*
> *My culture was militarized*
> *In the parlor rooms*
> *Of monarchs, popes, and liars*
> *But you can just lie with me*
> *And be free*
> *And we'll*
> *Listen to the land*

In my researches, I had talked to Arthurian writers in Glastonbury, and I recall one of them directing me to his non-fiction book which, annoyingly, I can't recall the title of today, even though I've Googled high and low for it. One chapter really resonated with me. Most of the book was scholarly, but this particular chapter had been channelled. I'm sceptical about channelling, especially as there are so many New Age charlatans out there, but this did have a ring of truth about it. It related how in Neolithic Times, tribes worshipped their ancestors. So when the King 'died' and went into the Earth he could still be communicated with inside his mound. He was still alive, only in a different dimension.

It left a profound impression on me and that's why Arthur has a similar role in *Treasures of Britain* as a kind of psychic transmitter. An enchanted Arthur sits in the Siege Perilous, staring out at us across time and space. Morgaine his sister tells him in the concluding pages, 'As Once and Future King, you will be an inspiration to generations as yet unborn.'

Ancestor worship seems such a 'primitive' concept in our modern monotheistic religious world where we are told 'religions of the book' have all the answers. But I knew it was a subject I would have to return to one day, because it is at the heart of most ancient peoples' religions and many tribal beliefs, including the Celts.

These mysteries of ancestry would eventually lead me to the conclusion of *Sláine*.

THE CLOAK OF FEAR

Illustrated by Steve Tappin, this twelve-page story appeared between *Treasures of Britain* Part One and Part Two. Bishop had suggested that the best way to sustain long-running characters, whether it was Dredd, Strontium Dog or Sláine, was to tell extra stories about them, where we can see the hero from another point of view. We get to know what the supporting characters think of the protagonist. It was a good idea, so I came up with a tale by Ukko written in verse. Dressed as a court jester, he relates the adventure at a banquet in the Eternal Fortress. Present are Sláine, Murdach, Nest and Mor Ronne the Dung Collector.

In the story Ukko descends into a dungeon and finds a mysterious case, which despite all his best efforts as a thief, he fails to open. Finally it opens of its own accord, and inside are magical grimoires written in a foreign language, and a mysterious green cloak. This comes to life as a Fear Demon, a formidable foe because the creature knows our darkest fears. Sláine fights and eventually destroys it.

The story was actually based on a mysterious real life event. It was the early 1990s and one of my best friends I'm going to call Kaz here, because I don't want to identify his house in Colchester, had made a most strange discovery in his basement. He had been digging out a huge pile of coal and found buried deep within it a suitcase with a combination lock. He patiently tried various combinations and eventually found one that opened it (no, the combination was not 666).

Possibly Kaz was hoping it was full of used bank notes, maybe the proceeds of a robbery, because why would anyone go to such great lengths to hide a suitcase? Instead, he found inside several very old books written in French – *ancient* French. So Kaz, who speaks French, could only make out some of the words. I never got to see the books because Kaz had already sold them to an antiquarian bookshop in Colchester. However, also in the suitcase was a mysterious green cloak with a hood. The kind of robe that features in *Dungeons and Dragons* or fantasy cosplay. Kaz thought it was the kind of weird thing I might like. He was right.

It was in pristine condition, it didn't smell fusty and there were no blood or other organic stains on it. If it was worn by Satanists, they were very clean Satanists. I knew the people who owned the house before Kaz, they seemed very respectable and there were no indications that they might be secret devil worshippers or, even worse, extreme *Dungeons and Dragons* roleplayers. So I wore it sometimes at events and eventually gave it to a girlfriend who was thrilled with it, because it gave her a romantic *French Lieutenant's Woman* look.

I once wore it at a candlelit banquet I held where all my guests wore fancy dress and agreed to do a 'party piece'. My Scottish friend Tony Skinner appeared in a kilt, playing the bagpipes, and I presented him with a wonderful page of pagan artwork that Glenn had painted – the witches scene from *Demon Killer* – as my thank you for all his invaluable help on *Sláine*. He had previously presented me with a golden neck torc, identical to the one worn by Sláine.

For my part, I'd nicked a traffic cone, planted it inside the hood and appeared as Torquemada. When it was my turn, I recited my 'party piece' in verse. Sadly, I was so drunk, I could barely read my words in the dim light and the damn cone kept moving about on my head. Such are the challenges of being Torquemada.

Anyway, it gave me the idea of Ukko appearing at a banquet and telling his tale in rhyme. It made me laugh, reading it the second time around, and it's wonderfully brought to life by artist Steve Tappin. He's painted it in a broad, caricatured style that suits the story so well. Steve uses strong bright colours; it's easy to read, yet very stylish and cool. Confirmation, if it were needed, that in the post-Bisley *Horned God* era, painted artwork *can* work with the right artist and the right story.

My favourite lines are where Nest explains she overcame her fear of vile and vulgar men by having a romance with the foulest man in the castle: Mor Ronne the Dung Collector, one of my favourite characters.

Nest: Happily, now I've defeated the foe... for Mor Ronne the Dung Collector is my beau. A man who works all day with muck, a man whose personal habits make me upchuck.
Mor Ronne: Yerrr! When it comes to foulness I'm the worst!
Nest: True, darling. But make your response in verse.

KING OF HEARTS

'The real underlying currency of our world is narrative and the ability to control it... The good news is that all we need to do to reclaim our world from the controllers is to reclaim our stories. The barrier between us and freedom is as thin as a fairy tale.'

Notes From The Edge Of The Narrative Matrix by Caitlin Johnstone

Caitlin's eloquent words beautifully describe one of my motivations in writing *Sláine* and for wanting proper control over my creation. And they apply so well to *King of Hearts*, which tells the story of William Wallace from a pagan perspective.

The movie *Braveheart* (1995) had recently appeared, so it was a given that Sláine would travel in time to join William Wallace in his fight for Scotland's freedom. The medieval manuscript by Blind Harry is the source of our knowledge of Wallace, but my story needed to say something new, pagan and esoteric. And so it covers Sláine's search for the Stone of Destiny, his battle with the Knights Templar, and explores the magical concept that Wallace was a King of Scottish Hearts, a sacrificial King who must, like Sláine, go into the earth after seven years so his country can live.

Painted by Nick Percival, it's a six-part story with the emphasis on action and adventure. Looking back, I wish I'd explored the magical subtext in more depth, risky as that would have been for the reasons I've previously described.

The minimalism in words is also reflected in the minimalism of content in the art. Even so, there are some powerful, thoughtful and emotionally-charged moments, such as in the sacred grove in Strathclyde where Sláine and Wallace meet and they acknowledge their trophies of the dead. Sláine tells a despondent Wallace, 'It was your soul cry that called me through time.' There's also a refreshing critique of the Qabala: the florid and pretentious magic that overshadows the magic of the Earth Goddess.

The story, like the film, has lofty claims that Wallace was important for the Celtic revival. It reminds me of the Celtic media festival held every year in different locations across the Celtic fringe. In 1995 it was held in Fort William and I went up there for the event. I recall being in a pub near the venue and admiring a magnificent and lethal double-handed sword hanging on the wall behind the bar. It had been used in medieval campaigns against the English. 'Aye,' said the bartender, noting my English accent, 'It needs to visit England more often.' It was a line I had Sláine repeating in *King of Hearts,* 'My axe needs to visit England more often.'

Sláine and Ukko are present at Wallace's execution in London, where he undergoes the Celtic and pagan triple death by being hung, disembowelled and beheaded. Their aim is to recover his heart to bury in Scotland to 'power the Scottish soul.' Ukko is sceptical of Sláine's magical purpose.

In response to Ukko's sneering, Sláine and I lay out our stall:

'Reality is *not* made by Kings, Emperors and dynasties ... you stupid dwarf! It is a subtle thing that flows through the hearts of men and women and never stronger than through the noble heart of William Wallace.'

And consider this view from Medievalists.net:

'The movie's effect in Scotland was even more profound, and spawned a new nationalism movement. Lin Anderson, author of *Braveheart: From Hollywood to Holyrood*, explained in an interview: "It has become part of the fabric of Scotland. There was anger that people didn't know who William Wallace was, and had been cheated of their history. But whether it is myth or reality, it created an aspirational national hero at a time when we needed heroes."'

William Wallace, like King Arthur, is important as a once and future King. It's a deeply emotional story that still resonates with me when I read it today.

I think Nick must have been given an impossible deadline, because the artwork is rushed and it also appears too dark in places. I say 'appears' because it looks so much sharper when images from it are reproduced in the *Sláine* roleplaying book. The Rebellion collections from this period have poor reproduction, as I believe they acknowledge and will doubtless improve on in time. But it's clear that Nick feels a passion for the subject and its heart is in the right place.

Even so, given the artistic shortfalls, that doesn't usually save creators from negative feedback, especially when Bishop was actively encouraging fans' dissent around this time. So I was bracing myself for fall-out to *King of Hearts* and to my surprise there was none that I'm aware of. This may be because Nick was seen as a new generation of artists, or maybe because fans saw him as one of their own, so perhaps Bishop backed off. In fact, I asked one such fan about this very subject. He admitted to me that certain creators

were always seen by fans as 'off limits', and would never be criticised, no matter what they produced. This doesn't, of course, say
much for such fans' objectivity or why we should pay attention to
them.

The next artist would not be so lucky.

Encouraging 'creator baiting' seems to have emerged around
1995. Possibly because Bishop wanted rid of what he saw as *2000AD*'s
'old guard' who needed to be swept away to make way for his superior *2000AD* New Universe with new editorial approaches, stories,
writers and artists. This was very much a feature of those times
before it went the way of the Marvel New Universe and is rarely
spoken of since. In fact, it's like *2000AD*'s New Universe never
existed.

But it was certainly very real to us at the time. In 1995, Bishop,
presumably confident his 'New Universe' of stories would succeed,
was at the *Judge Dredd* film premiere and turned to one of *2000AD*'s
most loved and most popular artists. He told him with a smirk that
his time was gone and he would soon be replaced. His exact words
were more unpleasant. The artist in question related this story to
Lisa and me. It was obvious that such a calculated insult, delivered
at the *Judge Dredd* premiere of all places, still hurt.

With the William Wallace connection, this is a good place to
introduce 'Braveheart', the second contender for my biological
father alongside 'Torquemada'. He becomes relevant as Sláine
searches for his own real father and the story reaches its conclusion.
And also for his effect on the *Sláine* story.

In my mind's eye, whenever I think of my possible father today, I
see him as 'Braveheart' with that huge spear charging into battle
against the English oppressors. This is because I recall him as a
trolley bus conductor, and they had wooden poles, over twelve feet
long, which they used to connect their buses to the overhead electric
tram lines. As a boy, in those pre-health and safety days, I'd thrill to
see the young conductors chasing and having incredible 'spear

fights' with each other. I'm convinced he was amongst these latter day warriors.

I remember him more clearly at Halloween, when our families would get together. 'Braveheart' was the life and soul of the Halloween party on 'Snap Apple Night.' We had to pick apples with our teeth out of a tin bath of water. I so desperately wished he could be my full-time dad.

He was 'Braveheart' in other ways, too. I had just started attending cubs, and fell foul of a predatory, upper-class priest, Father Wace. But from the age of seven, I'd already learnt the cathartic value and necessity of retaliation. I recall discussing with my brother the best way of dealing with him. Wace was a 'poverty-poseur' who wore second-hand clothes, sometimes his dad's old suits, doubtless to impress the congregation with his bogus poverty. His three-wheeler Messerschmitt – with its cracked and sellotaped cockpit – was as filthy as he was, so there was no point in coining it. He'd never have noticed. I wanted to slash its tyres, but my brother sensibly pointed out that would be incriminating as it was parked behind the presbytery, where only a few of us had access.

So, instead, I told 'Braveheart' who decided to have 'words' with Wace. That was not an easy thing for an Irish Catholic to do, especially in those days.

The exact nature of their physical confrontation I never knew. Annoyingly, adults don't think it appropriate to tell kids the lurid details. But I never went to cubs again. I suspect their encounter was mainly physical, because 'Braveheart' wasn't really a 'words' kind of guy.

Curiously, both men were products of the Benedictine Order of monks, but in very different ways. Father Wace had been a pupil at the elite Ampleforth College, the 'Catholic Eton' run by the Benedictines. Whereas 'Braveheart' was fond of Buckfast tonic wine, produced by the Benedictines, despite its notoriety for encouraging violence.

In a confrontation between these two alumni of the Benedictines, my money would be on the man who drank 'Bucky'.

It was well worth the aftermath, when Wace called me 'a wicked
little liar' in front of the other altar boys. I had to leave their Guild of
St Stephen. Judging by his red-faced fury, Wace had received a well-
deserved beating.

'Braveheart' showed me that people in positions of power can
and must be challenged, no matter what the odds. He confirmed my
own belief to never 'shut up and take it', even if speaking out gets
you thrown out. Whistleblowing, for me, is a useful form of retaliation if a physical confrontation is unlikely to have the desired
outcome. In fact, my original title for my *2000AD* series *Greysuit*,
about a rogue secret agent uncovering real life crimes, was *The
Whistleblower*.

'Braveheart' was a huge influence on *Sláine* and on me. He was
the role model I needed as a boy. Someone who would stand up to
the oppressors and charge into battle roaring, 'Freedom!'

26

MY MUSE WAS NOT AMUSED

The Grail story that followed came in two parts: *The Grail War* and *Secret of the Grail*, both illustrated by Steve Tappin. It was set in the South of France in the Pays Cathare: Cathar Country. If you're not familiar with it, check out Google images and you will see it truly is the ultimate in heroic fantasy, the real life counterpart of *Game of Thrones*, and a worthy setting for what would be the final *Sláine* adventure in time. Or look up *Castles* by supreme fantasy artist Alan Lee. Or check out the popular board game *Carcassonne*.

I've travelled all over this mysterious and magical land. Starting with Montpellier on the coast, where two French artists lived: Olivier Ledroit and the late Eric Larnoy, both of whom I worked with. Then west, towards the beautiful but touristy Carcassone, and beyond, to the grim and sinister Montreal. Finally north, to the mysterious Najac. It may look beautiful today, but there was a time when this faerie-tale, sunlit land was drenched in blood and the subject of a horrific massacre, as the Northern French Crusaders, led by the monstrous Simon De Montfort, wiped out the 'heretical' Cathars. With its mysterious Grail connection linking it to the Celts,

Cathar Country or Occitania surely ticks all the boxes for fantasy fans. And that includes, of course, *2000AD* fans.

My muse was also very keen for me to write it, because I'd – rather reluctantly – become drawn into my own real life mystery adventure about the Cathars. If I ever got around to novelising it, it would firmly be in the Dan Brown genre. I referred to it briefly in an earlier chapter: when I'd given talks about being 'haunted' by the Cathars at the Psychic Questing Conference.

So it's necessary here to give a brief summary of the Cathars, aka The Pure Ones, aka Gnostics. Regarded today as New Age icons, they believed reproduction was evil, as it meant another soul would be reincarnated on Earth, which they saw as Hell. A belief they are not alone in. They rejected the Catholic Church as Satanic and the Church said the same thing about them.

> They criticised the Church heavily for the hypocrisy, greed and lechery of its clergy and the Church's acquisition of land and wealth. *World History Encyclopaedia*

So nothing's really changed since the twelfth century. They also believed in reincarnation. There's considerable evidence that the Cathars were part of a 'black magic' continuum throughout history, although that doesn't in any way validate their Catholic persecutors.

Gnostic concepts, like believing reproduction is evil, leads inevitably, to strange and dangerous cults. Heaven's Gate, the suicide cult, was a modern day neo-Cathar UFO religion. Catharism was also the basis for Aleister Crowley's beliefs. His black mass is a Gnostic mass. It's a great pity, because the original idea of Gnosticism – once the earliest and gentlest form of Christianity – means we can find true knowledge and spirituality inside ourselves rather than from Abrahamic 'religions of the book'. However, it's also claimed that such self-knowledge is dangerous, and these and numerous other examples I could give you are hardly a good advert.

As a boy, I'd become involved with a dubious and scary Cathar revival cult, probably inspired by Crowley. Whatever else, my childhood was not dull. Later, that encounter would inspire my French series *Claudia: Vampire Knight*, following the writer's golden rule: write about your own experiences. Similarly, being 'haunted' by the Cathars in modern-day South of France, had to be useful background material for a *Sláine* story featuring the faerie world of Occitania.

And so to the Grail saga.

Let's begin with the art. Particularly because it was unjustly and *malevolently* criticised and a theme of *Sláine* is about fighting injustice. So I'm not going to ignore injustice when it's in my own backyard.

I'd seen Steve Tappin's *Cloak of Evil*, and I'm still hugely impressed by it. But it was humorous, and with a saga like *Sláine*, with readers' high expectations, I needed to be sure he was right for this story. Accordingly, Steve sent me a general heroic fantasy page of strip art: a scene of warriors fighting in the snow. It was a masterpiece. Easily comparable to the best of Simon Bisley and Dermot Power. It was like Frank Frazetta, come to life. I was blown away by it.

Steve's subsequent style on the Grail stories was fine but not in the same league as this excellent page. Of course it's quite commonplace for an artist's regular work to be different to their showreel art. Thus, I'm still mystified by one artist I worked with whose back catalogue showed he had a fine and delicate line, nothing like the rather crude black line on the story he drew for me. Similarly, a very popular *2000AD* artist introduced me to his good friend, who was a new comics artist. This artist produced two sample pages for me, which were brilliant. Then, when he got the gig, the standard of his artwork mysteriously dropped like a stone overnight, and looked amateur and stiff, disguised under a coating of thick paint. I'm pretty certain the

2000AD artist had, at the very least, 'helped him' with the sample pages.

Such are the perils of choosing an artist. It's really an editor's job to 'police' artwork rather than just accept it. So we have to add 'art detective' to the list of skills a comics editor needs.

In the case of Steve's art, there was no major drop. His work was highly professional. His storytelling was first rate. His attention to detail was good. Some scenes were incredibly imaginative. His historical accuracy was also good. Certainly better than the depiction of the Normans in *Lord of Misrule*, the Romans in *Demon Killer*, and the Knights in *King of Hearts*. Images could be boosted here and there, and it was a little stiff, especially at the beginning: hardly surprising with such a prestigious gig. But the art starts to loosen up from episode two. Sláine is not always as charismatic and expressive as he might have been, but that's true for other *Sláine* artists, too. And the readers generally accept this. Also the Grail Master – the Dark Phoenix – needed boosting initially.

But, all in all, Steve did a very professional job. Not in the Frazetta class of his sample page, but still very good. It's unrealistic to expect *The Horned God* or *Treasures of Britain* standard every week, every story, because artists like Bisley and Power were giving the publisher their art for a fraction of its true value. They were being exploited. Sometimes it will happen – when a new artist wants to make a name for themselves or needs something spectacular for their portfolio – but the rest of the time we all have to be realistic and recognise we get what the publisher pays for. Don't expect caviar if they're only paying for fish fingers. It's also clear Steve had put a lot of hard work and enthusiasm into his work. That was the positive feedback I got from ordinary readers and it's how I feel looking at the pages today.

So well done, Steve. I'm sorry it's taken so long for your pages to get the recognition they deserve.

A spoiler alert now.

In a moment, I move onto the story, which has some shock revelations. So if you're intending to read the Cathar story for the first time, you may wish to skip the next few pages.

Steve's depiction of the leader of the Guild of Varlets, Cutpurses and Mendicants is superb! A self-important, Fagan-like dwarf, even more crooked and twisted than Ukko, who has applied to join his Guild. And that takes us into the story as well. I laughed out loud at the interview where he explains most of his work is in marital investigation, checking on wives' fidelity:

'For this is the era of courtly love when troubadours sing of unrequited passions, of melting hearts and plighting troths. To put it bluntly, Ukko, they're all at it.'

Ukko proves troth-plighting is definitely going on and is then assigned the task of digging up the dirt on Simon De Montfort, the savage leader of the crusade. I thought all this was very *Blackadder*.

Meanwhile Sláine – now a mercenary – learns from a troubadour that the Grail stone is a seed from the womb of the Goddess used to fertilise the dead world of Earth where the Cyth were held prisoner. A stone that is sought by all sides in the conflict.

I'd forgotten so much of the story until I re-read it in order to write this book. It includes an earth-shattering revelation that Niamh has reincarnated in this world! There's a scene where her spirit appears to Sláine. Simon De Montfort has disappeared and Sláine asks where he has gone.

Niamh replies, 'I am Simon De Montfort'.

Wow! That took me aback.

She goes on to reveal that she needed a man's body 'to destroy the Cathars who are against life against Earth. Whatever I call myself, that's just *the name of my sword.*'

I could get behind Niamh/Simon De Montfort. I hated the Cathars with a passion that is hardly surprising, given my boyhood.

But Sláine tells Niamh that she wore the mask of the evil De Montfort too well, until she *became* the mask. This sequence dramatises an uncomfortable but actually commonplace esoteric truth about reincarnation that few of us will be happy with. Especially me. Namely that our lives run from:

Perpetrator to Victim to Perpetrator to Victim: Positive to Negative; Male to Female; Mother to Son, to Father to Daughter ... and so on.

Whether the principle of reincarnation includes bosses, friends and colleagues, I don't know. Or even – God help us – editors. I pray not.

But there's a constant cycle, reversal and interchange between lives and roles that makes reincarnation a difficult subject to fully absorb, and we're probably not meant to. It's made all the more difficult because there is no universally agreed grammar or vocabulary on reincarnation. Perhaps in Eastern religions, but not in the Western tradition. So we're left with endless questions and concerns. If you'd rather dismiss it all as complete bollocks, you've got my vote. Who needs that stuff in your life? Or the next life? And the one after that? Unfortunately, I would say from my own experience, it's still true. I often wish it wasn't. If you're looking for a good introduction to the subject, I'd recommend the late Roger Woolger's *Other Lives, Other Selves*, seen from a Jungian point of view. I've attended one of his seminars, and I can tell you Roger and his work are very grounded and sensible to read. There's no drippy New Age fantasies here. It will leave you wondering just how relevant it could be to your life.

Returning to Simon De Montfort: it must have been equally hard for this monster to have awoken from a hideous 'dream' where, 'I had the body of a woman!' Those are the kind of dramatic and dangerous challenges and betrayals that fantasy and science fiction movies are replete with, and it's why I like it. Transgender dramas are perhaps easier to write about today than two decades ago, but it was still a legitimate subject back then. I always wanted *2000AD* to push the boundaries and to challenge the readers.

I think Steve Tappin handles well the revelation and the dramatic fall out that follows. And Ukko brings some real *Blackadder* comedy to the scene.

The siege of Toulouse, the City of the Grail, follows. It's well portrayed, including an excellent and meticulously drawn siege engine, which was aptly named 'Bad Neighbour'! Esclarmonde De Foix, the last of the Grail Guardians, is also perfect. Steve hits just the right note with her. And with the comedy where the head of the Guild of Varlets, Mendicants and Cutpurses absorbs the shocking news that Simon De Montfort, Hammer of the Heretics, Scourge of the Saracens, Conqueror of Occitania, *dresses up as a woman!* No, his top agent Ukko corrects him – he *becomes* a woman. They discuss the opportunities for blackmail only to be overheard by De Montfort and Sláine! I laughed out loud reading this scene again.

They escape indescribable punishments by showing Sláine and De Montfort a secret way into Toulouse to do battle with the Grail Master. This is all classic and typical *Sláine* storytelling, there's nothing unusual about it, there's nothing remiss about the artwork, even if – as I have to stress once again, it's not *The Horned God* or the *Treasures of Britain*. It's all still in the same genre, it's the reason readers enjoy heroic fantasy and it's important to bear this in mind for later.

De Montfort/Niamh realises he/she has failed in his/her life mission. By exterminating the Cathars, he/she 'gave them the very death they craved.' Sláine reassures him/her: 'You made a mistake. Life's like that. Look at Ukko – he's one big mistake.'

The story reaches a powerful conclusion with the death of De Montfort and some esoteric twists and turns that lead us on to the concluding part of the saga entitled *Secret of the Grail.*

Negative reader feedback was now starting to appear in the

course of Part One, and we'll get to that shortly, but let me complete the second part of the Grail saga.

It was set in Montsegur, the legendary Grail Castle. A fabulous setting, if ever there was one, for heroic fantasy because it was here the Holy Grail was believed to have been hidden.

'A chalice chiselled from a magnificent emerald which came from Lucifer's diadem [...] This emerald chalice was used by Jesus Christ during the Last Supper [...] This sacred vessel, laden with extraordinary virtues, mysteriously disappeared after having been in the possession of the Knights of the Round Table, after which it was appropriated in some way by the Cathars.' *Legends of Montsegur Castle* - Melisande Moosong

In the Nazi era, Otta Rahn was recruited by Heinrich Himmler to find it. He has been described as the 'Nazi Indiana Jones', and the inspiration for Steven Spielberg's hero.

All this is fascinating material for a writer. Whatever you may think of it, there's surely a classic Dan Brown story in Montsegur Castle, and it's already inspired numerous novels. And there is also a *Sláine* story. Unless, of course, 2000AD is going through a phase where mystery, myth and magic are frowned upon and have no place. In which case, there is no place for *Sláine* either, because this is the very essence of heroic fantasy.

The story begins with a satisfying reprise of what has gone before, well executed by Steve with an imaginative and confident rendering of a typical *Dungeons and Dragons* scene, where key characters meet up in a bar. There's a reference to Ireland being over-run by bards because they don't have to pay taxes, clearly drawing on recent times for inspiration! In fact this concluding part of the saga really does feel like classic *Dungeons and Dragons,* very much in the tradition of those early black and white *Sláine Diceman* stories. Like other *Sláine* stories, I imagine this must have been used in many a gaming module.

Once again there is excellent comedy where the Guild Master is now planning to expand into the travel business with pilgrim package holidays, but Ukko turns down the job of being senior sales director to help save Sláine from Crom-Cruach. More action follows as Sláine seeks the Grail Stone, which will heal Niamh. It's in the centre of a mystical circular rose window.

Steve's art is really gaining in confidence now. Facial expressions are stronger. There are some beautifully painted images. There's a superb rendering of the Faerie castle of Montsegur at the beginning of episode seven.

Events lead to Sláine's trial for attempting to steal the Grail Stone while pretending to search for his eternal love. The trial was a useful way to reprise on key events in his life. It is interrupted by the arrival of the Crusaders, who besiege the castle. Under the command of their Bishop Engineer (a real life character) they hurl heads and bodies through the air from a stone gun known as 'God's Revenge'. Meanwhile, Sláine breaks free from his chains to prevent a sinister rival from taking the Stone.

The last two episodes Steve illustrated are ones I particularly enjoyed. Sláine, Ukko and co. sneak past the Bishop Engineer with sfx lettering Steve added: 'Tippy Toe' and 'Creep'. There's the intel-lectual climax exploring the subtext of the saga, followed by Sláine warping out to defeat the Dark Phoenix, now much more monstrous. Then an El Rider comes out of the Earth to reclaim the Stone on behalf of the Goddess.

The sacrificial death of Esclarmonde de Foix, the Chatelaine of Montsegur, a real life character, is a moment of deep emotion and tragedy in the tradition of the death of William Wallace.

It's followed by a painting of a beautiful blazing Phoenix, symbol of death and rebirth, rising from the ashes of its own destruction and towering over the Castle of Montsegur.

My wife Lisa had never seen the Grail saga before, but she looked through the second part as I completed this chapter. Her comments were:

> 'Wow! I really like it. It's incredible, beautiful and accessible. Inventive use of light and space and architecture so you never get bored. This guy's put a lot of work into it.'

However, this legendary saga, set in the magical world of Faerie – of Troubadours, Knights, Elves, Damsels, Chatelaines, Castles, Dragons and the Phoenix – had just one denizen missing, one creature I had overlooked.

Trolls.

And now they came crawling out from under their bridges. Orchestrated by the Troll Master Bishop, who ignored the golden rule: 'Do not feed the Trolls'. They set out to seriously burn both Steve and me on the 2000AD letters page, to the considerable surprise of ordinary readers. And to myself. My muse was not amused.

I'm not talking about constructive criticism, as I'm sure some valid points were made as well. As I've indicated, there are places where this *Sláine* story could be improved in story and art. There is always something that can be better. But a Troll is not genuinely interested in the story or how the writer or artist might improve it. The mark of a Troll is that he's angry with life and you can always recognise him in the abusive tone of his words. He needs to inflict his anger on someone or something. The Troll may have taken a particular dislike to a particular story or creator, just like we might all do, but, inflamed by his anger, he invariably crosses boundaries into personal abuse. And the Troll Master, too, was equally angry with life, so they made for fine bedfellows.

Trolls today are irrelevant because they no longer have such a platform. 2000AD is more sensible today.

But at this time, Bishop gave their derisory comments pride of place. He was doing a Gerald Ratner, who famously described his jewellery as 'total crap' and his earrings as 'cheaper than an M&S prawn sandwich but probably wouldn't last as long.' As a result, his company nearly collapsed. Bishop's hatred of his own commissioned stories is like Ratner featuring his jewellery on one page of his catalogue and on the opposite page printing customers' comments about how crap his products are.

I'm sure it was one of many factors responsible for the massive drop in 2000AD's circulation at this time.

Normal readers were confused and puzzled by the venom of the Trolls, especially *Sláine* fans who liked the story, even if it wasn't *The Horned God*. But they were actually being told *not* to like this story. It was a clear message: first, the editor does not like this story and second, he wants *Sláine* and 2000AD's creator out of the comic.

This was the third attempted coup against *Sláine*. But Bishop would succeed where the two previous coups had failed.

I was told that time-travelling *Sláine* sagas – with all their colourful splendour, richness of characters, complexity, not to mention opportunities for comedy, an essential ingredient for the saga from episode one – were to end forthwith. Sláine must return to his tribe.

Steve Tappin never worked for 2000AD again.

But he has risen up, like a phoenix from the ashes, to a great career in other media.

I was next on the Troll Master's list.

PART IV
RETURN OF THE KING

27

PAIN IN THE AXE

I
t might seem a good thing for Sláine to return to his tribe. I'd
covered the key Celtic themes and it was reasonable that the
Goddess would now send him home. Although, there were
still some Celtic historic stories that readers were suggesting to me.
The one I recall vividly, and was reminded of recently, was the
incredible story of Grace O'Malley, the Irish pirate queen. She came
from Mayo, my mother's county on the west coast of Ireland, and
made a legendary voyage up the Thames to confront Queen Eliza-
beth I. Discovering a connection for *Sláine* would have been an
exciting creative challenge, and if I found the right one it would have
brought out some new aspect of Sláine's character; just as it does
when Doctor Who meets different historical characters.

Anyway, it was not to be. And I could see a certain superficial
logic. Most *Dredd* stories are set in Mega-City, so why not have
Sláine back with his tribe? Yet there are huge differences between
the two series *signposted in giant capital letters* but which Bishop had
clearly overlooked. It's hard explaining to an editor who didn't really
understand the story or why the readers like it. But here's a reprise
of my reasoning:

I'd already made it clear at the beginning of *Demon Killer* that nothing – repeat *nothing* – happened after Sláine was High King and defeated the old Horned God, Slough Feg. Unlike Dredd, he is *not* at war with his own people or anyone else. He has *won* a Great Peace for his tribe. That's why he's such a hero: not by oppressing his people, but saving them. I'd even made a joke of how bored he was by peace!

That was *why* he moved on. So the character was now returning to stasis: he was not moving forward, not evolving, which the readers were used to – and expected. And the wide range of artists that editorial chose, all good but with strongly contrasting and different styles, emphasises how *directionless* this period was. Readers rightly look for continuity, not just in the writing and the world, but also in the visuals.

Even so, there could still be external and internal threats, although there was nothing as momentous as the events in *The Horned God*, which had been built up over so many years. So I decided I would make the best of it, play by editorial rules, and write to their flawed brief.

These stories (and *The Secret Commonwealth* that followed) have been reprinted under the title of *Lord of the Beasts*, the premier story by Raphael Garres. The script was inspired by a strange dream I had about a ferocious warrior, and editorial found the perfect match for my words with Raphael's art. He is a master of fully painted art, which undoubtedly resonated with readers, especially Simon Bisley fans. But his work is looser, actually incredibly loose here, which suited the warp spasm in the story.

It is still astonishing to look at. If we had continued with Raphael, it would have taken *Sláine* in a new direction, perhaps competing with Bisley's *Horned God*. But that style of story was heavily dependant on artwork as powerful as Raphael's.

Unfortunately, Raphael wasn't available for more episodes. And so there was a subsequent crunch of gears, with *Kai* painted by Paul Staples, though definitely funny and exciting and a pleasure to read.

I wrote it with Debbie Gallagher, a talented writer I had worked with on a very successful Games Workshop series called *The Redeemer*: a demented Inquisitor who had a blazing brazier of coals on his head!

I recall Debbie and I were inspired by a visit to the small estuary town of Wivenhoe near Colchester, and some eccentric characters we met there, including a lady in the local delicatessen who didn't know how to cut cheese with a cheesewire. We speculated that she was maybe a sea demon and her flipper couldn't grip the wire cutter. Later, we sat down in the large and empty village pub and were suddenly surrounded by locals sitting incredibly close to us. It's a scene we feature in the story. We fantasised that the Fomorians had come out of the sea and were disguised as humans, but didn't really understand human behaviour. Thus we had one sea demon wearing a human skin and disguised with heavy make-up as a human female. This demon was worried that Sláine, with his amorous reputation, might make a lecherous pass at her. Mercifully, her virtue was never in any danger.

I had high hopes that with *The Banishing* and *The Triple Death*, illustrated by Wayne Reynolds – our artist on *The Redeemer* – *Sláine* would find favour with the readers. I like Wayne's work a lot. And both stories still make me laugh when I read them today. Ukko is particularly on form! It requires good artwork to make a humorous script work. But feedback from editorial was lukewarm.

So I asked readers today what their thoughts were on Wayne's art.

Here's Jock Savage:

'That ubiquity and the sense that anyone could have a go at *Sláine* definitely affected the strip's prestige. The appearance of a new *Sláine* strip went from being an event - a rare show-case for the best *2000AD* had to offer - to something I took for granted.

'He had a really slick style but his figure work and layouts were still quite raw. I like his work, but it's definitely line-art that's been coloured-in. After the lush painted aesthetic of Bisley, Fabry and Power, that approach is only ever going to feel like a disappointment

'A prestige strip like *Sláine* wasn't the place for anyone to be ironing out the wrinkles in their art. But that's an inevitable consequence of the questionable editorial decision to make *Sláine* a permanent fixture in the comic for three years.'

Anthony Lewis: 'Totally agree with the comments I've seen. Reynolds' figure work wasn't good enough and the faces didn't seem right to me.'

Other readers were more positive. Markpa Jackson:

'I thought his work was a little eclipsed by some wonderful moments of otherworldliness around that time, especially Garres and Siku. But the high-contrast style worked particularly well with the skeletal warriors in Triple Death and the time worm, and told both stories cleanly.'

Dr13thebeast: 'I remember a lot of hype about his work in *2000AD* and I enjoyed his *Sláine*, I'd love to see more.'

Andrew McIlwaine: 'Wayne Reynolds was Sarmaith (top notch) like a gritty British Rich Corben.'

I think everyone makes valuable points. But Jock is absolutely right: *Sláine* had become a victim of its own success and we could not always match the readers' expectations.

If it had been up to me, I would have stayed with Wayne. He was a safe bet at a time when the character and the comic desperately needed safe bets. He is known and respected as an established sword and sorcery artist, he had a commitment to *Sláine* that the other artists lacked, and continuity and good storytelling are paramount. But after choosing Steve Tappin, I was in no position to insist, and my recollection is that editorial felt otherwise and they were now guiding *Sláine's* destiny.

Next, I was told by editorial that the readers loved the following *Sláine* story *The Swan Children*, based on the pagan story of Children of Lir. The ending where the beautiful swans are baptised by a priest and turn back into ancient decaying humans still makes me angry. Its success was all the more remarkable because it was beautifully painted in a radically different style by Siku, who is a Christian minister. Siku declined to do more *Sláine* because it wasn't in tune with his beliefs, which I understood and respected. But I suggested to editorial that I could write more emotional stories like the Children of Lir. There's hardly any shortage of them in the Celtic mythos. No, I was told emphatically, despite its popularity, they didn't want strong emotion in *Sláine*.

This kind of feedback made me wonder then and now at their peculiar motivation. Why would you want to dilute the power of a story? Was it *too* sad? Perhaps they really were determined to move *Sláine* – and presumably the whole comic – away from the strong emotions for which it was famous, and which were certainly my hallmark.

Macha by Paul Staples, a very funny, exciting and poignant tale, and the excellent *Beyond* by Greg Staples, a different style again, completed this phase. Greg's fully painted art is of the highest possible standard, but the contrast with other artists' styles couldn't be greater. It's like lining up a Rolls Royce alongside a Volkswagen – both excellent vehicles, fit for purpose, but they really should not be compared with each other.

The result is a mishmash of a collection. If there was any logic to the wide variety of artists, it must have been whoever happened to be available, whoever had the time to fit it in into their busy schedule, which is definitely not the best way forward with a premier character like Sláine.

It was all smoke and mirrors and I found it impossible to make sense of their story vision for *Sláine* and the comic, despite meeting up with editorial to try and understand them. I took Bishop out to lunch at my expense and asked him outright what I needed to do, what I needed to change, to tick all the boxes with him. He told me I used too many ellipses in my dialogue ...

I formed the impression that whatever I did, they were not really happy and – perhaps because I was the creator of the comic – they were easing me out slowly, so there could be no complaints from the readers or from their Egmont bosses. If you find that strange, it's not. This kind of thing happens all the time in comics, in media, or as indeed, anywhere in life.

But perhaps I'm being unfair and these constant shifts in direction were really about editorial desperately, searching for 'The One'. The one story and the one artist that would finally be a smash hit with the readers.

Finally, Dave Bishop announced triumphantly he had found 'The One'. The answer to all our problems. An artist with an exciting, radical new look that would bring new energy to the comic. An artist who, he proudly and confidently assured me, would eclipse all the other heroic fantasy artists I had worked with and was *born* to draw *Sláine*!

Dave certainly knew how to pitch an artist to a writer! I remember excitedly looking forward to examples of 'The One', this amazing new talent that he was crazy about.

It was David Bircham.

28

AXED!

'In the late 17th century, a Scottish minister went looking for supernatural creatures of "a middle nature betwixt man and angel." Robert Kirk roamed the Highlands, talking to his parishioners and other country folk about their encounters with fairies, wraiths, elves, doppelgangers, and other agents of the spirit world.' From *The Secret Commonwealth of Elves, Fauns and Fairies* by Robert Kirk

In his famous book, *The Secret Commonwealth*, Kirk describes how a sorcerer may make contact with the creatures of the El Worlds:

'The usual method for a curious person to get a transient sight of this otherwise invisible Crew of Subterraneans is to put his left foot under the Wizard's right foot, and the Seer's hand is put on the Inquirer's head ... Then will he see a Multitude of Wights, like furious hardy men, flocking to him from all quarters, as thick as atoms in the air.'

Kirk describes many of the denizens of the underworld, such as

'The Reflex Man, a Co-Walker, every way like the man, as a twin brother and companion, haunting him as his shadow...'

It's a complex account, hard to read in the original, and I once had a modern day translation that made it more accessible. It was a book I'd been thinking about for years and how it might be dramatised. At a Celtic film festival, a Scottish documentary filmmaker and I even had a meeting with a leading Scottish TV producer to discuss it. We explained the premise of *The Secret Commonwealth* and talked about putting together a proposal for a TV documentary. The producer sounded keen and we went away to consider it further. I spent some time really studying the material but I just couldn't get the right angle to make it fly.

So when Bishop finally realised that Sláine needed to come out of stasis and feature in the kind of classic long-running *Sláine* saga the readers wanted, rather than the less satisfying shorter stories, I thought immediately of the fantastic world of Robert Kirk. But, like the Cathar story, it would require great artistic sensitivity; a feeling for – and even a profound knowledge of – the world of Faerie. It would be the comics equivalent of artists like Brian Froud, designer of *The Dark Crystal* and *Labyrinth* or Alan Lee, designer on *Lord of the Rings*. To aim that high would, of course, be impossible – but that was the style, the tone, *the look*, that was needed.

And it was feasible. Comics do *not* have to settle for third best. Despite that being the subliminal message British readers get to this day. There were a number of *Games Workshop* artists around at that time who could have been approached. For example, Adrian Smith, the co-creator of my French fantasy series *Broz*. He had previously painted some excellent covers for *Toxic*. He is well worth a look, as his art is amazing.

But there was no way I was going to suggest *any* artist to *2000AD*, not after the Grail debacle It would be unfair to the artist, whose career could be destroyed by their unpleasant Trolls. It had to be an artist they chose.

The artist Bishop was enthusiastically behind as his 'hot, brand new discovery' was David Bircham. He was 'The One'.

When I saw sample pages, my heart sank. David is a very talented artist and we would later talk about doing a crime comic series together, but he did not seem right for classic heroic fantasy like *Sláine*.

If Steve Tappin and Wayne Reynolds' work, two established fantasy artists, was 'wrong', how could David Bircham's approach possibly be right?

Aware that if it went down badly with the readers, the story and even the character itself would be dead in the water, I felt I had to intervene. I made a special visit to *2000AD* to discuss it.

I was not reassured. Bishop told me with a grin that Dave Bircham had not even looked at past *Sláine* stories, like episode one by Angela or *The Horned God*. You cannot possibly build on and improve a successful fictional character unless you first study its *foundations*. Where and how it all began.

Dave Bircham, fired up with encouragement from Bishop, intended to find his own unique path. And he would be painting it on computer – still unusual at that time – which would somehow make it 'revolutionary'.

Bishop not only thought Dave Bircham's disinterest in looking at previous *Sláines* was a good idea, but was also highly amused by it. When I questioned his judgment, he dismissively waved aside my concerns.

'Trust me,' he said, grinning.

Writing the scripts was not a happy experience. Editorial sought to impose their supposedly superior storytelling skills over mine. Thus, I wanted to open with a strong epic scene, like the opening hook in an action movie, but they wanted more build up. I believe they were referring to text novel rules, perhaps from some writer's guild, but that doesn't apply to a weekly comic where the reader needs story satisfaction within the episode.

The typically strange Celtic ways that Robert Kirk made contact with the Secret Commonwealth – such as looking backwards between your legs – were lost on editorial and they regarded them as stupid. There was really no point in trying to explain that *Sláine* is based on its own unique *real* magic and not on the followers of Lord Dunsany: the magic novels and tales that editorial was familiar with. Those writers are all brilliant, but it's emphatically *not* Sláine's path. *Real* magic gives the story its own unique frisson, which the readers will sense, even if it's beyond editorial's comprehension.

In writing the story, I remember being inspired by the magical characters at *The Green Gathering* festival. In particular, the images of Medb with cloven hooves. And just soaking up that joyous pagan atmosphere and bringing it into *The Secret Commonwealth* made a difference. With Medb as the villain, the stories hold up and are generally well regarded. They somehow survived the bruising editorial intrusions and the art debacle.

But reader reaction to Dave Bircham's art was everything I feared. As one fan reviewer put it,

> 'It is jawdroppingly awful. No kidding, friends, this is the one that nobody can stand. Four months of eyekicking artwork burying what might have been an interesting plot somewhere. It earned the instant derision of fandom when it first appeared, and my kids immediately cried foul when they saw it. David Bircham is the art droid responsible for this mess.'

I can't quarrel with this description, one of many along those lines. It's harsh, but it's valid. So there's no point in going through the individual episodes and commenting on the stories and the art and talking about what might have been. The whole thing is an expensive write-off. A waste of everybody's time, money and energy, including the readers.

But the reviewer is missing an important point that he was not aware of. It's *the editor* who is responsible for this mess. Emphatically not the artist.

Dave Bircham was the patsy. He's an *extremely good* artist – but he was not properly briefed and directed.

Let me stress an important point: Dave Bircham, Steve Tappin and I were all professional freelances who made a precarious living by our wits. We were not there to be the catspaw of a salaried editor with a vindictive agenda.

Bishop knew *exactly* what the readers wanted art-wise from feedback on Raphael Garres, Wayne Reynolds, Siku, and Paul Staples. *Exactly.* Why choose an artist that is so diametrically different? Why not, at the very least, provide him with the past stories that he needed to absorb? Or test him out first on a short story and get reader feedback, just to be sure?

Okay, if he made a mistake, why not acknowledge it? Just as I acknowledge I made a mistake in trusting Bishop. I should have refused to continue. Maybe exited the series, although it's entirely possible *that* was they wanted. They might well have continued with Dave Bircham working with a new *Sláine* writer. It's one of the ways these things are done.

There are only three explanations for this new debacle.

Firstly, it was an error of judgement. That could be put down to a lack of training. John Wagner and myself were trained as sub-editors at publisher D.C. Thomson's. We were taught to be professionals, to be encouraging in our dealings with freelances and were reprimanded when our letters to creators were too cold, too curt, or too aggressive. We were taught to pay great attention to what *the readers alone* wanted.

Secondly, as the comic's sales continued to drop, Bishop was planning to leave.

Thirdly, that it was a way of killing off *Sláine* and getting me out of the comic. Presumably so he could still pursue his new-look or

New Universe *2000AD*, free from the legacies of the past. He may have still genuinely believed in his new vision for the comic and felt what he saw as 'the Old Guard' were a burden who were holding him back from success. After all, as I mentioned earlier, he had previously told one of *2000AD's* most loved and most successful artists that his days were numbered.

I actually think it's healthy that I can't figure Bishop out. I'd be worried about myself if I could. So let the facts speak for themselves: Dave Bircham never worked for *2000AD* again.

And *Sláine* was axed.

I had submitted another serial to Bishop, called *The Resurrectionist*. It went through several versions, which he actively encouraged me to write, so I thought he was genuine and serious, but he then stalled endlessly on making a final decision.

That's every freelances' nightmare: being given 'busy work' when the editor has no real intention of buying and is stringing you along, deliberately wasting your time for whatever dubious reason – which can include pure vindictiveness.

It happens more often than you might imagine.

But freelances are usually good at sniffing out time-wasting editors. The danger comes if you are too hungry for work or too keen on your story. Then you ignore those warning signs at your peril – as I did. Bishop is not alone, I can think of at least two other editors who pulled this stroke. When I finally pressed him hard, he said quite casually that he was rejecting *The Resurrectionist* because it featured time running backwards, a concept that had already appeared in science fiction novels and was therefore not original.

Retitled as *Requiem: Vampire Knight*, and with art by Olivier Ledroit, it has gone on to be a bestseller in France, still in print to this day. It sells in various European editions and in Brazil, too, and there is a spin-off series *Claudia: Vampire Knight*. Olivier and I own the English language digital comic strip rights to *Requiem*, and I am pleased to say that the digital edition sells well, too.

The royalties I receive on *Requiem* exceed *all* the royalties for a lifetime's work on *2000AD*, because Rebellion do not pay proper royalties.

I see this through pagan eyes as balance being restored. If you prefer, you may see it as a happy coincidence.

But, where *2000AD* was concerned, I was finished, too.

29

BURYING THE HATCHET

I really thought my time on *2000AD* was over, and I concentrated on work elsewhere.

But once Dave Bishop had gone, there was an unexpected and welcome change of direction.

Andy Diggle had taken over as editor and remarkably, he seemed keen to get *Sláine* back in the comic. I think that speaks volumes about what had happened and the readers' ongoing love for *Sláine*, which had clearly survived *The Secret Commonwealth* and Bishop's coup.

Our past differences in the Bishop era were behind us. Instead, we had a long and positive conversation in which we explored the various challenges on *Sláine*. He acknowledged that what the readers were looking for was another epic *Sláine* saga, rather than the miscellaneous stories that Bishop had commissioned.

I told him that I'd now covered the principal Celtic legends and the cupboard was bare. It was why, I explained, I'd featured the historical dramas. They alone had the majesty and power that the readers were looking for. But there, too, the key Celtic dramas had been covered.

So it looked like we really had reached the end of the road.

It really felt like it was over.

But as Andy was so keen on *Sláine* returning, I found myself thinking, as writers do, maybe, just maybe, there was a way. There were two Irish legend possibilities, I told him. Both were long shots that would require considerable developing to work.

The first was the Phantom Island of Hy-Brasil, a mysterious disappearing island said to lie in the Atlantic Ocean, west of Ireland. It is Ireland's Atlantis and there are even theories that the country of Brazil is named after it. That kind of legend is in the same genre as *The Lost World* by Arthur Conan Doyle, *Pellucidar* by Edgar Rice Burroughs, or *She* by H. Rider Haggard. It is usually beloved of science fiction fans, but has rarely been a success in *2000AD*, as far as I know. It's a journey into the unknown and thus the dramatic pitch is different to *Judge Dredd: The Cursed Earth* where the world is still established beyond the walls of Mega City. There have been successful exceptions in *2000AD*, like *Meltdown Man*, but for the most part that sub-genre is too risky. Not least because it's taking Sláine and his readers from the familiar that they like, into a strange new world that they have to be persuaded to like. The last thing either Andy or I wanted after *Secret Commonwealth* was to take any risks.

There are various voyages to magical islands in Irish legends, usually inhabited by fantastic creatures: the voyage of St Brendan, for instance, but I decided in the end not to pursue it. Although I still hanker after Hy-Brasil and find myself thinking about it from time to time, trying to make it work. Looking for the right angle. This is not a cue for a *Sláine* wannabe writer, I hasten to add. *Sláine* is off-limits to other writers (see later).

The same applies to Tory Island, the Fomorian sea demons' portal on Earth, where the vilest, cruellest monsters emerge to wreak havoc on the world. It would be fascinating for Sláine to visit Tory Island and encounter these demons in their own world. But I would have to resist the temptation to turn it into a broad satire –

with poorly disguised demonic versions of Boris Johnson, Michael Gove and David Cameron – which would, of course, ruin *Sláine*. And *Sláine* has already visited the similar world of the Cyth, so it was better if the Fomorians invaded Ireland.

This was the subject of the second legend I decided to look at: *The Books of Invasions.*

Andy and I also agreed that it would need a new artist for this epic undertaking. It made a great difference actually having a supportive editor at *2000AD*. The first time in a very long time. After some hunting, I finally found a likely possibility: Stefano Cardoselli who worked with writer Tzvi Lebetkin. Tzvi, a long time *2000AD* fan, generously agreed to stand aside to let Stefano draw *Sláine*.

By now, Rebellion had taken over *2000AD*, Andy had moved on, and Matt Smith was the editor. Matt and I both liked Stefano's *Sláine* designs. He's a very cool artist but the real test, of course, was to try him out with a Future Shock. It's always a tough test because the Future Shock may not resonate with the artist and I think that's what happened here.

We might have tried Stefano out on a one-off *Sláine* next, but then Jason Kingsley, the co-owner of Rebellion, intervened. He preferred Clint Langley to paint *Sláine*. It was tough telling Stefano the bad news, because he had really put his heart and soul into his work, but it was a good call from Jason and absolutely the right decision.

Clint would turn *Sláine* around and give the character a fantastic new lease of life.

THE SWARMING

From a continuity point of view, *the Books of Invasions: Volume 1,* could run directly after *The Horned God.* And it certainly has the epic quality of the latter, although I miss the subtexts of *The Horned God* and the historical sagas. But exploring the complexity of the Sea Demons and the challenges Sláine must face more than makes up for it. There are the different Fomorian breeds from all over the world who have arrived in New Troy for the Swarming. There, they are officiated over by Moloch, a truly repulsive Fomorian, enhanced by a golden tear eye-ring, a great idea of Clint's. He's a character so horrendous, I actually had a nightmare about him while I was writing this chapter.

The art in the opening part, entitled *Moloch,* just gets better and better. Clint gives the saga a particular digital look that gives it the depth of painted artwork, but a clarity that it is important for comics to appeal to a wider audience, rather than just aficionados. There's a beautiful burial scene that is pure pre-Raphaelite, but which I won't elaborate on here, just in case you're not familiar with this series and are intending to read it. And Sláine looks cooler as the series develops, almost certainly because Clint is basing our hero on himself.

This was quite commonplace where *Sláine* is concerned. Thus in *The Horned God*, Sláine is easily recognisable as Simon Bisley.

Before the Swarming, Sláine says goodbye to Ukko and it will be some time before we see him again. Ukko was the mainstay of the saga up till now and he always had a valuable role where he could be used effectively: initiating nefarious schemes; challenging Sláine; providing comedy and making complex ideas accessible. But in the story that lay ahead he would have seemed 'stuck in'. Alternatively, the plot would have needed altering to accommodate him. Their parting is quite emotional because Sláine calls the dwarf his 'friend'.

Thanks to digital art, Clint was able to add extra pages for the collected edition.

Thus at the Swarming, there are two additional pages of build-up, which improves the pacing and gives the scene a real movie-style flow. A weekly comic must, by definition, give value for money. If it's too aesthetic, too slow, the readers would have said we were just producing the story for the collected edition. So this was an ideal solution, although it involved Clint in extra unpaid work. Moloch was a name I came across in a Celtic legend, but he appears to have been a villain across the whole of the legendary world, with a modern day counterpart in the Cremation of Care ceremony at Bohemian Grove in California. There, today's world leaders also worship an owl statue named Moloch. No matter what the conspiracy theorists say, I'm sure it's all harmless fun and nothing to worry about. Members have included Ronald Reagan, Herbert Hoover, Richard Nixon and George H. W. Bush.

Anyway, I drew on both ancient and modern traditions for the Swarming. Moloch is using child sacrifice to summon a monstrous creature from the Stars – the Aten. I was basing the being on the Aten, the Sun God of the Pharaoh Akhenaten, husband of Queen Nefertiti. Akhenaten (meaning 'Effective for the Aten') was a physically strange creature with a distorted head and an almost female body. Suggestions that he suffered from some genetic condition have proved inconclusive. There is great potential in his weird appearance for a fantasy writer and his ugliness contrasts with his wife's renowned beauty. He certainly acted oddly. During his reign he attempted to do away with the multiple Gods of the traditional Egyptian religion and replaced them with just one deity. Atenism is a rare example of a monotheistic religion in ancient times and it's possibly even the forerunner of the God of the Old Testament. Thus Freud believed that Moses was an Egyptian priest and that Yahweh was the Aten. I return to this Egyptian connection in Part Two of Volume I.

Sláine saves the children, and Part One concludes with a savage battle between Sláine and Moloch and a deeply emotional and savage ending. I so wanted to see Moloch die!

But I had to wait for Part Two – *Golamh* – where Moloch gets what he so richly deserves. Sláine's expressions are a joy to behold. Clint is acting out every pose – I believe his partner took photos of him – and it really pays off. The potential for artists to become actors in their own strips is something that Clint pioneers, certainly for this generation. But before Moloch dies, he prophesies that there will be a new wave of Invaders of Ireland. They are the children of Atlantis come to reclaim their ancestral home, the dread of Europe!

There are references to Golamh, the monster of this story, in Celtic lore. Thus there is Golamh Head off the coast of Galway, suggestive of a possible Atlantean connection.

When the leaders of the Invaders appear, the mysterious Gael and the beautiful Scota, they are both visually striking. Gael has a strange hood over his head, but Scota steals the show. She has a sumptuous look that is extraordinary to see in a weekly comic. She has a glamour that I've previously only seen in Hollywood epics like *Cleopatra*.

And rightly so, because Scota is Meritaten, the daughter of Akhenaten and Nefertiti, after whom Scotland is named. I used *Kingdom of the Ark* by Lorraine Evans as a key source. I'd previously written about Scota in my French series *Biankha*, illustrated by Cinzia De Felice. Biankha is a play on the Egyptian word 'ankh'.

Scota's story – her name means 'pirate' – underlies one of my objectives in *Sláine*, which is to romanticise the legends of Britain and Ireland that all too often fail to reach a wide audience. King Arthur is an exception, but the other stories of Celtic myths don't have the wider following they deserve. Cuchulain, Brutus of Troy, Scota, and the Mabinogion, are all the equals of Hercules, Jason and other Greek myths. Yet even today, it would be easier to get a comic book or a film about Hercules or the Greek Gods off the ground than one on Ireland's greatest fantasy hero, Cuchulain. Because we are conditioned to believe our own culture is secondary, actually *inferior* to the dominant establishment Greek and Roman culture.

To take this saga as a case in point, Gael is described in the original sagas as a 'Golamh', an unnatural creature, and relates how he was bitten by a serpent while fighting as a mercenary in Egypt. That is what inspired my story. It's surprising to me that Gael – the father of the Gaelic nations of Irish and Scots – has never been commemorated in fiction before.

Fantastic extra pages added by Clint for the book edition really bring out the cinematic and 'wide screen' nature of the saga. Gael's cloak is thrown back and we see he has a sea devil parasite living on his back, turning him into a Golamh! The earliest Babylonian legends show such fish-men as bringing humans 'civilisation'.

It was an ambitious saga, because it featured Atlantean weaponry such as 'fire-staffs'. I'd previously featured them in the Dark Gods, but they need colour to really do them justice. I'd originally been inspired by the Brothers Hildebrandt fantastic art in *Urshurak* to see the visual potential in magical 'guns' but now at last, Clint's art was finally a match for them.

The volume concludes with an epic battle between Sláine with his Tribes of the Earth Goddess, and the Atlanteans, directed by their Golamhs. Sláine has ignored his corrupt King Sethor and taken control. There looks like a cast of thousands involved! That is no easy task in a comic, unlike in a movie such as *Braveheart* where Mel Gibson can call on the Irish army as extras to create a vast battle panorama.

Looking through these brilliant pages, there is only one thing missing: a soundtrack! The ubiquitous *Carmina Burana* by Carl Orff is the obvious contender, but it's been so over-used in movies now, alongside similar rousing music, that it's lost much of its impact. I'd favour an adaption of Carl Orff's *Triumph of Aphrodite*, or some Heavy Metal music to enhance these pages further.

THE PARTING OF THE CLANS

Volume 2 begins with Part Three: *Scota*. The epic battle continues with the Treasures of the Goddess being used against the Atlanteans. But there are still close-up moments of emotion and comedy. One of my favourites is where a wounded warrior has to eat porridge mixed with garlic. If the arch-druid can smell garlic in his wound, it means it will not heal and therefore the patient will be consigned to the Cauldron of Rebirth to re-emerge as a zombie! We feel the relief of Fergus when the arch-druid gives him the all clear.

Sláine makes an arrangement with the Atlanteans that his clans will go into the earth, to another dimension, where they will be free of the Fomorians forever. He and Scota work together and gain access to the sea devils' serpent staffs. Once again, battle is joined but by now Scota's husband, Gael, has been turned into a dribbling wreck by his parasite Odacon. The Fomorian orders him to command his Atlanteans to destroy the barbarians. Instead, despite his agony, he calls out, 'Death to the Demons!' He pays for his defiance when Odacon murders Scota. His twisted relationship with his parasite is chilling to read. As he cries out for his loved one, Odacon responds, 'Do please continue your wailing. The pain of a dry skin is like the most intoxicating drink to me.'

Sláine, honouring a promise he has made to Scota, forces Odacon to heal Gael and have King Sethor take his place. The parasite orders Sethor to bend over in a grotesque scene that is darkly humorous, yet also gruesome beyond words. The cowardly Sethor is pleased to have communion with a God and Odacon is equally pleased to have found the perfect Golamh.

Clint's photo-realism is worthy of comment. It results in some great facial expressions, but I found myself sometimes really wanting to see this as a movie, rather than as a comic book. There is a mental adjustment involved in viewing a comic in this way. I can recall photo-novels of films like *Invasion of the Body Snatchers*, and my recollection is they never really took off, perhaps because they are a hybrid form. I think in *Sláine* the readers accepted it as a necessary compromise – firstly because it didn't exist as a film, secondly because there are amazing imaginative scenes which take our minds into the heights of familiar comics fantasy, and thirdly because it is a way to make full-colour, huge comicbook epics economically viable for a creator to produce. Let's not forget we all need to eat.

As the saga continued, I had enthusiastic feedback from most fans, but some raised this criticism, not always objectively and not always fairly. Mindful of past problems on the Grail stories and *The Secret Commonwealth*, I touched base with editor Matt Smith for his thoughts. He was very reassuring and supportive. He rightly took the view that Clint was pioneering a new type of comicbook art, he needed our encouragement and readers would get used to it over time. Matt was right – Clint's pioneering work here would lead to his astonishing digital work on *ABC Warriors*, which has been an equal success. And to his work on *American Reaper*, where it is even more innovative. I doubt Bishop would have had Matt's courage and perception. Instead, it could easily have become a Troll-fest, with the Trolls let loose to rip the heart out of comics photo-art until Clint had gone the way of Steve Tappin. Matt instead dealt with the issue with a commendable restraint: the mark of a good editor.

What I personally took away from this was that no story can appeal to all of the readers all of the time. Some fans will always find something to complain about – after all, they even complained about the art on *The Horned God*! This is why an editor's backing is important to creators.

Part Four of Books of Invasions, *Tara*, is particularly sexy and has a sequence that made me laugh when I read it again. Gael's previous love, Fais, Princess of Atlantis, says she will happily let him go without making trouble, so he admits his lust and love for Scota. The expression on Gael's face is perfect as he thinks he's gotten away with dumping Fais without any grief. It's hard to see how an art depiction could improve on the photographic expression here. But then, having walked into a far from tender trap, Fais goes absolutely nuts and tries to kill him!

Similarly, when Gael is saying how Scota was always faithful to him, Sláine replies with a sceptical 'Yes...' With so many conventional artists that 'Yes' would have fallen flat and the dialogue would have been dead in the water. Far too often, if an artist can't get the expression right, they'll just draw a silhouette or have the character with his back to us. Which makes my dialogue absolutely pointless. But the expression on Sláine's face here brilliantly but subtly conveys his doubts and his memories of Scota. Once again, the artist is literally the actor. When I see acting this good in a movie I applaud it, and I do so here. This photographic sub-genre of comics really needs further development and encouragement, rather than negativity, suspicion and hostility. Currently, it feels to me like a neglected, even a lost art, as the industry often remains within its most cautious and safe tramlines.

At Tara, under siege by the Fomorians, Sláine meets the warrior Daughters of Danu and enters the Cauldron to investigate the Otherworld his clans have agreed to retreat to. It's not quite the haven he had expected it to be and there are curious and magical dangers he encounters. Visually outstanding is the evil Morholt, leader of the El Riders, who wields a huge pair of 'battle shears'. He looks meaningfully at Sláine as he says, 'Your size?'

Finally, Sláine is victorious: he knows the Otherworld will be safe for his tribes and returns to Tara.

But he's too late. Tara has fallen.

32

MAGENTA CHILL!

Volume 3 commences with Part Five: *Odacon*, where a warped Sláine yet again saves the day. Now his Tribes of the Earth Goddess will 'go into the Otherworld and become invisible to this one. You will share Ireland with the Atlanteans, but in a different density.' Some head for Hy-Brasil. Most agree to enter the Otherworld.

But the dangers are not yet over, because Odacon intends to infect Ireland with his spawn and turn a new generation of humans into his slaves!

Here Clint adds some silent spreads for the book editions, which act as excellent transitions. They're his best yet, the comics equivalent of a David Lean film creating a sense of time passing and boundless landscapes. Notably, he has a snow scene on a double page spread with just small figures crossing a vast, white wintry terrain. I always felt such cinematic scenes have huge potential and I would have loved to have seen more of them. We really feel we are in the cinema. They create a different mood to anything else I've seen in comics, but are invariably in the hands of the artist and so out of my control. Also, they're okay in a reprint collection, but for origination publishers would understandably be nervous at paying for numerous silent landscape spreads.

Thus in *Sha*, Olivier and I had *six spreads* of the night sky representing the transition from a witch burning in the medieval past into the horrors of a future city called New Eden. We see the heroine's soul as a pulsing light crossing through the darkness and then reincarnating, descending down through the clouds into New Eden. I remember the French publisher looking nervous at the prospect of six 'empty' pages, but he reluctantly agreed to it. They are very moving and powerful. For book collections, I really think such sequences should be experimented with, as they provide extra value to the weekly comic edition.

A classic wide-screen movie scene follows where Sláine arrives in a village and has to check the villagers for demon infestation. We learn he has already killed thousands, and for the first time Sláine admits: 'That was too many.'

He discovers that this village is also infested with the spawn of Odacon and everyone must be killed. For me, it's the most outstanding sequence in the whole trilogy of *The Books of Invasion*. The pacing and storytelling is perfect. Above all, the drama is deeply emotional. Once again, Clint's wide-screen, stunning art shows the cinematic potential of comics.

Using Sea Devil science, Sláine and Gael descend into an icy lake and discover, far below, Odacon and a vast breeding creature, the Mother of all Fomorians, who occupies a full two pages to emphasise her colossal size.

She introduces herself as Magenta Chill!

She is ultimately vanquished, but meanwhile Odacon has defeated Sláine and intends him to be his new Golamh!

Extra pages in the book edition explore the full enormity of what this means and allows us to linger on Sláine's dreadful plight. In this final volume of the trilogy, this is surely the worst moment of Sláine's life!

With Gael's help, Sláine breaks free and Odacon escapes on horseback. His fellow Sea Devils tell him it is only five miles to the sea, where he can descend to the bottom of the ocean and plan his revenge: 'Goodbye, my lord, dive well, dive deep.' He thanks them and says, 'I will remember you in my curses.'

Reaching the sea, Odacon rides off a cliff. It's a fantastic movie scene: an alien monster riding a horse! But it's Odacon's misfortune that the tide is out and they crash down onto the shore.

The dying sea devil is so close to the sea and yet so far.

For a moment, we feel his love of the ocean and just what that means to him. He is desperate for water... water... water.... And a sneering, triumphant Sláine looks down and urinates on him before he kills him.

Gael is pronounced High King, and Sláine goes in search of his son Kai in Book Six, the final part of the Books of Invasions, entitled *Carnival*.

A carnival of Celtic monsters is crossing Albion. They were a formidable range of characters and I think I was overly ambitious in devising so many: The Bog Mummy; The Shoggey Family; The Burning Man and his Amazing Corpse Candles; The Sleepless Beauty; The Changeling Children who laugh when bad things happen and cry when things go well; Skullduggery; Anger Management; Anguina the Lady of the Skirt of Snakes; Crom Dubh, the Headless Man, And Shock Head Red – 'the less said about him the better!'

And finally, the master of magic... Kai Mac Sláine!

All presided over by Ukko, the Carnival Master.

All of them superbly designed by Clint.

One of the monsters is killing the others using 'Dragon's Breath' poison. Kai realises from the first murder victim, 'Someone held the bag of Dragon's Breath over his mouth until he suffocated.'

Sláine joins the Carnival and he and Kai eventually track down the murderer in a sinister whodunit tale.

There are some superb dark moments, such as the battle between Sláine and Crom Dubh, but, overall, the photographic approach and the numerous cinematic 'wide screens' don't work so well here. The photorealism and the natural lighting on the characters' faces contrasts with superbly painted dark horror scenes, which is distracting and disorientating. Also, as I've said, perhaps a carnival of monsters was too ambitious to begin with and/or the pacing is too intense. If I'd paced it slower, so we linger longer on the characters to establish them better, and I'd doubled the length of the story, it would have worked better. Given the ingenuity of the murderer and their particularly cruel murder weapon – Dragon's Breath – I'm annoyed with myself that I didn't. A lost opportunity: my bad.

Despite its faults, there is a dark menace about the whole story that still chills me and makes for uncomfortable reading. There is no physical movement to relieve the carnival's claustrophobic world of unrelenting evil. The ending is grim and dark, sustained by Clint's art, which confirms that he is a master of horror as well as fantasy. In some ways, this story is more horror genre than heroic fantasy.

But perhaps there are some stories that are too dark, even for *Sláine*.

33

'THE SQUEAKY WHEEL GETS THE GREASE'

I'm indebted to *Sláine* reader Dan McDaid who made the following valuable suggestion for a *Sláine* movie. It provides a quick litmus paper test for wannabe directors:

> 'I could see the teaser trailer, two beautiful actors in a forest glade, clad in fantasy garb, talking lovingly to each other; in walks Slaine, covered head to toe in blood, axe in hand. "Hello. Have you seen my dwarf?"'

If a director doesn't understand this teaser, they're wrong for *Sláine*.

A black sense of humour is required and there's plenty of it about with many HBO offerings, some of the Marvel films, *Peaky Blinders* and – back in the day – *Blackadder* and so on. My biggest fear is that a *Sláine* movie will be given a po-faced treatment and be a watered down version of one of the 'old school' sword and sorcery movies, ending up reeking of Lord Dunsany elitism. It's the unique comedy that makes some of the best *Sláine* stories, because it laughs at its Celtic craziness. Something the stony faced *Conan* never could (sorry, Simon). You're unlikely to find subversive humour in the works of any of his Lordship's devotees. Maybe that's why none of them light my fire. It's also why *Asterix* works, because it mocks authority. Given how *Dredd* was stripped of its core humour in both movies – to its considerable detriment – I think my fears are justified. There are a lot of humourless people out there in movie-land and because they lack a sense of humour, they don't understand why we, or a cinema audience, would feel differently to them.

As Cuchulain was the prime inspiration for *Sláine*, I should really talk about that, too. But let's go through it in chronological order first.

The first interest in a *Sláine* movie came through Egmont's ill-advised Fleetway Film and Television, where the *2000AD* publishers were actually *paying* Hollywood movie producers to try and get their IPs made into films. Anyone who knows anything about the movie business knows this is nuts. We knew the Hollywood people concerned, because Kevin O'Neill and I had successfully optioned *Marshal Law* for a substantial sum of money. We saw the dangers and tried to warn Egmont, who refused to listen. I think the best deal they got was optioning *Strontium Dog* for a quid.

But one good thing came out of it. I was paid to do a proposed TV bible for *Sláine*, which – remarkably for me – I still have. Although time has moved on, its detailed structure is still of value; it's relevant, and shows one way it could be done. As I'm not a pushover like Egmont, I'm afraid it's not free, should anyone in the film business wish to peruse it. The figure I have in mind is rather more than a quid.

I'll give you a preview just now, to whet your appetite. In my treatment, Niamh becomes 'Deirdre' because one of the Hollywood producers – a character with an impressive movie CV – asked me to change those 'fucking weird, unpronounceable Irish names' and make them more accessible.

Of course no one ever says, where Odysseus, Achilles,

Aphrodite, Archimedes or Aeneas are concerned, to change those 'fucking weird, unpronounceable Greek names.'

In fact, the tragic legend of Deirdre of the Sorrows, 'a tale of beauty, lust and death', who was kept locked up, away from the eyes of men, was the basis for Niamh, so the name change is not quite as heretical as it might have been.

The treatment begins with Slough Feg and Maeve (changed from Medb) planning the destruction of the Tribes of the Earth Goddess. Then we cut to Sláine and his tribe battling Slough Feg's Shadow Warriors. The Shadow Warriors try to capture Deirdre, who fights back fiercely. Sláine comes to the rescue. He has a warp spasm and defeats the Shadow Warriors, but he has gazed upon the forbidden beauty of Deirdre and he wants to see her again, even though her marriage to the King is imminent.

His warp spasm means that despite his questionable parentage, he is the Chosen One of the Goddess and he meets the Earth Mother in a magical initiation ceremony.

Meanwhile, we see Ukko and his nefarious deeds in the South of the Land of the Young, in Gabala.

Then, back with Sláine, he returns to Deirdre. They sleep together; are discovered; he's sentenced to death by a furious King, breaks free and flees. As Feg and Maeve make further sinister plans, Sláine arrives in Gabala and meets Ukko.

Sláine is looking for work and Ukko tells him that there's always work for young heroes in these troubled times – as a mercenary, bodyguard or prizefighter. But, of course, he'll need an agent to represent him. Sláine wins a spear-throwing duel, using his power to salmon leap, and then has an encounter with the Time Monster from the very first episode of *Sláine*. As in that episode, he defeats the Monster by throwing a toad into its mouth, causing it to suffocate (Ukko's idea).

But Sláine and Ukko are caught by Maeve and her Skull Swords and are sentenced to be sacrificed to her Elder Gods. A gruesome Elder God, directed by Feg, starts to manifest!

This is a summary of the pilot episode described in my treatment. As you can see, the pacing and structure is different to the weekly comic story. The principal supporting characters need to be introduced – Feg, Maeve, and Ukko – and they feature in all the subsequent episodes. Plus we see the inciting incident of the whole saga, where Sláine sleeps with Deirdre.

In the first season, all the classic early *2000AD* episodes are featured; *The Beast in the Broch*, *Sky Chariots*, *The Bride of Crom* and much more. Looking over the treatment today, it's probably enough for three seasons, rather than one. But my brief was to provide material for twenty episodes for the American market, rather than the British market (six episodes) and for subsequent seasons.

It certainly demonstrates the cinematic potential of *Sláine*. But, like everything else from Fleetway Film and TV, it got nowhere. Cynically, I wonder if it was just an exercise in 'busy work' to justify the whole enterprise and its funding.

Next came an important short fan film on *The Horned God*. Created by Miguel Mesas as a 'trailer for a movie that never was', it is professional, enthralling and emotional. I cannot recommend it highly enough. You can check it out on YouTube (it's in Spanish with English subtitles). Miguel totally understands the character and the story. He makes the character and the theme look effortless and easy. By comparison, many film writers and directors seem to struggle when they adapt comic book characters. Miguel's work is there to show how it *should* be done. It's had at least a quarter of a million views.

With the Rebellion era, there was considerable movie interest in *Sláine*. I'm aware of at least three film production companies who – in fairly recent years - wanted to option *Sláine* as a movie or for television. At least one company was serious and had an excellent CV.

Two production companies dropped out and they possibly

weren't that serious. It happens and I can understand how time-wasting and annoying that can be, so I sympathise when this happens. But the third production company was extremely serious. I can't say more on this matter without breaking a confidence, so let's move on.

At this stage, it's worth defining the movie 'jungle' as I understand it today:

1) Big studios with big money that want *everything*. This means a studio buy-out of everything, short of the comic. That's supposedly one reason why it's never happened with a *2000AD* intellectual property. In such circumstances, Rebellion tell me they are actually protecting creators' interests as well as their own by turning down buy-outs. However, Marvel got around this during their own pre-studio days, and so did Egmont with their first *Dredd* movie, where the IP wasn't affected outside of the movie. Doubtless there are other examples where the voracious demands of studios have been addressed to everyone's satisfaction.

2) Smaller production companies with limited money. They are never going to demand a buy out so that's not the problem. But then it won't be a big budget movie. So – even if they have a brilliant CV – that may yet be a reason to turn them down. But you can only get a big budget from a studio...

3) Developing a movie in-house, possibly with an external partner and probably with independent financing. That has a set of entirely separate issues, which require considerable skills to navigate. It's my recollection that this approach has been in operation since 2017, hopefully eventually paying off.

But you can understand why – after twenty years – the prospect of a *Sláine* or other *2000AD* film feels to me like being in a catch-22 loop with no way out. But – as I discovered when a film was made of my *Accident Man*, and *American Reaper* was optioned by Spielberg's company Amblin – endless patience can be rewarded, so hope springs eternal.

In recent years director Duncan Jones has shown an interest in making a movie of *Sláine*, possibly after directing *Rogue Trooper*.

In February 2018 he tweeted about it. It had 22 thousand Twitter impressions in *six hours!*

Subsequently, Duncan tweeted his interest again (with a similar enthusiastic response):

> 'Sláine is a character known best from the comic 2000AD that riffs on the warp-spasming Celtic hero Cuchulain, written by the legendary Pat Mills and drawn by the ineffable Simon 'the Bis' Bisley. I love it to bits. If Rogue (Trooper) goes well... you never know.'

That would, of course, be brilliant. Not least because Duncan grew up reading *2000AD*. A reader responded: 'If you ever manage it, you'll have my money. The only thing I ask in return is Cythrons, leyser guns and dragons with crystal skulls. It's not much to ask, when you think about it.'

Significantly, another reader also pointed to those early, pre-Bisley stories, perhaps mindful that they might be overlooked:

> 'It's epic, I love the run of early stories too – Angela Kincaid's opener, Belardinelli's incredible backgrounds and the warp spasm, and Mick's battle between flying boats and his creepy Drunes.'

At the time of writing, I'm not aware of any movement on *Rogue Trooper*, so I rather fear it may not happen. And that's a great pity.

This is probably the right place to make a plea to any prospective film director who is thinking of throwing their hat in the ring: *please* do read the stories. And, in particular, study the subtext of episode one by Angela Kincaid, *The Horned God* by Simon Bisley, and the final series by Leo Manco. There's an important continuity of theme there – relevant to making a movie – that should be so bleeding obvious, I'm not going to spell it out here.

A second plea would be to look at Sláine's unique hero-harness and explore its *'Incredible Hulk'* possibilities as its straps and cords stretch and lengthen to accommodate his warp spasm and prevent him turning around in his skin. The cinematic possibilities are *new* and considerable, but it's something that is almost impossible to make work in comics. It would be too easy for a director to ignore because it's 'difficult' and that would be a pity and a great disappointment to fans.

Over time, several directors and producers have contacted me in the hope that I may be able to smooth their path to Rebellion's door because of the challenges I've described. Not a hope, I'm afraid, except to offer them tea and sympathy. I'm only the writer-creator, so I'm at the bottom of the food chain.

At the time of writing, the most likely way forward now seems to be an in-house development, either solo or in conjunction with an established film or TV production company. On the face of it, that sounds promising and I genuinely wish them well. After all, it is to my and other creators' advantage for something to finally happen on *2000AD* characters. I'm told the whole Covid business hasn't helped. Now the worst is over, maybe things will get better.

However, my past experience as a consultant on a Rebellion solo in-house development on *Flesh* was not a happy one. I believe the *Flesh* project has been shelved, although no one has told me as such. Once again, let's just move on.

One positive piece of news here, though, which I wasn't aware of before, and which somehow got lost in all this complexity. The Rebellion deal on character licenses – 40% to writer and artist creator – is close to industry standard, unlike Rebellion book royalties, which are certainly not. So that's encouraging at least, should a film ever happen.

Finally, I'm afraid there are further challenges on a *Sláine* movie if it ever gets the green light. There's the question of writer and artist creative *developers* being rewarded on films and merchandising featuring their work. It's a gorilla in the corner that no one talks about. Apart from me.

Currently, writer and artist developers are not rewarded in Rebellion's financial model, unlike the Egmont deal on the first *Dredd* movie where developers – such as me, and artists such as McMahon and Bolland – most certainly were.

As it stands, the issue is completely hypothetical, but you can be sure that if a 2000AD movie or TV series ever happens, it will become *very* relevant. The prospect of big money on a movie always brings everyone out of the woodwork. On a movie like *Sláine*, it could be argued that it would need the judgement of Solomon to evaluate and pay artist developers. It was one reason I went out of my way to ensure the principal design elements were all contained in Angela's episode one. But there will still be additions. For example, the design elements in *The Horned God*, which could well be used. As Egmont did successfully apply the judgement of Solomon on the first *Dredd* movie, and all creators were happy with the sums awarded, it's clearly possible to sort it out in an amicable way.

Remarkably, Egmont applied the principle of *full transparency* and *full consultation* with creators and it really worked! I thoroughly recommend this as a business strategy.

At some stage, this nettle of creative developers will have to be grasped, as is already happening in the States. See the examples of Marvel and DC Comics, below.

Recently I raised a merchandising query involving artist developers. It was suggested to me that if this was a concern, creators might sort development fees out amongst *themselves*. Creator artists might apportion sub-percentages to developers, thereby voluntarily reducing their own royalties. But that's clearly never going to work for reasons that surely need no elaborating here. So let's move on once more.

Until there is serious money involved, no one is likely to care. Here's the most up-to-date information on our fellow comic creators across the pond for when or if that time ever comes.

A recent article in *The Hollywood Reporter* entitled 'Marvel and DC's "Shut-Up Money": Comic Creators Go Public Over Pay' (July 16, 2021) covers developer dissatisfaction when seriously big bucks are involved and they aren't financially rewarded.

A few relevant highlights:

"... companies such as Marvel viewing these (development) payments as thank-you gifts – and a way to avoid the bad publicity of warring with a creator. "It's 'shut-up' money," as one Marvel creator who receives such payments [...] likes to call it."

"After Starlin's airing of grievances, Disney renegotiated his deal for Thanos, the villain of *Avengers: Infinity War* and *Avengers: Endgame*. Those films went on to gross $4.83 billion globally, and Starlin, while not sharing details of his deal, walked away happy. "The cliche is that the squeaky wheel gets the grease," Starlin tells *The Hollywood Reporter*."

"Since the 1970s, DC creators who added a new character to the mythos have been entitled to payments from film, TV and merchandising, an idea spearheaded by then-publisher Jenette Kahn."

"Levtiz had a similar viewpoint at DC. "It's really good business," says Levitz... If you act in a fashion where you treat people in a way that they think they've been treated fairly, the next creative person is more interested in working for you.""

Would Rebellion follow Levitz's wise words and the encouraging examples of Marvel and DC? I guess we won't know until a big budget *2000AD* movie or game finally happens.

Until then... I shall squeak away.

34

'WELCOME TO THE WOUND FEAST!'

Clint's artwork on *Sláine* was a key factor in the two of us getting a film gig about Cuchulain. Together with producer Jeremy Davis, we had formed a company, Repeat Offenders Ltd, and I was commissioned by the Irish Film Board to write a screenplay on Cuchulain. Clint drew some amazing film designs for the character.

By comparison with *Sláine*, film progress with our company Repeat Offenders Ltd has been smoother and clearer. Our IP *American Reaper* has been optioned by Steven Spielberg's Amblin Entertainment. The director's screenplay version is complete and under review. At this time of writing (June 2021), it's been announced that Amblin and Netflix have gone into partnership, which is encouraging news. Whatever the final outcome, it was still a coup to have a story optioned by Spielberg's company.

Similarly, Jeremy optioned our version of Cuchulain with Subotica (one of Ireland's leading film and TV production companies) and the Irish Film Board. We all got well paid for our efforts, so, even though it eventually didn't fly, we're all happy bunnies. Indeed, as I said earlier, the guy at the Irish Film Board did warn me that he had a shelf load of previous screenplays of Cuchulain.

If I'm looking for a reason why we've made some progress in the movie jungle, I'd say it was down to Jeremy's incredible patience and perseverance, which not everyone possesses (certainly not me), and to practising full transparency.

There's an aspect to this that's relevant to *Sláine*, so I should say more on this subject. There is no copyright on Cuchulain, that's why it's never happened and why the Irish Film Board have a shelf full of screenplays about him. We had our first indication of this with our chosen and well-accredited director, who had some great American studio connections. We had some positive meetings and I recall he wanted my screenplay to go in a pretty wild and Tarantino-like direction. He felt the key to Cuchulain was that he was 'a fame whore'. Sláine would relate to that because he says, 'I'll do things they'll talk about forever'. But, next thing we know, our director has departed to do his own *rival* version of Cuchulain! That also didn't fly.

Subsequently, we didn't have the star line-up to overshadow other Cuchulain film projects out there with famous actors' names attached. Michael Fassbender, for example. That was some years ago, so I assume that didn't fly either. And so it will go on. At any one time there's probably a couple of Cuchulain film projects in pre-production. I've talked to film production companies and they were nervous that if they started work on a Cuchulain movie, it would be quickly trumped by another company. It famously happened with Robin Hood and two disaster movies. To quote *Business Insider:*

> 'It's not uncommon for multiple movie studios to have similar, rival projects get made around the same time. "*Armageddon*" and "*Deep Impact*," which were both about an asteroid hitting earth, came out in 1998. Two Truman Capote biopics came out within a year of each other.'

In 2015, there were *six* Robin Hood films in development, plus a television series. So that's the minefield through which Ireland's greatest legend has to navigate.

It also has to overcome the literary 'burden' of expectations from the intelligentsia, who I suspect would be less than impressed by a Hollywood approach. Our comic book treatment was one of the reasons we got the gig. We were making Cuchulain accessible to a popular young audience who had never heard of him. And, incidentally, I *did* retain all those 'fucking weird, unpronounceable Irish names'.

There's another problem with Cuchulain as well. Like all Celtic legends, the stories about him do *not* obey the rules of drama. The tone varies and they meander in ways that do not suit a modern audience. So it needs an action writer like myself, not an academic, to make sense of them. I recall my opening action scene went down extremely well with our producer. The ending of Cuchulain was also a challenge. In our case, a most ingenious and original ending was suggested by Subotica, which I still carry a torch for. I hope they guard it well.

Any historical or legendary film has this same problem getting made. Thus there's the proposed TV series on *The Lion of Ireland*, Brian Boru, who defeated the Vikings at the Battle of Clontarf. It was announced in 2019, but there appears to be no news about it since.

So, by comparison, *that* is the attraction of the fictional *Sláine*. Dramatically, it's more straightforward. There are no literary pretensions. And there are no fears of rival *Sláines* turning up. Although it's worth noting that *Sláine* himself has his own status in Irish mythology. He really was the first High King of Ireland.

Clint Langley's art on Cuchulain was amazing and I'm sorry that, at the time of writing, it's not on public display anywhere. It's different to his work on *Sláine* and has an energy and a magic about it that brings the Cuchulain legend to life as never before.

One day, either Cuchulain or *Sláine* will finally get made into a movie, possibly to the detriment of the other. That would be a great pity, as we really can't have enough Irish fantasy homicidal maniacs on our screens. But, if I had to bet on which film would get made, my money would be on *Sláine*.

So if you're a producer or director and you're seriously thinking about either of them, what can I say, but, in Sláine's own words: 'Welcome to the Wound Feast!'

DROP THE DEAD DONKEY?

After the *Books of Invasions*, it made sense for Sláine to be a wanderer again, at least for a while. It also gave me an opportunity to better explore Brutania before embarking on another long story.

So the plan was for Clint and I to tell a number of shorter stories, entitled *Sláine The Wanderer,* commencing with *The Gong Beater*. We open with a truly awesome Tower of the Cyth that still takes my breath away! Sláine is attacked by Gardar, a Gong Beater, who needs money. An action sequence follows where Sláine explains to Gardar that there are Twelve Doors to Eternity – a blow to the head, to the breast, to the leg and so on – and asks which door would he like to take? Inevitably, it ends with Gardar's death. His female friend Sabrina explains it is all the fault of the mysterious new owner of the Tower. He had laughed at her fears about the evil of the Cyth, so she beat him up, but he actually enjoyed it!

Sabrina: 'I like your swearing and slapping.' He told me he was beaten for years by some evil brute and that is the reason he is mentally sick.

Sláine discovers the owner is Ukko, and he is in the process of converting the Tower into luxury apartments: *'Only one left!'* Ukko's evil ways always amuse me; he is the very embodiment of corrupt capitalism! He needs a gong beater to summon his work force and he persuades Sláine to take on the job. It's a strongman image I've loved since seeing the gong beater introduce the Rank movies, and Clint draws it to perfection.

Inevitably, the gong summons the Cyth, and Sláine uses it again to get rid of them. Then he continues his wandering with Ukko clinging onto his leg once more, as he did all those decades ago back on Angela's episode one.

The gong originally came from a story I had hoped to write for the celebrated American fantasy artist Mike Kaluta. My French publisher on *Requiem*, Jacques Collins, like myself, is a huge fan of Mike's art. So when an opportunity came up, Jacques and I flew to New York to talk over a storyline with Mike. I remember several story meetings sitting on a bench in the middle of Broadway with Mike and Jacques. Mike found it an inspiring location for creative jamming sessions and, I have to say, it worked for me, too. So the book finally looked like a goer. But so many creative projects don't work out, for one reason or another, and this one eventually didn't happen. When that occurs, it's sensible to defray the development costs by recycling the story elements in other ways and that's what happened here.

Next is *The Smuggler*, where Sláine gets caught up in an illegal trade of smuggling and selling a magical form of amber. It warps time, so dinosaurs are trapped within it! When they are released, Sláine is caught up in a battle with the smugglers. I try to ring the changes with the action, so here he uses a war quoit as a lethal frisbee and does a spear feat – running up a spear to axe its holder!

He has arranged to meet Ukko in the port of Bethlusion, the centre of the amber trade. At the city gates, he sees smugglers trying and failing to get stolen amber past security. Indifferent to their fate, he wanders into the city, shooing away a donkey that insists on following him. He tells the donkey to be gone, and find its master.

The donkey replies, 'But *you* are my master. Hello, Sláine.'

It's Ukko.

It's a long story, as you might imagine!

Ukko and a female accomplice, Sorcha, were caught trying to steal from Lord Ogma, an amber merchant and noted taxidermist. Ukko had behaved like an ass, so Ogma had him sewn up inside a dead donkey and made him behave like one.

Ogma has previous: he once sewed up a man inside an apeskin and an ape inside a man's skin. He's always looking for new twisted diversions. He keeps on beating Ukko until he behaves like a real donkey.

Fortunately, Ukko is befriended by a genuine donkey, Domnall, who he meets in the stables. Domnall and Ukko become *close* friends. The donkey shows Ukko how to walk and bray, so he is no longer beaten. Domnall eventually helps Ukko escape, although, 'there was a price I had to pay for his assistance...'

'Please,' says a scowling Sláine. 'Spare me the details'.

I think of all the Ukko plots, this one I found the funniest even if the donkey scenes are drawn rather neutrally by Clint and don't exploit the comedy potential sufficiently.

Ukko's plan is to smuggle amber out of the city using his Trojan Donkey! Sláine is persuaded to help him because Ukko has told him Sorcha is a dead-ringer for Niamh, and might finally stop his grieving.

They have to overcome the guards who are Ambroids, reptile men from millions of years ago who were also caught in the magical amber. Its qualities make it like the Tardis: small on the outside and vast within.

Finally they catch up with Ogma, who is planning to miniaturise Sorcha in amber and add her to his collection of human beauties trapped in the mysterious resin. 'I have their beauty forever and they can never leave me.' Sláine thinks he is an evil bastard, but Ukko replies, 'Eh? *Why?* I can see where he's coming from.'

Ogma is surprised to see Ukko again: 'I had thought Domnall would have finished you off by now.'

In the ensuing battle, Sláine and Ukko become enveloped in amber, too, but eventually escape and Ukko disguises himself again to get out of the city, laden with amber in the belly of the donkey. Unfortunately, the amber is contaminated by... well, if you're not familiar with this story – it's well worth a read. There's so much more to this story, including the way Sláine and Ukko speak to each other in humorous Irish triads at key moments!

I would say *The Smuggler* is classic, textbook *Sláine*, beautifully illustrated by Clint. Very much in the tradition of Angela's episode one, which should be a template for the entire saga.

It's in the top ten of my all-time favourite *Sláine* stories.

But did the readers feel the same way? I have no way of knowing for sure. Perhaps they loved it, perhaps they hated it? With so many different stories in *Sláine the Wanderer*, it may have been possible to finally identify what the current *2000AD* 40-something audience prefer, which could be totally different to the original 14-year-olds who read *Sláine*. I think this is where the Rebellion system falls down, and traditional feedback is necessary to really get a handle on the current readership and for a writer to give of his best.

In the absence of feedback, I will say that *The Smuggler* has all the right beats of a three act drama and all the elements of a classic sword and sorcery tale: heroes; heroines; villains and monsters, combined with some wonderful moments of *Blackadder*-style comedy.

So, assuming the Penguin audio dramatisation of *The Horned God* is a success, I would recommend *The Smuggler* as a future hour-long comedy audio episode. And *The Gong Beater*. In both cases, sound effects would hugely enhance the story. I recommend it particularly because it comes from *later* in the *Sláine* saga. It's far too easy to just focus on a few early classics like *The Wickerman*, which left such an impression on young readers at the time, and forget that there's a whole body of later work of similar quality, read by other readers of different ages.

What I can say with certainty is that *The Smuggler* will appeal to a general audience whose tastes are so much easier to gauge than a specialist audience. You do not have to be marinated in the *Sláine* mythos, Irish legends or comics to understand it. That hugely neglected audience, sadly now lost to comics: the boy or the girl, the man or the woman in the street, who have never heard of *Sláine*, I know would still 'get it'.

MURDERBALL!

In the next story in *Sláine The Wanderer* we meet *Sláine The Exorcist*. 'Doctor' Ukko has bought an exorcism business and is removing demons from Cordelia, a possessed patient. Sláine then does the 'heavy lifting' and kills them.

This is another dark and sinister tale, and reads like a modern day version of a *Hammer House of Horror* film. Unlike *Carnival*, there's a limited number of characters and the pacing and the story-telling is first rate. It's wonderfully Gothic and the scenes with Cordelia inside a glass coffin are truly memorable. Here the photographic images work well and I would say this is amongst Clint's finest work. Plus we get to see the Guledig in all his evil glory! I thoroughly recommend it.

It's followed by *Sláine The Mercenary*, in which we meet an old friend and an old enemy. There is Quagslime, the Fomorian Collector of Taxes, introduced in Glenn Fabry's story *Sláine The King*, and now back in full colour and looking all the more evil for it. Plus Nest, who is also a sword for hire here and looks beautiful – I always preferred this Fabry version of her, which has that red-haired, freckled, fay Celtic quality to her. She's *still* an eternal student: my riff on people I've known who seem to study for one university degree after another and never finally complete their studies.

At the heart of the story is a game of Murderball, designed to raise passions before the battle begins. Sláine leads one team, and the bald and tattooed warrior Phelim the other. I'd long considered Sláine playing hurley – like Cuchulain – but I could never find the right story angle. When Clint and I were regularly going over to Ireland for talks about our film version of Cuchulain, somehow we ended up in a Dublin pub in Temple Bar where we met Phil O'Brien, a celebrated tattooist.

Phil told me there was an even more savage game the Celts used to play: Murderball!

He described how, in ancient times, Irish warriors played Murderball before a battle as a way of terrorising the enemy. The last known occasion was probably before the Battle of the Boyne in 1690. Naturally I was hooked, Murderball is perfect for a *Sláine* story! It also bore out my suspicions that there is so much else academics have removed from Irish legends and history, because it's dark and savage – like Murderball. Lady Gregory, for instance, who admitted that she had cleaned up her account of Cuchulain for her readers.

Even better, Phil was perfect to play Sláine's opponent in the game, so Clint took lots of photos of him. Clint is there himself, of course, as Sláine, and our original producer on *American Reaper*, Alex, is also there in the guise of Locrin the Cautious, the human ally of Quagslime: 'They say he won't touch a meal until four hours after his food taster has eaten the same dish and is still alive.'

So when I look through this story today, I'm meeting lots of old friends, real and fictional!

The ball is a newly decapitated head (needless to say). And, regarding the rules of the game, there are no rules (needless to say). It's all in the worst possible taste and is exciting, funny and has once again a touch of *Blackadder* about it – plus the film *Rollerball*. Clint and I are both huge fans of the movie and you can feel an echo of the bitter subtext of *Rollerball*.

It's all excellently summed up by Quagslime who says, 'Let the Fianna waste their energy on this disgusting exhibition of barbarity. Only mad Celts could play such a pointless and revolting game.'

But the 'balls' are quickly damaged and Nest, a prisoner of Phelim, is about to be beheaded in order to provide the next one. However, as established in the previous tale, Sláine has an alternative. 'Here's one I beheaded earlier. My enemy Crom Dubh!' The demon from *Carnival*. Phelim warns Sláine: 'We get through six balls at least. You're only delaying the inevitable.' Nest's time will come.

Events degenerate from there. Clint is really into this story and it's one of his finest and goriest works. There's an epic 'scrum' involving at least *a thousand warriors* fighting for the ball! You have to see it to believe it! I can understand why academics decided not to include Murderball in their accounts of the ancient and historic Celts way of life. It is a complete gross-out, a celebration of comic bad taste, and a way of defending our industry from being taken over by the *Guardian*-loving literati, who would love comics to be transformed into 'nice', respectable – and, all too often, crushingly dull – middle-class graphic novels ('Fat comics with bits of cardboard around them', as one comics creator put it).

For me, as an example of popular culture 'bad taste', this story takes its place alongside *Mars Attacks* cards, the infamous *American Civil War* cards, and the early issues of my comic *Action*. In fact, it commences with what looks to me like collector cards of the star players in Murderball: Goll Garb the Rough; Blod Ironjaw; Murder Face; Hy Blood; Finnachta of the Teeth. And, of course, Sláine the Mercenary. I would dearly love to have collected the whole set.

And it's fitting that Murderball should end *Sláine the Wanderer* and Clint's tour of duty on *Sláine*. It's a most exhilarating conclusion.

Also in the collection is an introduction by the late, great John

Hicklenton, and his drawings of Sláine are spread throughout the book. Johnny loved *Sláine*, and I always felt we should do a story together one day. We had worked on *Zombie World* for Dark Horse Comics, and featured a similar fantasy character in that horror series, so I was aware of his potential.

Thanks to Clint, Johnny finally got his chance.

Sláine The Wanderer is dedicated to Johnny and his partner Claire.

THE BOOK OF SCARS

To celebrate *Sláine's* 30th anniversary, we produced *The Book of Scars*. Each scar on Sláine's body tells a story and his greatest enemy, the Guledig, attempts to change those stories with an ending where, this time, Sláine will be destroyed.

So some of the classic tales are revisited with new insights, and commentaries by the artists. Clint drew *Bride of Crom* in an art style that closely resembled Belardinelli's amazing original. Sláine breaks out of the Wickerman and climbs up the side of it to rescue Medb, but *this time* she is prepared for him. A spell of binding is put upon Sláine so he cannot warp out. And we learn that Medb was drugged by Slough Feg – this was the reason she accepted her fate to be burnt alive. Drugs were hardly a subject that could be written about when the original *Bride of Crom* was published, although it was obvious even back then she was under Feg's spell.

Finally Sláine makes Medb see sense, she releases him from the spell, and he wins the day. It's a sad and beautiful tale that benefits from its retelling. Particularly sad, because we see the terrible effect the evil Feg had on Medb, and how it will direct her life from now on.

Mike McMahon agreed to draw a scene from his classic *Sky*

Chariots. Drawn in his new art style, it still reminds us of the splendour of his original. This time, the Drune Lord Slough Throt blunts Sláine's axe and makes a deal with the Norsemen to protect him. But Sláine is saved by the Goddess and prepares to behead Throt. The Drune Lord is not afraid to die because the Guledig has promised him everlasting life.

Sláine says he is 'happy to help'. He tests the edge of his blunt axe. 'But it could take a while...'

Just as Mike had moved on, so too had David Pugh. I had hoped to persuade David to contribute to the anniversary book, but he replied to my invitation:

> 'Maybe I'm not the right person to revisit *Sláine*, it's been twenty-eight years since I last worked for *2000AD*. I'm not sure I can generate the anger needed to pull off the fight sequence convincingly. I'm trying to be a much more mellow and happy person, I'm enjoying living the adventure more than I ever did drawing it. It's very flattering to be offered the chance to do these pages and part of me is really interested to see how I'd tackle the character now.'

I'm sure Dave would have done a brilliant job, but I totally understood. He was travelling the world and having fantastic new adventures, which sounded as amazing as Sláine's adventures, so good luck to him.

Glenn Fabry was up for revisiting his El women story and it was great to do a comic remake of them. Sláine looks leaner and meaner than first time around, but still devastatingly handsome. And the El women look even scarier and more beautiful than before. Elfric joins them and the Guledig has given these faerie creatures protection against iron this time. But Sláine uses a magical tathlum to defeat them: 'A concrete ball – no soft missile – hardened with lime and the blood of toads and vipers and furious bears.'

Next is Simon Bisley's *Horned God*. The Lord Weird Slough Feg was swallowed by Crom-Cruach, but now – thanks to the Guledig – he is magically brought back to life. He proclaims to Sláine, 'Let there be a rut between us to discover who shall be Horned God.'

In the battle that follows, I note that Feg asks Crom to 'bind this upstart of *uncertain parentage* with your tentacles.' Sláine's father – and my own – was clearly on my mind.

Feg removes Sláine's hero harness so he cannot impale him with its boar tusks. It certainly looks like the end for our hero now. So much so that in the Castle of the Ever Living Ones, Nest orders Ukko to rewrite the end of *The Horned God*. Ukko is reluctant but then he's told the story is so popular, with a goatskin edition, vellum calfskin edition, a pocket squirrelskin edition and a deluxe version on clay tablets 'for serious collectors'. Therefore, Nest tells the dwarf she can afford to pay him in gold. This persuades him. *Gold...?!* Alas, that was wishful thinking on my part.

Sláine defeats Feg, but all my interest was on Ukko, who is then told that there will also be a *Horned God* oral fireside edition. This audio version will be *free*. The shock is too much for him and he passes out. I know the feeling.

Clint Langley's *Moloch* follows. In a new spin on the original story, Moloch will spare the lives of children due to be sacrificed in return for Sláine's life. Sláine agrees, but Moloch, predictably, is lying. Sláine sheds tears for their impending deaths while Moloch eagerly collects these valuable 'hero's tears'. But it's just a ruse for Moloch to get close enough for Sláine to kill him.

Thus the Guledig's plan has been outwitted. But he tells Sláine that the religion of the Cyth, celebrating his sacrifice, separating humans from their true animal nature, will grow and prosper. 'I have left the greatest scar of all.' A chilling thought.

A gallery of *Sláine* covers follows to complete *The Book of Scars*. Plus comments from various artists such as Duncan Fegredo, Leigh Gallagher and Jock. And also from fans. Looking through the covers,

Glenn Fabry's are outstanding. And, of course, Simon Bisley's. And, of course, Clint Langley's. And, of course … Okay, the list could go on *forever!*

But Clint's are definitely amongst my favourites. For example, the cover with a close-up of Moloch with just his name below. No stupid jokes. That has a cool quality that I prefer. I find some of the 'humorous' Thargish lines on other covers mildly irritating, but I assume the readers must like them, so I usually keep my mouth shut. Originally, I had an agreement with McManus that *Sláine* covers would be different and you'll see the result of that on most of the early covers. They have an epic rather than a 'comicky' quality. Those jarring and intrusive 'Tharg notes', which affect the tone of the story, were once excluded. But, over time, as so often happened on *2000AD*, agreements get eroded. And there's only so many battles with them I can fight.

Of course there are exceptions: Clint and I talked about the cover for *Murderball* being based on a famous *Rollerball* poster. The caption we chose, 'It's not a game, it's Murderball' feels entirely appropriate.

I should also mention my preference for slow, brooding images such as a pin-up by Dave Kendall, where Sláine is looking down at a dead Skull Sword. The lighting is excellent, but I especially liked the look on Sláine's face and found myself wondering just what is going on in the barbarian's mind? It leaves a slow-burn aftertaste, which I think is a measure of the quality and the potential of full colour art.

With an afterword by Graham Linehan (*Father Ted* writer), this is an excellent collection for fans.

I think Sláine has the best line in the book when he asks the Guledig, 'How's the neck?'

THE THROWBACK

The most remarkable feature of the Brutania Chronicles was the astonishing number of references artist Simon Davis and I exchanged during out discussions on the visuals for *Sláine*. It was 2012, Clint was illustrating *The ABC Warriors*, taking it to new full-colour heights, and Simon had expressed an interest in taking over the series. He was particularly inspired by Sergio Toppi, who had a great feeling for fantasy, and he wanted to give *Sláine* that European sensibility.

I too love Toppi's work. Although I was cautious, as I said to Simon at the time:

'Funnily enough I had a chance to use Toppi back in the '70s and I turned him down – rightly I think – because at that time he didn't have many images on the page and also he wasn't engaging the reader. You're being told the story, rather than being in it. That still comes across in the black and white pages, which I think date from that era. His figures don't make eye contact and I remember worrying about that and deciding not to risk him.'

Simon successfully resolved that problem in the *Brutania Chronicles Book One: A Simple Killing*. His Sláine certainly does make eye contact with the reader and draws you in. Originally, his Sláine had a McMahon influence, but I explained that there needed to be visual continuity with Clint's version. And every new saga should still connect with the creator's vision in episode one – Angela's handsome rendition of Sláine – rather than a later and controversial version of the character. Accordingly, I also sent Simon a copy of *Conquering Armies*, the visual bible Angela and I used in the creation of *Sláine* and which would remain relevant right through to the conclusion, as we shall see. It's a book that I've praised so strongly that the publishers, Humanoids, asked me to write the introduction for a new edition.

Another key reference I sent Simon was Virgil Finlay who – uniquely – brought mountains 'alive'. And, in return, Simon showed me his designs for giants and mermaids, both of which would feature in the new series. They were risky because they could be seen as the stuff of fairy tales, rather than heroic fantasy, but Simon made them work. The mermaids, in particular, look astonishing: truly malevolent. They were all part of creating the new world of Brutania. Simon also came up with the wonderful auroch Sláine rides in this adventure, easily the visual counterpart of the mammoth in his early black and white stories. The setting for most of the story would be the Isle of Man, known as Monadh in Sláine's time.

The backgrounds were equally important. I had discovered a superb reference of a reconstruction of the Neolithic village of Lepenski Vir, which inspired Simon to portray the skull village of Bladnoch. I'm sure at some point – especially now I'm identifying the source – Lepenski Vir will turn up in some future sword and sorcery film. It's a visual gift to any fantasy designer. Remember you saw it in *The Brutania Chronicles* first!

The city of the Drune Lords had to be particularly powerful. I based it on the rock caves of Cappadocia and collected references from *nine websites* to capture their fantasy potential. Here's an evocative passage from Deborah Petersen's blog post *The Bizarre Underworld and Lunar Landscape of Cappadocia*:

> 'In the middle of modern-day Turkey lies a unique lunar landscape of caves, tunnels, and hundreds of entire underground cities that span for miles, which were first carved out by the pagan Hittites over 3,000 years ago. Called Cappadocia, this land of lost cities has secrets inside every cave and around every corner — from honeycombs of tunnels rigged with booby-traps to the clandestine routes of fierce battle.'

The world of Brutania was taking shape. These and other sources would provide the basis for Simon to produce some remarkably beautiful double page spreads, too numerous to focus on them all here. I was following a system I'd used in the black and white era of *Sláine*: introducing new visuals, seeing what worked and what didn't work, so they might be returned to again in the future. I had also designed two maps: Brutania and the Island of Monadh, so this new world was firmly established in the readers' minds.

My belief on spreads is that, in many instances, we are looking at them as works of art and they need appreciating in that way, just as we stare at a painting in a gallery for hours on end. For this reason, I like to keep the words to a minimum, so they don't intrude or distract from the art. There are similar spreads in *Requiem: Vampire Knight* and the artist, Olivier Ledroit, believes that there *should* be plenty of text, primarily to slow the reader down as they look over the pages. I don't entirely agree. I feel that, with beautiful art, the reader will naturally slow down and pore over the detail or simply step back and allow themselves to be engulfed by its magic. Of course, every spread is different and sometimes it would work better with additional words. There are no absolute rules. For example, there's a great sequence where a Giant's Causeway rises up out of the ocean. You can almost hear the waves crashing against it as Sláine uses it to cross from Albion to Monadh. But, in that instance, it needed more text, which I added after it was painted.

By comparison, there's a centre spread of Sláine riding through a lush green forest that needed no additional words. It's not especially detailed, but the richness and the mystique of the terrain is such that I found myself utterly lost in Sláine's world. I *have* stared at it for hours. In fact, I'm continuing to do so as I write this chapter. For me, it is one of the high points, not just of the Brutania Chronicles, but of the entire *Sláine* saga. It's a scene straight out of a movie, yet, unlike a film, the reader can linger on the scene for as long as they want. One of those wonderful moments where comics actually have the edge over cinema.

Story-wise, this adventure, *A Simple Killing*, was inspired partly by *The Fear Teachers*, a short-lived series Tony Skinner and I wrote for *Toxic!* (illustrated by the late John Hicklenton). The premise that Tony had inherited from his pagan tradition is a powerful and an important one. If this story had been written back in the days of *The Horned God* or the historical sagas that followed, which also explored complex and pagan ideas, I would have laid out my stall with wordier exposition. Not least because I knew there were so many more pagans reading *2000AD,* before the Bishop cull. But the scars from that era and the victory of his Trolls, had not entirely healed. So I throttled back on the explanations and focused more on the drama.

It is a meaningful story with far-reaching implications that, as far as I'm aware, isn't covered elsewhere in sword and sorcery, perhaps because the genre was originally inspired by Lord Dunsany with his largely imaginary worlds. By comparison, this story comes from a real-life pagan tradition. It is *not* the product of imagination alone. Also, I always felt when I read Dunsany-inspired works that they were well written, but on the opposite side of the fence to me.

The muse that drives me discouraged me from reading them for this reason. Whether it's easily recognisable or not, most fantasy has a subtext which tells us where the author's loyalties lie. In her view they were often hierarchical, elitist and even neo-Christian, which did not please her. 'They're not for you' is a polite version of what she had to say about the books by the disciples of Lord Dunsany.

Here I can be a little wordier about the premise of this *true* sword and sorcery tale. That humans are 'different' is in no doubt. This story is one explanation for the reason why. Of course there are other possible explanations but this is the theory that – in broad brushstrokes – I believe.

In essence, we humans are 'not right', we have been modified in some ultimately injurious way, so we are remarkably different and more destructive than other animals. There are also various anomalies about us that may be explained away, yet I remain unconvinced by. For example, only *Homo sapiens* have survived and Neanderthals, Cro-Magnons, and other human species are long gone, yet there are endless variations of other animal species. There are other unexplained oddities about humans that most of us have come across and thus don't need exampling here.

At the heart of being 'not right' (neurotic, if you will) is that we are more fearful, above and beyond the natural fear that any animal needs in order to survive. This, according to pagan tradition, is the product of genetic engineering: of science, but not 'our science', from an era where science would have been indistinguishable from magic. In *The Fear Teachers* it occurs in the age of the Old Testament, where humans are herded into camps to be experimented on and changed. In *Finn*, the end result was powerfully described by Tony Skinner as, 'Look at what's wrong in a man and you'll see the webbed footprint of a Newt.'

The Fear Teachers – the Gods – taught us to fear.

In *Sláine*, it was time for me to look at this again, to see just how that fear might have been induced in ancient times. *The Island of*

Doctor Moreau surely demonstrates its dramatic potential. In fantasy, we all of us love mad scientists and their insane experiments. On the Island of Monadh, weird species of humans are being created in the tradition of the H. G. Wells classic. The 'mad scientist' is Gododin, the son of the Lord Weird Slough Feg, who seeks revenge on Sláine for 'murdering' his father.

Sláine's father, Roth, is also referred to, and the theme of Sláine's ancestry is explored in subsequent volumes.

Meanwhile, Sinead, Sláine's companion, has been 'improved' by Gododin so she is afraid and will never challenge authority again. And Sláine needn't think he is exempt. As Gododin says to him, 'You don't think you're natural, do you? Where's your fur? Your tail? The Gods took them away aeons ago. Without their intervention, we'd still be apes. The Cyth improved us all. Even a throwback like you.'

So we should be grateful to our 'Creator' Gods or God, as the various Abrahamic religions endlessly exhort us. Whether we're happy to be 'improved' is open to considerable debate.

And, in particular, the Fear Teachers want us to be afraid of *them*.

One of my abiding memories of childhood was the fear that Catholic worshippers seemed to live with. From my position as an altar boy, I would endlessly scan the faces of the congregation as they knelt in fear, surrounded by images of torture and horrible death, begging their angry God to be merciful with them. *Mea culpa, mea culpa, mea maxima culpa.* 'It's all my fault.' Classic guilt-tripping. Some of them may have been faking it, but not the poor devils I was watching. They were in a subdued state of constant terror, a terror I failed to feel. I guess the Gods did a poor job of 'improving' me.

I think I'm a throwback, like Sláine.

'PAPER WILL NEVER REFUSE INK'

There are some dazzling visuals in this second volume of *The Brutania Chronicles: Primordial*. In particular, a scene where our hero and Sinead leap off a cliff, which has to be in the top twenty *Sláine* scenes of all time.

Sláine and Sinead have escaped Gododin and approach the mountain of the Archon, the celestial jailers who have imprisoned the Cyth on Earth. A pagan interpretation of the biblical 'War in the Heavens'. I had expected the mountain to be animated stone, as in the celebrated Virgil Finlay's living mountains. But instead, Simon had covered it in lush green vegetation. This is where editing the story against the art is invaluable. I was able to change the dialogue, so Sláine comments 'It's said the Archons possess only inanimate objects, like stone, because they hate living matter. The trees growing on the mountain must be like a *disease* to it.' Every problem is an opportunity!

There then follows a sequence that still makes me smile where Sinead replies only in clichéd phrases taken from traditional and wonderfully rich Irish sayings. Such as 'melodious is the closed mouth', 'never bolt your door with a boiled carrot', and 'the man with the boot does not mind where he places his foot'.

I'd grown up with these often-obscure phrases that were used by Irish relatives as a kind of psychic defence. So I might say there was a book out exposing the crimes of the Vatican and a relative would defend the Church, not with logic or with evidence, but by saying, 'Paper will never refuse ink'. I love that.

Or I'd talk about the injustice in the world and my relative would respond, 'The poor will always be with us'. This requires no further explanation, but another wonderful saying she used is barely decipherable, 'Live horse and you will get grass'. I think that took me at least an hour to figure out! Hearing them used so often, I realized these comforting phrases block out conscious thought or soul searching and may produce, in extremis, human zombies: Stepford wives, like Sinead here.

But the soul searching does continue in *Primordial* and leads to Sláine fearing he will join his father Roth in the icy world of Ifurin, a Celtic Hell reserved for criminals, traitors, and outcasts, where he will never sleep, never be at peace, because 'like father, like son, that is an inescapable law'.

A Hell not unlike the Wickerman, which was always on my mind and which I'll return to later.

Meanwhile, the Trojans pursue Sláine and Sinead. Their mantra is 'We obey like a dead body obeys' – originally a Jesuit command. That doesn't bear too much thinking about. And Sláine fights back, striking them out of nowhere in a guerilla war action sequence we've never seen before in the series. I watched *First Blood* again to get in the mood. Suitably inspired by Rambo, I tried out some action ideas here that I would develop further in a more urban setting in the final *Sláine* story *Dragontamer*.

A spoiler alert just now: I don't think I should say more about one of the central characters in *this* chapter, just in case you haven't read *The Brutania Chronicles* and are intending to. However, I do have to discuss this character in the two chapters that follow, so you will need to skip over them to avoid revelations.

As the story continues, I found myself feeling Sláine's rage at the way the Drune Lords have drugged Sinead in order that they can use her as a breeder. She is desperate for sleep flowers and will do anything for them. Drugs must have played a huge role in the Celtic era, arguably their knowledge of their different effects would be at least the equal of our own.

Sláine fakes his defeat in a desperate bid to bring her to her senses, but fails and I felt his despair as he is surrounded by the Trojans. But then the knowledge that she is to be used like a dog to produce obedient future generations finally lands and she is transformed into a warrior again! I felt Sláine's exhilaration as he exclaims, 'Sinead! Good to have you back!' They fight their way out and jump from a cliff in a beautiful action scene that is the equal of any movie. It's in scenes like this that fully painted art really comes into its own and I doubt we could be drawn into the world with line and colour *quite* so successfully.

Slough Foy – who wears the mask of the Salmon of Knowledge – has a conversation with Slough Gododin as they prepare the Primordial. Slough Foy was based on Father Foy, a legendary priest from Mayo (my mother's county) who was defrocked, probably due to drunkenness. But he had mysterious magical powers: it was claimed he could even walk on water. My cousins described him as a kind of druid who would curse those who displeased him. I've recently seen his grave in the churchyard outside Ballina Cathedral and it's covered in pagan-style votive offerings.

Then Sláine emerges from a blazing forest, warped as never before.

Foy is concerned that this could enrage the Archon – Yaldabaoth – who only allows the Cyth to experiment on humans when they can be controlled. And Sláine is surely out of control! The Archon will be even angrier when he discovers the Drune Lords are creating the Primordial, the ultimate warrior, greater even than Sláine!

But Gododin reminds Foy that the Archons think in geological time. 'By the time Yaldabaoth decides to act, an Ice Age will have passed.'

Finally, Sláine comes face to face with the Primordial, a creature even more hideous than his warped persona, and an epic battle follows!

THE PERFECT MURDER

The zest and the power of the battle between the Primordial (revealed as Gort) and Sláine is unmatched in *Psychopomp*. And then it becomes even more savage as Sláine becomes warped again. I'm not sure my words always kept pace with the fight; words complimenting action are always a challenge.

The character of Gort, as the Trojans' commander, was firmly established in the previous volume. There I explored what I regard as an important truth, namely that Gort had a death wish. This is something I believe is prevalent in many modern day heroes, but is rarely talked about because of its disturbing implications.

Gort has partaken of the Salmon of Knowledge and realises the Cyth and everything they stand for are a lie. *This* is why he wants to die. It's why he agreed go under cover and become the Primordial. But his comradeship with Sláine has also affected him, so the outcome is that he changes sides and joins forces with our hero in this volume.

I thought about and researched Gort's character very carefully before I wrote Volume One. It was inspired by several British army heroes, usually risk-takers who may have had a death wish. Or were believers in 'the noble sacrifice'. In particular, Robert Nairac, the

British army officer who went undercover in Northern Ireland and was eventually discovered and killed. Also the TV drama *Harry's Game*, where a fictional British army officer has a similar role. Nairac, a dedicated soldier, had come from a privileged background and was highly educated. Similarly, Gort had studied at the University of the Lord Weird Slough Feg where his tutor gave him the Salmon of Knowledge.

I had planned from the very outset that Gort would be an agent of the Drunes and a Trojan army officer. I think it worked well in Volume Two, but here at the end in Volume Three, somehow I don't think it had as much impact as I would have liked. I didn't feel the pang I was expecting when, after being together for three books, these two 'blood brothers' finally go their separate ways. Visually it felt distant and emotionally non-engaging to me.

By now, Sláine is bloodied, beaten up, bearded and showing his age. I hadn't written Sláine to be bearded and ageing, but over-directing an artist can be constricting for them, and counterproductive. In subsequent episodes he becomes even more world-weary, and his features change so that he is barely recognisable as our hero. Arguably it's realism after all he has been through, but it's too extreme for my personal taste. I would draw your attention to *The Life and Death of a Druid Prince: How the discovery of Lindow Man revealed the secrets of a lost civilization* by Anne Ross A sacrificed Celtic man has been reconstructed and he looks stunningly handsome. In fact, he looks remarkably like Sláine.

As the Gort story comes to a close, the story of Macha takes over and we see Simon's superb interpretation of Sláine's beautiful mother. I had only featured her briefly in the past, where she had tried to outrun the King's chariot; now we finally get to know her. She is an adventuress and a free spirit, who sweeps aside a young Sláine's anxious questions about his paternity, refusing to name his father.

If you consider the powerful Celtic women of legend, she is very much a woman of her times and our own times, too. She is also the greatest archer of her generation, which explains Sláine's skill with a bow. Hence, there was a scene in an earlier *Sláine* adventure where Ukko has an apple *in his mouth* and Sláine successfully fires an arrow through it, without it coming out the back of his dwarf's neck! This was a classic Celtic feat, totally over the top, and eclipsing the more 'sensible' or rational feats to be found in Anglo-Saxon, Greek or Roman legends.

But now there are even wilder archery scenes where, in a flashback, Macha fires fifteen arrows at high speed. This was based on a YouTube video I'd seen, which I passed onto Simon. Then Macha shows a young Sláine how she can fire a special arrow – with feathers at both ends – that swings around and returns to sender, shooting a Fomorian demon who has been creeping up on them. I actually found this 'boomerang' arrow exploit in a book describing the feats of Arabic archers, and experts have seriously considered its credibility. True or false, it is classic *Sláine*.

As Sláine connects with the memory of his mother, she guides him against his present enemies, with a series of dazzling archery skills: The Eagle feat – seizing an arrow in mid flight and firing it back. And the Falcon feat – splitting an arrow coming towards you with another.

Sláine knows that 'The Dead never die'.

The Lord Weird Slough Gododin tries to destroy Sláine by taunting him that Macha had at least three secret lovers, any one of whom could be his father. Or was there also a *fourth* lover? 'So who was he? I don't think you're going to like the answer.' There's a sense of dread here, powerfully conveyed in Simon's art.

Then there is the terrible revelation that Roth's boasting that his wife could outrun the King's chariot was *deliberate*. So he could get rid of his faithless wife who had made a cuckold out of him.

'It was the perfect crime.'

The perfect murder that Sláine had witnessed as a boy and had been powerless to prevent.

So many heroes have the death of a parent as their inciting incident, and now the horror of this event, established early on in the black and white era of Sláine, comes into its own. It makes a tragic and murderous sense, and once again, points towards the conclusion of the saga.

The knowledge causes a defeated Sláine to break his bow and fall to the ground as Gododin summons his own father, Slough Feg, from the Otherworld to witness our hero's final humiliation.

Then Sláine draws on the power of Zana, the Mother of all Humans, who he has helped escape. She is how humans were, before we were 'improved'. I'd always been fascinated by the story of our oldest ancestor *Lucy,* brought to life in a stunning book by renowned comic artist Liberatore. I chose the name Zana after the strange early human discovered alive in Russia in the nineteenth century. Neanderthal? Yeti? Throwback? No one knows, but she undoubtedly existed. Brown Lotus published an article, *Zana's Story*, on the online platform Medium:

> 'Zana's unique features rapidly earned her celebrity status. No one had seen anything like her. She was six-and-a-half feet tall, with black skin cloaked entirely in thick auburn fur. Zana also had more stark musculature than even the strongest men. Her sheer strength was legendary, and she did not seem to be affected by the frigid winter air, even though forced to sleep in the outdoors.'

Hardly has Sláine regained his strength when the Mountain of the Archon opens and thousands and thousands of Archons pour from it, intent on Sláine's destruction! I used the famous Chinese Terracotta Army as my inspiration. There were said to be more than 8,000 figures buried with the Emperor Quin Shi Huang. I would say there are a similar number in Simon's panoramic final scene.

But momentous as this finale was, there was one question uppermost in my mind. Macha had three lovers. Sláine's uncle, who bears the same name. Trego the Sword Master. And Duban the Druid.

Who was the Fourth Man?

THE WICKERMAN AKA THE MILK BAR

From the early *Sláine* story of *The Dark Gods*, it had been established that the Cyth lost the War in the Heavens and had been sent to a prison planet called Earth. But who were their jailers?

It was time to focus on them in Simon's final volume *Archon*. Inspired by the animated mountains of Virgil Finlay, I'd always wanted stone monsters to appear in *Sláine*. After the animated trees of *Lord of Misrule*, animated rock creatures were equally challenging. But I think the concept has great potential, especially after seeing the *Doctor Who* episode *Blink*, in which stone angels appear. Simon did an excellent job on the Archons, he brought out their robotic quality and I enjoyed seeing their defeat. Sinead melted them with a magical horn featured originally in the black and white *Sláine* stories. Then Gododin is made their prisoner for failing to defeat Sláine, confirming their identity as monstrous jailers.

The Archons are villains with great potential and I would have loved to have featured them again. So I'm sad that this is their only battle with Sláine. But Sláine and Sinead leave the Island, defeating the mermaids who attack once more as the Causeway sinks beneath their feet.

The Archons give Gododin one last chance to destroy Sláine, killing his fellow magicians as a demonstration of what will happen to him should he fail. *'Be sure, this time, Sláine is undone.'*

Meanwhile, Sláine is communicating with his dead mother. This culminates in the revelation that the Fourth Man might be an El Lord, a creature as odious as Elfric! The thought that a demon could be his father almost destroys Sláine.

I breathed a sigh of relief myself when it's finally revealed that Duban the Druid is his father! I had an emotional stake in it because I was drawing on my own search for my biological father. There were the three contenders I've previously mentioned: 'Jack the Lad', 'Torquemada' and 'Braveheart'.

But, unlike Sláine, I would not know the answer to my own quest until I wrote the final chapters of this book.

That said, I suppose 'Torquemada', as a Knight of St Columba, has a certain resemblance to Duban the Druid, but he's not an exact fit by any means. All three contenders were still real possibilities for paternity.

'Torquemada' certainly inspired those constant taunts by Sláine's greatest enemies. Namely that our hero is an outcast and will end up in the Wickerman filled with low-life, just like his legal father, Roth Bellyshaker.

As a boy, 'Torquemada' took me to the modern day equivalent of the Wickerman to give me a 'short, sharp shock'. This equivalent was the 'roughest', cheapest café in Ipswich: The Milk Bar. According to 'Torquemada', it was filled with the dregs of society. We sat in the fluorescent-lit, dingy café, looking at bored bikers playing the fruit machines and down-on-their-luck customers in demob raincoats nursing lukewarm tea in Styrofoam cups. I remember feeling rather ridiculous in my blue, gold and red school uniform. I think he liked me wearing it because it was a reminder that the Knights of St Columba had paid for both my brother's and my education. They 'owned' us.

He sneered at the other customers. 'They're losers. They'll never amount to anything. They'll never be anyone important.' ('Torquemada' himself was a paint shop foreman, no less) 'This is where you'll end up, unless you pull your socks up, laddie. Do you understand ... *laddie?'*

I wanted to say, 'I can't, because I don't wear sock suspenders like the Knights,' but I wisely kept my mouth shut. His 'short sharp shock' left a deep impression on me. It's why there are endless references to the danger of Sláine ending up in a Wickerman, aka The Milk Bar, throughout the saga. It was clearly highly symbolic that Sláine *breaks out* of the Wickerman with the rest of the 'losers' and *defeats* the equivalent of the Knights, before going on to become High King of Ireland. And now, in this final volume by Simon, he has even defeated Galactic monsters in the shape of the Archons. So much for the dire predictions of the Knights.

The Archons and Gododin make one last bid to destroy Sláine. This time the Earth Goddess, beautifully painted by Simon, vanquishes them. It would seem that Gododin is killed by the vengeful Archons, but we don't actually see him die. The door is left slightly ajar for his possible return in the future. Good villains should never be wasted!

As the Brutania saga concludes, I set the world up for the next serial. And so for the first time we meet Brutus – visually based on Oliver Reed and verbally based on Churchill – and his two pacifist sons Locrin and Kamber. The legendary Brutus, King of the Trojans, also known as 'Brute of Troy', is a fascinating character rarely featured in heroic fantasy and I looked forward to exploring him and his dysfunctional family in the future.

I also had Simon visualise the Trojans' city of New Troy or Llandin. There are mysterious memories of 'Troy Towns', labyrinth mazes, throughout Britain, and they provided the basis for this primal version of London.

The city has the scale that I was after, although I would have liked the land areas to have been more than just causeways in the water, with more details, streets and buildings to fully appreciate its grandeur. I was inspired by and, I freely admit, thoroughly spoilt by the European comic book tradition. Thus on *Requiem: Vampire Knight*, Olivier has painted similar fantastic cities: Necropolis for example, but he can then sell those double page spreads for thousands of pounds and he often designed pages with an art gallery in mind.

The British 'all rights' system means artists cannot take the same time, even though they often have the same talent, like Simon. We are conditioned to see ourselves as third best, somewhere behind the Europeans and the Americans so everything is still about speed – the curse of our British comic tradition – and not about quality. There is no incentive for an artist to spend weeks drawing a fantasy city anymore. In the past, there were artists who did: Glenn Fabry on *Tomb of Terror* or Kevin O'Neill on the fantastic underground cities of Termight, endlessly toiling over amazing fantasy architecture. But it was to their financial detriment.

The most fascinating aspect of those final pages is the 'telegram' system of our ancient ancestors, whereby a message could be sent from the north of Brutania at sunrise, transmitted from Caller to Caller, to reach New Troy by sunset! This is based on an account by Caesar in his *Conquest of Gaul*, which suggests the Celts could quickly communicate over vast distances.

I came across it in a remarkable book entitled *The Ancient Paths: Discovering the Lost Map of Celtic Europe* by Graham Robb:

> 'Graham Robb discovers how the roads of Europe were laid out – long before the Romans – according to Druidic calculations. Inspired by a chance discovery, Robb became fascinated with the world of the Celts: their gods, their art, and, most of all, their sophisticated knowledge of science. His investigations gradually revealed something extraordinary: a lost map, of an empire

constructed with precision and beauty across vast tracts of Europe. The map had been forgotten for almost two millennia and its implications were astonishing.'

I'm imagining the final sequence of this book in a movie as Sláine's message is passed up hill and down dale. Sláine wants Brutus to know that he's coming for him. Like the yodellers who call from mountain to mountain, his communication is passed from shepherd to ploughman, to washerwoman, to blacksmith, to priestess. Via baritone, tenor and soprano, it crosses Albion and finally reaches Brutus in New Troy. It's a message that Brutus's nervous first minister is understandably afraid to pass on to his Emperor.

It consists of just three words, which are the title of this book.

PART V
DRAGONTAMER

SIN CITY

Sláine the Wanderer and *The Brutania Chronicles* had enabled me to set up legendary Britain before exploring it in detail. That process now began in earnest with *Dragontamer*. New Troy, aka Llandin, is firmly based on the City of London. According to legend, Brutus founded the capital in 1070BC and the 'Stone of Brutus' can still be seen today in Cannon Street in the City.

William Blake tells us it was on this stone that the Druids carried out bloody sacrifices.

> *Where Albion slept beneath the Fatal Tree,*
> *And the Druids' golden Knife*
> *Rioted in human gore, In Offerings of Human Life...*
> *They groan'd aloud on London Stone,*
> *They groan'd aloud on Tyburn's Brook...*

An ancient saying claims, 'So long as the Stone of Brutus is safe, so long will London flourish.'

So, too, can be seen the magnificent heraldic dragon statues guarding the City and hence why living versions of them, complete in every detail, feature strongly in *Dragontamer*.

The City's history and its power certainly stretch back in time. William the Conqueror made a special agreement with the City in 1067, upholding its rights and privileges.

In the 1600s, the City rewarded Oliver Cromwell with gold for selling out the English Leveller revolution and the soldiers' fight for freedom. Cromwell had crushed the army mutinies and sentenced its leaders to death by firing squad. An important story you can be sure is missing from most schools' history curriculums. Events I covered in *Defoe*, because we need to know about the City's perfidy.

In World War One, these events remarkably repeated themselves. There was the great British mutiny at Etaples, where soldiers went on strike for freedom and to end to mass-murder. An event endlessly minimised by our shameful establishment historians. The mutiny was crushed by the City of London's Honourable Artillery Company. A regiment of 'Ruperts' who would have no sympathy with the suffering of the common man. Events I covered in *Charley's War*, for the same reason as *Defoe*.

The City was the capital of the British Empire (whose crimes are all too well known now), and today it is a global financial power, its continuing crimes not so well known. See for example *The Spider's Web: Britain's Second Empire*, on YouTube. The film paints a disturbing picture of its modern-day greed and avarice, perfect for incorporating into my barbaric Kingdom of Brutania. A Sin City indeed.

Nothing has changed over the millennia. This really is an *eternal kingdom*, and evil does repeat itself, as a medieval poem suggests:

> *Brutus! there lies beyond the Gallic bounds*
> *An island which the Western Sea surrounds,*
> *By Giants once possessed, now few remain*
> *To bar thy entrance, or obstruct thy reign.*
> *To reach that happy shore thy sails employ*
> *There fate decrees to raise a second Troy*

And found an Empire in thy royal line,
Which time shall ne'er destroy, nor bounds confine.
Geoffrey of Monmouth, History of the Kings of
    Britain

I based its legendary King Brutus on Winston Churchill, a detail I would have been reluctant to admit at the time I first featured him. But now, when police have to mount guard over Churchill's statues, it's clear the truth is slowly emerging: the public are finally becoming aware of his endless crimes – which amount to mass-murder – and weighing them alongside his agreed role as the nation's saviour. It's well overdue. I gave Brutus a dysfunctional family affected by the Web of Weird and ancestral curses. That's why Brutus drinks metheglin, a strong form of mead, which dulls his senses to the horror of his crimes. Whether Churchill was affected by something similar, with his 'Black Dog' depressions and 'alcohol dependency', I couldn't possibly say.

The Web of Weird – Karma – features in the story. Thus, it's rather more than coincidence that Brutus, inordinately fond of war as was Churchill, has two sons who are pacifists. We've probably all seen such paradoxes. A friend of mine, who was an anti-establishment pacifist, had a son who joined the British army and loved every minute of it. I fear that's sometimes how Karma – action and reaction – works.

Alongside the Web of Weird, there is also the impact of ancestry, something our modern society tries to deny, but is all too pervasive. Family curses such as those suffered by the Kennedys and the Windsors are well known. History seems to endlessly repeat itself. There are Bible references to the sins of the fathers being visited upon their descendants to the fourth generation. The DNA and psychoanalytical basis for this phenomena now has a name: epigenetics. It has even entered popular culture, for example with the TV series *The Affair*, where an epigenetics scientist makes sense of dark family secrets. But science still has a long way to go to catch up with our Neolithic ancestors, who knew far more than we do about the mysteries of ancestry.

Ancestry affects both Brutus and Sláine in *Dragontamer*, and has great potential for future stories, not just in the *Sláine* saga. We are talking real-life magic here – or epigenetics if you prefer. I've also featured it in my new comic *Spacewarp*.

If the subject is of personal interest to you, there is the Family Constellations system – a powerful method because of the number of participants involved, each one representing a relevant family member. It was devised by Bert Hellinger, who wrote a book on the subject called *Acknowledging What Is*. Hellinger based his Family Constellations system on his experiences with Zulu tribes. Or, for a more Irish connection there's *Wood You Believe It: The Ancestral Self* by Father Jim Cogley. These system have a serious purpose – principally to acknowledge missing members of the family tree. Missing members can be miscarriages, adoptions, family members cast out, or – in my case – a missing biological father. If they're not acknowledged, it creates a kind of energy blockage. The family tree and the power of the ancestors is awesome and it is not the product of a vivid imagination. I've felt it, and really wished I hadn't.

There is also the University of the Lord Weird Slough Feg, maintaining links with past stories. If Feg seems an unlikely choice to have a university named after him, consider Oxford University's Rhodes scholars named after Cecil Rhodes, who was also a monster. Only now are his statues being taken down. Feg's university is also there so I could dramatise the druids' magical systems. For instance, readers recently told me about the 'memory palaces', the systems by which tribal cultures can remember their histories going back thousands of years. It's likely the druids would have used a similar system because they jealously preserved their secrets and despised books.

Then there is the strange labyrinthine layout of New Troy,

clearly designed to make the city accessible to the Trojans' aquatic Fomorian 'allies'. I'm left wondering who or what is really at the heart of the labyrinth and the mysterious connection to 'Troy Towns' – turf mazes – that are still found throughout Britain.

Finally, Ukko has a bar in New Troy. His life's dream is realised at last. So he's there whenever the saga needs some levity.

With all these new elements in place, I looked forward to writing *Sláine* in legendary Britain for many years to come.

But Fate, or the ancestors, had other plans for me.

UNFINISHED BUSINESS

There was a break after *The Brutania Chronicles* and I wasn't sure when or how I would return to *Sláine*. I had other writing projects that were taking priority. Simon was keen to continue, but I didn't feel inspired to write the next saga, although all the characters and Sláine's world were set up for the future.

Then, following the death of an Irish relative, as I looked into the records of my ancestry, something compelled me to continue. There was unfinished business: the search for my identity and Sláine's search for his identity were somehow still enmeshed.

I felt the story and art needed to move at a different pace to *The Brutania Chronicles*. I decided to make it frenetic, all-action, with more images on the page to hold the reader's attention, feeding the exposition into the drama in such bite-sized chunks that the audience would be barely aware they were swallowing it. Keep it short and sharp (ten episodes), with ascending drama that doesn't give the reader a chance to draw breath. With a younger Sláine and some new action concepts to keep the story fresh. If my story style sounds compressed, you would be right, but I'd worked with Simon on *Black Siddha*, where the story was even more compressed and he did a fantastic job, so I knew it was feasible.

After some months, Simon decided to pass on illustrating the story. He will be missed by many, such as reader Paul Banville who said: 'I really like Simon Davis's work. It's his art on *Sláine* that kept me reading *2000AD* after returning to the fold with Prog 2050.'

Colin Miller agreed:

'Simon Davis is one of the very best - top three without a doubt - Davis, McMahon & Bisley. And, probably more important than my own opinion, my 12-year-old son is completely blown away by it. It's been his transition point from reading Marvel to *2000AD*.'

And so began the search for a new artist. Editor Matt Smith came up with Argentinian artist Leo Manco – a truly inspired choice – who was to make a huge difference to the saga and ensure it ended on a high note.

Here's what I had to say to Matt in July 2018 when Leo was first suggested:

'Looking at his art, I would say he could bring to *Sláine*: The original feeling of *Sláine* episode one (by Angela), with a touch of *Conquering Armies* (her role model), a touch of Simon Bisley where it wasn't too Conan, and especially Clint Langley.'

What makes Leo's work on *Sláine* so especially impressive is that the story was written for *Simon*. So Leo, an Argentinian, had to make sense of notes and descriptions written for a *British* artist! But my initial thoughts about his work were correct. His black and white inking style reminded me of a more exciting and dynamic version of *Conquering Armies*, the much derided bible I'd insisted on using as my role model for *Sláine*.

Like *Conquering Armies*, Leo transforms black and white art into colour. We'd finally returned to my original dream of how *Sláine* should look. We'd come full circle.

In fact, I urged Matt to run the story in black and white, because it's such a joy to see. But, mindful of the long legacy of *Sláine* in colour, Matt felt it should stay in that way, and I'm sure that was safer. Even so, I think there's a case for a black and white edition of *Dragontamer* at some stage, possibly a collector's edition.

What I especially liked about Leo's work is that it is sharp, detailed and real, and you can see exactly what's going on. All too often, fully painted *Sláine* artwork wasn't this effective.

Colour was a challenge for Leo but I think he masters it. It can be a problem colouring black line art, but Leo's experiments in that direction came up with the perfect palette. Curiously, *Conquering Armies* also needed to be in colour for a new edition and their version is fine, but safe. Too safe for my taste. Consequently, I still prefer it in black and white.

But do not assume that this process was simple or brief. It bears out my view that to properly develop a character it can take six weeks of unpaid work. I won't go into all the detail on the endless art development phase between me and Leo. I would encourage a particular direction and then he would come up with a new approach, followed by another, and another ... It was clear he was totally in love with the character.

It was just like the early days of *Sláine*, where artists gave their all, because they loved drawing the character and were indifferent to the money.

To give you just a taste of the work behind the scenes. Leo's first colouring was too warm, suggestive of a hot climate story, like *Conan*. Even Sláine's axe was gold coloured.

So this is what I wrote back to Matt at the time:

'Leo's colour palette should be muted, North European. Dave Kendall did a *Sláine* pin-up, you'll recall where you could almost smell the damp. Might be useful as a ref?? Colours should have the feeling of Britain and Ireland. Soft wet greens of Ireland. And also as this is a DARK URBAN story, the muted colours that create a 'noire' feeling. Like Dark Knight.'

That green, green grass of Sláine's homeland was so very important. At first Leo tried acrylics, and these were my thoughts:

'Firstly, his beautiful black line work is getting lost under the acrylic style. This is a shame because it's his line work which is the appeal of his art. Even with cool, muted colours, correct axe colour etc, if it's done in that acrylic style is unlikely to be appealing. In order to lose that heavy-handed American comic book look, which I know our readers will hate, it needs a similar colour approach to Dark Knight.'

And so on.

All this is perfectly normal and a natural part of the creative development of a comic strip. Even though publishers hate to admit it, because it would mean acknowledging creators are *working for nothing* during the development period. None of us get it right to start with, and that should be financially acknowledged with a suitable bonus. In the past, there were ways this was done, because it was recognised how *devastating* this could be to a freelance's budget. The alternative is fast-food, third-rate comics. Or stories drawing heavily on another creator's work – such as Gerry Finley-Day – so there is less need for development time. The new writer benefits from all the foundation work of the original writer, who is never remunerated.

I counted a total of 67 emails between Matt, Leo and myself between July and December 2018, discussing different aspects of the art!

And it was well worth it. Leo has produced a masterpiece.

Nothing was too much trouble for him. The effort he put into the art was simply mind-boggling. All too often, creators eventually *have* to cut corners and use a McDonalds approach, knocking the pages out in order to pay the bills. But Leo never did. He even made further considerable improvements for the book edition for *free!*

I have a reputation for being painstaking, which does not make me popular with every artist, as you can imagine. But, for the first time, I've encountered someone in the industry who is even more painstaking than me.

I've finally met my match. No, actually, I've been beaten at my own game.

44

HOW A NEW SLÁINE STORY IS CREATED

R eaders sometimes ask me how stories are created and constructed, so I thought it would be useful at this point to demonstrate a little of what is involved, and why I chose not to continue *Sláine*.

So this is *The Sláine Story That Never Was*.

Or rather it's a visit to its construction site with all the building materials, scaffolding and plans that would have enabled me to create it. Like all construction sites, it may look like a jumble, but hopefully you'll see the sense of it. And all that jumble of new ideas, it should go without saying, remains the copyright of this writer. Like all construction sites, there's a security guard on duty – and trespassers will be dealt with.

If you're a new writer, looking for insights into storytelling, I hope it's helpful, but please don't be intimidated by your visit. Your own muse will guide you. And you may build a completely different house to me. Just make sure it has firm foundations, whatever your design.

The process usually takes at least six weeks unpaid development time, including interacting with the artist on his visualisations.

Below is an approximate breakdown of those six weeks because

– just like any artisan – a job needs *costing* before I start. We don't expect builders to work for free when they build houses and we shouldn't expect writers when they build their imaginary edifices. Here I'm referring to *planning* the building, *designing* it, not just turning up at the building site with a concrete mixer and a lorry load of bricks. This period of time would not necessarily be in a block, but sometimes spread out over several months, particularly the interaction with the artist.

ONE WEEK: Developing *the new villains* I had planned if *Sláine* had continued. In fact, I originally featured them at the end of *Dragontamer,* but cut them out for reasons of space. The villains are what usually make a story click with the readers. Reading ancient accounts of their evil exploits. Getting inside their heads. I find them really exciting and sinister, so that would have been a most enjoyable process. Seeing how they relate to Brutus and co. Looking for a prime villain amongst them to focus on. And how he might relate to Sláine as a powerful adversary.

Finding visual refs. Finding modern-day equivalents, ideally someone I know of personally. Considering satirical personal elements to the new villains. That makes it cathartic for me, and gives the villains a memorable edge. Most of my villains are partly based on someone I know. New villains like this are likely to go through at least two iterations, with various name changes, as they are further refined. As I'm hoping to use the historical basis for these villains in a comic story elsewhere, I can't be more specific about them here, or the original sources I've found.

ONE WEEK: Researching dragons to develop them further. In particular, the dragon statues of the city of London. There's something about them that I don't feel either Leo or myself have quite captured. I need to take a fresh look at them. Probably also drawing on modern birds of prey as well as Celtic legends. There's a lot here in Spain to inspire me. Eagles and vultures fly overhead every day.

This is something to talk over with an artist. If it's not really gelling, I could marginalise them.

There's so much else in the story. Developing New Troy, including its Atlantean maze, Ukko's bar and the University of the Lord Weird Slough Feg. It may need a map of the city with its unique waterways and how they work. Reading accounts of life in ancient cities. The darker and grimmer the better. Looking at the historical crimes and the (ongoing) sinister secrets of the City of London. They are the heart of New Troy, but there's not that much useful or relevant in print about these 'bankers', so I'll need to dig long and hard to discover the truth about them.

ONE WEEK: Developing Brutus and his dysfunctional, drugged and horribly haunted family. How to make them even more *Gormenghast-esque* (an early source of inspiration). How they might interact with each other without becoming a digression. Looking again at the people I based them on to see if additions or replacements are required.

Considering whether Brutus and Sláine meet yet, and under what circumstances. New examples of oppression from Brutus for Sláine to combat. Drawing on British colonialism and the struggles of First Nations for inspiration.

Researching original accounts of Brutus, Albion, and the mysterious Troy Town mazes (which are all over the UK) to provide an original Celtic backcloth. Brutus's relationship with his Drune Lords, the Fomorians, and his past genocidal crimes against the Giants. How much evidence is there of genocide in ancient times in Britain? Something there I could adapt.

We may never see all this, but it helps to deepen his character to know how he feels about his fellow villains. Reading a negative, true history of Churchill who is the modern day counterpart of Brutus. Churchill 'relied on alcohol' and Brutus relies on metheglyn (mead) to deal with his inner demons. Brutus is the very embodiment of all that is dark, corrupt and wrong about our country and its sinister –

and ongoing – history as a Dark Empire. There may be an esoteric continuance of this theme of evil Empire, so will need to look at Geoffrey of Monmouth's account again.

ONE WEEK: Looking at Sláine's character: where is he going personally? What is his deeper response to Brutus? Will his tribal background remain shut down? What about his druid father – can I take that further? Even though I passionately hate such 'wise old git' magicians with beards because of their superiority. Who is he based on, beyond my own family background? Maybe look at one of the popes. Perhaps Sláine hates him as much as I do, even though his father helped him. Nice ingratitude and conflict. Maybe the druid turns up in Ukko's bar? Perhaps Sláine disgraces himself – that could be fun. But then his father reveals something momentous – some new magic – that drives the plot. Ukko making sarcastic comments about Sláine's different dads could also be amusing and he could take the piss out of the druid. That feels like a strong scene.

What about the comedy? How far can Ukko feature without dominating or skewing the story? Can his tavern play a central role, just as the Eternal Fortress did in the Horned God? It takes up a lot of space, but Simon Bisley was a fast artist and so is Leo. It would mean a longer story, so I would need to clear that with the editor.

Celtic martial arts – new action elements and comic strip techniques to keep the story and art fresh. Visuals to shock the eye that we've never seen before in comics. New angles on the warp spasm – already entering new territory in *Dragontamer*. Ensuring Sláine dominates throughout. The role of magic. To further develop ancestral magic or the hauntings by the dead, or more likely, to look at an entirely fresh aspect of Celtic magic and Goddess worship that may not have featured in *Sláine* before.

ONE WEEK: One or two angle concepts or characters will jump out from the above as the prime ones that will light the readers' fire and my own, and direct the serial. Probably the villains and how they harm ordinary people and new magic introduced by Sláine's annoying dad. I then focus on them exclusively, researching and developing them further, taking away the scaffolding and the debris, disposing of other elements or putting them on a back burner for later volumes. So a strong, simple, accessible story emerges.

ONE WEEK: Decorating time. Post-mortem on existing art. How to evolve the art further. The artist's views. Or it may not be necessary. Either way it requires thought. Emphasising the non-*Conan* quality of *Sláine*, certainly. Looking at the dragons and seeing how they might be more scary. Designing the new villains and the world of New Troy. I would need to find new Neolithic city sources for further reference, so it's not just beehive buildings. We need to retain our sense of wonder at the fantasy world of New Troy.

Leo also likes ongoing feedback on his episodes as he draws them, which is fine, but rather than a quick, 'Yeah, that's great', it's far better to take the time to study them and suggest tweaks. This was certainly how it was done with Angela Kincaid, Glenn Fabry, David Pugh, Simon Bisley and other artists. On occasion, scripts were rewritten or later episodes modified to take account of the visual direction the artist was taking it in. And even new ideas that occurred to the artists that I might incorporate, or be inspired by their insights. All that needs factoring in financially. This is not a free service that the builder provides for his client, and it's not one that can be ignored either.

There are numerous sources I would consult, so let me mention three of them. *Scarred For Life*, which is a good anchor to the past when 2000AD was in its hey-day. I'm always concerned that the comic's original energy can get lost in the wretched times we live in and *Scarred For Life* is a good primer to ensure *Sláine* remains faithful to its roots.

Then there's the *Hookland* website, which captures the magic and the mystery of Britain and Ireland. Including the world of Faerie. After *the Secret Commonwealth* disaster, and all that wonderful magic wasted, I backed away from the more subtle and low-key magical world of folklore. But now could be the time to revisit it. It would mean a darker, creepier more nature-orientated story and would put considerable visual demands on the artist. Belardinelli would have got it, and so would Angela if she had still been drawing *Sláine*, but it could be a tougher proposition for any other *Sláine* artists and would require a great deal of thought and discussion and interaction with the artist. The inspiring material in *Hookland* is truly unique. Reader Sarah Harris recommended if I was perusing, to 'set aside a month or seven.'

And moving on from the themes in *Hookland*, there is *The Book of Trespass* by Nick Hayes. The whole point of Brutus is that he is a symbol of *eternal* oppression by our British ruling class, from the monarch down, and this book would get me in the zone and remind me that this is an eternal war. The tyranny exposed by *The Book of Trespass* – our land stolen from us – would fit well into the story of *Sláine*. Our hero's battles need to be relevant to us *today*. This is a source I will have to use to inspire me to write a story elsewhere.

Whatever the final design of this imaginary *Sláine That Never Was*, one thing is certain: Sláine must win. And not just because that's the nature of comics. Although it's why comics are so important as a genre. But because all too often, exposes of evil in other media end on a negative note. I'm a huge fan of Ken Loach's work and it's absolutely valid, for his audience, to portray failure (e.g., *Days of Hope*), or Chris Mullin's *A Very British Coup*, which culminates in defeat. But a younger audience may well conclude that the evil bastards these films brilliantly expose will always win. So in all my stories the hero usually *wins* – because the establishment *can* be defeated. That's not a comic fantasy. On a personal level, outside the scope of this book, I've had two important successes against establishment figures, which everyone told me when I started were absolutely impossible. And I've not finished yet (I refer to it briefly at the end of this book). So we are conditioned endlessly to keep our heads down and our mouths shut. Not to be 'troublemakers'. And to believe that the establishment, in whatever form it takes: politics; religion; education; medical or business – will always get the better of us. Not true. Conversely, we are conditioned to believe it is a force for good and should not be challenged. Still not true.

Sláine is the embodiment of defeating such establishment oppressors. The more we fight them, the more we see just how vulnerable the oppressors really are. They are not the strutting demigods they like to think they are. They can and must be taken down.

So that's my six weeks. Of course, like all builders, I'm likely to run over on time.

Once all this is done, I would then write a synopsis for the editor's approval. Usually in the form of an episode breakdown. The subsequent writing and payment for those episodes is currently cost-effective, no more and no less, but that is an entirely separate costing to this initial development time.

Returning to the development: the only chance of getting that time paid for would be when the book finally comes out. A book edition on *Sláine* is likely, but not on my other *2000AD* stories. But it could still be eighteen months after publication before I receive any royalties, as Rebellion pay once a year in arrears. Other comic publishers pay every six months or quarterly. Because the royalties are so low – see next chapter – it will defray some (but certainly not all) of my time costs creating a building, an intellectual property, which *I don't own*. So it could be *three years* after the development before it's *partly* compensated, if I'm lucky. And sometimes I haven't been lucky – see the next chapter.

No builder I know waits that long for his money.

In the preferred fast food world of British comics, where quantity rather than quality is the rule for as long as I've been in the business, it's usual to short cut through such development time because of economic necessity. On occasion it may even be beneficial – it can keep a story sharp, superficial and instantly appealing, which can be attractive to some comic readers. On occasion. Of course there is a danger of 'over-thinking', as defenders of fast food comics will tell you. But this planning time is why *Sláine* has been around for forty years and the 'short cut' story is likely to be around for a whole lot less. I used a similar planning approach on *Charley's War,* endlessly researching along the above lines, and that is why it too has longevity. My other stories, too, were devised with this approach.

All these areas of development come under the banner of what Mick McMahon once memorably described as 'staring out the window time'.

If a publisher wants *classics*, that will be remembered for a lifetime, like the stories from *2000AD's* golden age, and like *Charley's War*, then I'm afraid they have to *pay* us for 'staring out the window time'.

Of course how far they actually *want* classics anymore is open to question.

45

A PERFECT STORM

I wrote *Dragontamer* in early 2018, and it appeared in 2021. Much was to change during those years and everything finally added up to a perfect storm, where I asked myself in 2021: just what was the point in continuing to write *Sláine*?

Coming up against irreconcilable differences with a publisher, freelances have just two choices. You either put up with the problems or you move on, as most of my peers – 2000AD's early and greatest writers and artists – did long ago. Often with a heavy heart. Don't let snide supporters for today's status quo tell you that their departure was all about economic gain and prestige, as if they were somehow wrong and even disloyal to 2000AD by leaving. That's unfair; they had no choice and for most it was a huge wrench parting with characters they had created and loved. If the deals had been better the majority would have stayed or at least kept a significant presence in the comic from time to time. It's why many of them won't talk about 2000AD: the subject is still painful to them.

I too should have departed long ago, but having started a comic like 2000AD, it's so much harder to let go of your baby. Especially when it includes *Sláine*.

I naively believed there would eventually be positive changes if I just held on long enough, or explained to publishers the huge bene-fits *to them* of applying industry standard rules.

Unfortunately, no one was listening. The subliminal message I take away from this is clear enough, to me at least: If you don't like it, there's the door.

And that's why I've got my coat.

In fact, it was unrealistic of me to expect international comic standards of copyright and quality from a publisher with overlap-ping but ultimately different objectives. Just as it was unrealistic for me to continue to go on producing a story to international standards to my own economic disadvantage. After 40 years of writing *Sláine*, that would be extremely dumb.

Other elements that comprised the storm were not negative; on the contrary. Leo had produced a great saga, so perfect in every way, that this was surely the right time to finish *Sláine*. To go out while we're winning, with a story that harks back to the very beginning of the character.

After all, *Sláine* had to end some time.

Plus, I have been given a firm assurance by Rebellion that no one will take over my stories or re-imagine them, adapt them, spin-off subsidiary characters, or use the world as a springboard for their own ideas.

I'd had previous firm assurances to this effect but, ever anxious that the goalposts might yet be moved as they had been in *2000AD's* dark past, I have editor Matt Smith's assurance to me, on 1st September 2020:

> No, there'll be no plans for any other writers to use your
> characters or worlds, or spin-offs thereof.

That undertaking is as clear as it can possibly be. It is not quali-fied in any way whatsoever.

So that's good enough for me, for the readers, and for the Suits.

It had been a possibility, albeit a remote one. After all, no creative team has ever touched Alan Moore's stories for 2000AD, like his *Halo Jones*. Or Grant Morrison's stories. Gerry Finley-Day was not so fortunate. His stories have been relentlessly strip-mined by other writers, generally to their detriment. It would be reasonable to construe that the underlying reason for the difference between how the three writers have been treated is ultimately about power: who has it and who doesn't. Gerry clearly doesn't – thanks in part to a relentless campaign to attack and undermine his work, prior to it being appropriated (no coincidence there), which is why I champion him at every opportunity. But there would rightly be a huge negative reaction from readers should any other writer *dare* to attempt to continue Alan's *Halo Jone*s. Or Grant's *Zenith*. There would, hopefully, be a similar reaction if a writer tried to do the same on *Sláine*. With luck, it will never be put to the test.

The reasons for preserving my legacy on *Sláine* also need stating. The most important is that it rarely works when other writers take over a character. To put it crudely – they will fuck it up. My anti-war saga *Charley's War* is a case in point, but there are many others. When *Charley* continued into World War Two with another writer it bombed in record time because – despite Joe Colquhoun's ongoing brilliant work – the readers didn't like the 'safe' storytelling. *Judge Dredd* is the possible exception to the rule because it was developed by several of us. But even there, creator John Wagner's writing stands out head and shoulders above everyone else's.

It's understandable that some fans would like their favourite stories to continue forever, even if it's only a shadow of what it once was. Better '*Sláine*-lite' than no *Sláine* at all, might be their argument. I know some readers feel that way about other 2000AD stories, but thankfully not mine, as far as I know.

There is a remedy, if that is what readers really want: a financial reward to the creator if another writer takes over. This is industry standard in France and elsewhere, and it works. So if I stopped writing *Requiem: Vampire Knight*, another writer could be appointed, but I would receive a share of their royalties. Publishers Glénat would definitely seek my approval on this, because they have similarly consulted me on a possible *Requiem* film.

That seems like a reasonable and fair solution to me, but it's not one that's followed on *2000AD*

In any event, *Sláine* is an intensely personal quest, and I believe Rebellion recognise the impossibility of sustaining the unique hallmark of the creator with another writer. Like so many others, I was never interested in reading *Conan* by different authors after Robert E. Howard. Rebellion seem to understand that another writer, even with talent and a good reputation, would be unlikely to successfully continue *Sláine*. The financial rewards wouldn't be sufficient, the opprobrium from *Sláine* fans would be considerable, and there would be so much better uses for their talent. Besides, for the character to go where, and to what purpose? It would be far easier to create their own brand new character, so they don't have to constantly look over their shoulder at the past. That's what a writer with genuine talent would do.

Despite all this, the threat is still real enough in recent years. Usually it starts with a 'nibble' around the edges of one of my stories to test the water. A small unauthorised 'guest appearance' by one of my characters in another story, perhaps, to see if I will complain. I always do. Letting it go or turning a blind eye doesn't work, because boundary breakers only see that as weakness. Once you let one in, others follow. I guess such writers are short of work, not to mention talent.

Thus, one new writer stated in a Rebellion publication in response to a question by an interviewer that she *knew* it was wrong, but she was *still* going to find an artist and submit a *Sláine* proposal to *2000AD* anyway! I complained to Rebellion, who warned her off, but they spun it to me that it was actually a measure of her great *love* of *Sláine* that she wanted to write her own story about him. Oh...

really?! That tired old excuse of 'homage' is still being used after all these years? Come on!

It's what opportunist writers usually say. Alongside: 'I know you're very protective of your stories, but Rico was only a *little* character. So I didn't think you'd mind.' This was Michael Carroll's justification to me after writing *three* novels about my creation Rico, who was central to the first *Dredd* movie. It's a wonderful piece of Irish blarney, which I'm sure Ukko would greatly admire. Blarney matched only by Rebellion telling me that it would not be *practical* to inform me of similar novel plans on my characters in the Dredd world, should this ever happen again in the future.

To sum up, the financial model Rebellion use is benefiting its owners and its salaried staff; but it is not, in my opinion, sufficiently benefiting the freelance creators with industry standard arrangements. Yet those creators are actually responsible for the long-running and well-loved comic characters that have generated the bulk of their income through comic sales, book sales, options and merchandising. They are the source of that wealth.

It's a subject Rebellion would prefer me not to talk about in public. Their defensiveness reminds me of comic publisher D.C. Thomson, memorably filmed in an amusing 1970s documentary by (I think) BBC2, called 'The Red Lubyanka', due to its HQ's forbidding red sandstone exterior. In the film it was portrayed as an impregnable fortress where the staff pulled up the drawbridge, and defied and ignored their critics, looking down on them all with a dour and stony silence. In some ways, it feels like comics have come full circle, back to those dark days.

Despite my best and recent efforts to find a solution acceptable to both of us, Rebellion and I have reached an impasse, so it's not possible to accommodate their request. And that's a pity, because there are many positive aspects to Rebellion's reign over *2000AD*, which I applaud. The staff's dedication to the comic. Their understanding of the characters and its history. Their successful commercial exploitation of the various intellectual properties for merchandising. That's all to be commended. But, as I've had to remind them on numerous occasions, freelances are emphatically *not* staff, and that isn't taken on board. Being treated on occasion like staff did not sit well with me. Because one of the few benefits of being a freelance is that we are actually *free*. It's why, when I was offered the permanent editorship of *Battle*, *Action* and *2000AD*, I said no, because it would have meant becoming staff and having to put up with the restrictions and control that go with it. I need to be free. In particular, free to speak my mind when I feel we freelances are not being treated correctly.

The Little Sisters of Absolute Misery – with all their power – were unable to silence me when I was seven years old and spoke out against what was going on (see Chapter 2). So I don't think there's any chance of anyone else succeeding today. It's hardwired into my DNA.

A good example of a core problem was in 2019, when *Sláine The Horned God* (Hachette edition) launched the *2000AD* Ultimate Editions on the newsstand. Price: £1.99.

At the time of the launch, I raised my concern that this full colour, deluxe hardback was being sold for such a small price – as a 'launch loss leader'. And other full-priced books that followed would benefit financially from *The Horned God* being 'the fall guy'.

Here's what Ben Smith at Rebellion had to say in response:

'There's definitely no sense of HG subsiding the other books. Rather it's leading the charge with the Crown Jewels. The low price on the first book ensures that it sells in substantially greater quantities than any other subsequent issue. By a large factor of difference, up to ten or more as I recall it being explained to me... There's no disadvantaging of Pat or Simon by being first out of the gate, quite the reverse.'

So I spent time and energy promoting the book and the series. For example, I went on an extended *2000AD* promotional podcast with Simon Bisley to talk about *The Horned God*.

But my concerns were completely justified. I received £129 in royalties for *2000AD*'s 'Crown Jewels'.

The 'disadvantage' was huge and has not been remedied since, despite my bringing it to their attention and suggesting a token payment that would acknowledge the disparity so we could all have closure on the matter. There was no response.

The number of units sold of *The Horned God* was also withheld, despite my requests for information. But the revenue Rebellion received on it was listed on my royalty statement as £2587.30. Due to Simon Bisley and myself was a total of £258. This means Rebellion takes 90% of the profits and passes on just 10% to creators. This is far below industry standard, which is 50% to publisher and 50% to creators.

Checking on other titles on my royalty statement from Rebellion, this percentage breakdown appears to be universal across all books.

Leo Manco was shocked and disappointed that I was leaving *Sláine*. But this was just one of the elements in the perfect storm. This is how I explained it to Leo:

'Like Connery, I should 'never say never again' - but I don't see how I can return to writing *Sláine*...
'This is because it's uneconomic. Each *Sláine* book takes weeks to develop before I write it and I can't afford to do this anymore, when I have other books that pay better and fairer. Unfortunately, Rebellion relies on its creators to subsidise them – and keep a disproportionate amount of the royalties – which I'm not prepared to do anymore.'

I also had to think about my writing motivation – or rather my muse's motivation – which has always been subversion. Influencing younger readers was her objective, but could that really apply today? Now that *2000AD* mainly appeals to older readers? Just how far can you subvert a fifty-year-old? My muse doesn't think it is possible.

Finally, I really like to encourage *new* talent. That was often a motivation for writing *Sláine*, going all the way back to Angela's episode one. One talent in particular stands out: Charlie Gillespie, who produced *Sláine* sample pages that I loved, but, alas, I couldn't get him into the comic, even on a one-off story.

Here's Charlie on *Sláine*:

'In a nutshell I'd like to marry the heyday of the painted strip with some of the epic/detailed digital quality of the Langley years in a digitally painted version. Depending what the story was it would be interesting to study Sláine's noble side vs his manic side. I've often fantasized about a book where Sláine has lost his connection to the Goddess and becomes the worst that he could be, called *Sláine the Tyrant*.'

That is so inspiring, and you can see how I could be tempted to continue, despite the stormy weather. I've put up with challenging behaviour from editors in the past, and by comparison, my differences with the current publisher are not as bad. Surely I could put up with them again and just focus on the creativity? And use stories outside of Rebellion to fund and subsidise the development time on another *Sláine* saga, as I'd done so often, over his forty years of existence ... The substantial royalties I receive on *Requiem* often compensated for the far lower royalties on *Sláine*, for example.

But one other factor had changed. The subconscious reason I wrote *Sláine* in the first place. My other prime motivation for exploring all those extraordinary Celtic legends. It was always about understanding my ancestry, my roots. And now I was about to have some final answers.

Sláine's parentage had been confirmed in the final volume of *The Brutania Chronicles*. Now it was my turn. I'd sent off for a DNA ancestry test for myself and I knew I would receive the results very soon.

And then ... my Quest would be over.

DRAGONTAMER: THE EPISODES

Before reaching the end of my Quest, let's take a closer look at the last book in the series.

It had been a while since I looked at *Dragontamer* episode one, and when I did so in order to write this chapter, which is a commentary on Leo's artwork, I was blown away all over again. Leo and I exchanged a total of 17 *emails* as he endlessly tweaked and refined his colour system for the first episode.

Thus, there's *at least* three different, beautifully coloured versions, just of his page one!

I'm especially pleased with the action scenes. Sláine is moving so fast, all we see is the result of his axe-work, never the weapon itself. I introduced this concept because I realised that showing the axe can slow down the action. This approach also stirs the reader's imagination and draws them deeper into the story.

Episode two show a mysterious build-up leading to a sensational warp spasm. The detail on the scenes is of the same high standard as *Conquering Armies*. We see endless Trojans falling to Sláine's axe, and Brutus's throne room is designed and depicted with absolute conviction. All this is normal enough in European comics, where detailed backgrounds are de rigueur. In fact, the lack of them in

French comics can be a deal breaker, as I know to my cost on my French series *Broz,* illustrated by the brilliant Adrian Smith. But not in British comics today, because of the desperate need to cut corners in order to pay the bills. We are the poor comics relation and that's the way some professionals in our industry seem to like it, actually sneering at my bid to reach our lost youth audience with my own comic *Spacewarp.* One individual called it 'fucking risible'. It's *always* been like that from the beginning of my comics career. Some strange flaw in the British comic psyche that I've never understood. Competitiveness goes into reverse: it was how quickly you could *sink* to the bottom of the pond. Failure often led to promotion. Publisher John Sanders once said to me, when I complained about losing major talents like Brian Bolland and Dave Gibbons, 'We cannot compete with the United States and France.'

We have to know our place.

Fortunately, Leo and I do not agree, and the standard here is uncomfortably high for celebrants of the failure of British comics.

Episode three features Duban the Druid in a stunning underwater scene. Leo expanded this scene into a spread over two pages, and he was absolutely right to do so. My original script was too compressed as I overreacted to previous *Sláine* stories where the visuals could be too loose and empty.

There's also a classic scene as a bloody Sláine grins with a 'Here's Johnny' expression: a reminder of why Angela and I chose Jack Nicholson as our visual template. It's a relief to come back to the roots of the character established all those years ago. It only took four decades. I think this 'Here's Sláine!' scene, where he rips out of the water and leers at his enemies competes well with 'Here's Johnny!'

The mad axe-man theme is sustained in episode four, with a full-page scene of Sláine doing what he does best. It's a gem! Duban is a powerful character here, although, subconsciously, I was probably drawing on one of the contenders for my biological father:

'Torquemada'. Consequently, I'm not sure I did Duban justice in the writing, because I couldn't think of anything positive to draw on from his real-life role model. So I probably defaulted here to bog-standard Gandalf, Obi Ben, or *Dungeons and Dragons* wizards.

I love Leo's Brutus in episode five: a troubled Emperor with a dysfunctional family. I found myself liking him as a character and that's also down to Leo's interpretation, which makes him three dimensional and not a stereotypical villain. His wife, Innogen, was inspired by a friend telling me about a woman who always checked that the soft lighting in a room made her look good, and used her hair to hide her features. Leo took this further: we see her eyes scarily staring out *through* her hair! That has iconic comic-book potential and is something I would have played up if I'd continued with the saga.

The little dragons were inspired by Pine Processionary Caterpillars we encountered here in Spain. Incredibly toxic, they spend part of their life cycle in nests high in pine trees, and when they come down to the ground their poisonous hairs can be lethal for pets and harmful to humans. Lisa and I found they're the very devil to destroy!

Episode six is a high point for me. I never thought I would ever again see artwork as detailed as Joe Colquhoun's *Charley's War*. I've heard some fans shamefully dismiss Joe's detailed art as 'old school' and 'of its time'. But here is Leo, drawing a similarly detailed opening picture. This is just how Joe would have depicted it! Lots of people, and everyone is a character. Nothing fudged: an authentic Celtic chariot; beautifully drawn horses, and a gloomy British wet landscape. You can see that, like Joe, Leo's thought about this scene with a film director's eye. As a result, we are at the movies here.

The fantasy archery scenes that follow are superb. They go far beyond the rational, 'Robin Hood' style of archery we see in movies. And yet, surprisingly, they are based on accounts of medieval bowmanship.

I've always been fond of the shoggey beasts, who first appeared drawn by Mike McMahon, and here they provide a metaphor for anyone who is victimised for being different. I was drawing on a story about a distant Irish ancestor of mine in the 1930s. He was a young, strong swimmer, a member of the Gaelic Athletic Association, and yet he ended up drowned in the River Moy at a place where salmon fishermen stand in the river, wearing waders. Verdict: accidental death. It's possible he met his death because he was 'different'. That was the view of my ancestors and I discovered they weren't just interested in motivating me to write about my current lineage. They were also motivating me to write about old wrongs, too. It was surprising how much passion I felt when I read about this tragedy, soberly reported in the local newspaper. A passion that is transferred to this shoggey beast story.

Episode seven sees Sláine playing music in Ukko's bar. Here are some excerpts from the script and my description of ancient musical instruments, to give you an idea of the detail with which I normally approach the saga:

'Sláine is leading the prehistoric equivalent of a band like Corvus Corax. See youtube below. The detail on the costumes is perfect. I think Sláine has to play a primitive bagpipes??? It needs a mad drummer, a snarling singer and a horn player/s. The horn in his band could be a carnyx. It could be an alternative for Sláine to play, giving him the charisma of a sax player, but I have a feeling the bagpipes have the edge?

'Crotales (hand bells) made of bronze or wood as well as terracotta rattles are known since the Bronze Age, some of which came in the shape of birds. Closed bells were sometimes built with a ring and could be strapped to the player's apparel.

'Whether the Celts used drumming instruments like the Roman *tympanum* is unknown, but very likely, because other forms of hand drums like the ceramic German *Honsommern Drum*, which was similar to the African djembe, are known since the Neolithic.

'The bodhran is probably more recent, but you might feature a primitive version.'

The result, according to Sláine's enemies is, 'A harsh, unpleasant noise, unworthy to be described as music.' Leo carries it off to perfection.

In episode eight, Leo draws the most powerful full-page image. In his words: 'Here we go with the son of Brutus, this is the most gothic image Doré style as you suggested and that came to my mind.' I find the dragon boy even more disturbing than Gustav Doré's work.

The colour on this episode is terrific, but I find myself time and time again often preferring Leo's original black and white, which is wonderfully Gothic. I know Leo is modifying his colours for the collected edition, so I may not be alone in my opinion.

Episode nine maintains the high standard Leo has set himself. There's a truly iconic shot of Sláine surrounded by dragons. Often art can be rushed at the end of a story because of the deadline, or the artist is already planning his next job. That never happened here. The dragons reminded me of the eagles, vultures and hawks that circle over a ruined castle where we live, sometimes mobbed by smaller birds, anxious to protect their young. It's going to be hard not to turn all that into a future dragon story. Especially as I look out from my office at a mountain known as El Hacho, *Axe Mountain*, with raptors soaring overhead.

As usual, I edited the script against the art, which gives a final polish to the story. This is something that is not commonplace in modern comics because of the economics and, like any system, it doesn't always work, but here it's worthwhile, even though Leo's storytelling is exemplary.

Normally, I set the *Sláine* sagas up so final episodes have cliffhangers or elements that definitely require answers in future volumes. I came close to doing so in episode ten. In fact, I had the next threat planned, and was intending to show the new villains as the final image.

But there wasn't space to do the ancestors justice as well, so I held the new threat back, not knowing at the time that this would be my last *Sláine*.

There are some remarkable images in episode ten: the view of Duban in classic sword and sorcery mode, repelling arrows, fired from some spring-loaded gun. Brutus's loathsome 'spin doctor' Slough Gorm. The urban dictionary describes a gorm as a complete moron, a popular insult in my teenage years. I like to think it's as unpleasant a word as Slough Throt or Slough Feg.

But my personal favourite is the Guledig. He's been drawn impressively before, but maybe he looked too much like the Mekon, because I was inspired by Belardinelli's original Mekonesque view of him. It was based on Manannan, king of the sea, and was also symbolised as the triskele, the ubiquitous sign all the villains bear from Angela's episode one. So all the British artists who drew the Guledig were doubtless also thinking of the Mekon, and that may have held them back.

Here Leo – who may not have been aware of the Mekon – redesigns the Guledig, whilst retaining the original premise, and I think his version tops them all. As the supreme villain in the *Sláine* saga, above even Slough Feg, he deserves greater recognition in the pantheon of villains. Imagine this creature walking on two or even three legs towards you! And Leo is probably right to make him huge, although the Guledig can vary his size, of course. Remember that he spins like a wheel, something it was unreasonable for me to ask the artists to convey, although I think I tried! But if there's ever a *Sláine* movie, I would expect to see the Guledig spinning as well as scurrying across the ground, Alien-style, towards us. With the incredible film sfx today, we should expect no less.

At the end, Sláine flies off into the sunset, young, powerful, pagan, ever ready to take on the oppressors of freedom. For me, that is the best way for a comic saga to end, rather than broken and disillusioned, or dead, or mission accomplished – or that contrived and overworked ploy of the 'noble sacrifice'; laying down his life for others, with all its establishment and neo-Christian associations.

I also love the final view of the ancestors. Leo was originally planning it as a double page spread, so we would see more ancestors receding into eternity, but he ran out of time. I'm curious to know readers' favourites here. Do let me know! You can find my social media and contact details at the end of the book.

I think Macha stands out the most for me. There's something in her face that tells us she is bad news, and yet ... Roth is a close second. He's wearing an expression that seems very Celtic to me. He looks a real hard case. I'll come back to Roth in the final chapter. Duban also looks good and I think that's down to a certain darkness and arrogance in his face, that is missing – for me, anyway – from Obi Ben, Gandalf and the usual good-guy wizards.

Finally, as I look out on Axe Mountain from my office, I read Sláine saying for the very last time, 'Kiss My Axe!'

The definitive punk expression. A verbal gift from our rebellious Celtic ancestors, two thousand or more years ago, to help us cope with the modern authoritarian times we live in.

To remind us that our ancestors really are with every one of us.

THE AXE FALLS

A s Leo drew the very final episode of *Sláine* in March 2021 and I was writing the first draft of this book, my DNA results arrived from *Living DNA*. I would finally discover: was my father 'Torquemada'? 'Braveheart'? Or 'Jack the Lad'?

The DNA report displays percentages of maternal and paternal recent legacies, but doesn't distinguish between the heritage from the mother and father; however it's roughly 50% from each parent. My mother came from Mayo on the west coast of Ireland, so her DNA endowment to me would probably be 50% Irish, give or take the odd Viking.

Therefore, if my father was 'Braveheart' – who was born in Dublin – my DNA result should show a high percentage of Irish DNA: at least 70%.

But if my father was 'Jack the Lad', it would have a high East Anglian percentage.

And if my father was 'Torquemada', it would have a high Scottish percentage, as *he* was born in Glasgow.

The following story demonstrates just how much was at stake for me.

Years ago, I was at an Irish wedding, and one of the guests became exceptionally drunk, even for an Irish wedding. This was rather surprising, given that he worked in an Irish brewery: you'd think he could have paced himself better. Under the influence, he started to warp out in the direction of his mum, bringing up old grievances, and becoming extremely aggressive towards her. He was all ready to attack her, and I had to step between mother and son in order to protect her from his wrath. The next day, he apologised profusely for his behaviour and his odd flying fist that I had to block. I said that it was no problem from my point of view and the only thing that *really* upset me was that he called me an 'English bastard'.

So this 'English bastard' now reviewed the possibilities. The DNA test would finally show my heritage, beyond all reasonable doubt.

There was Dubliner 'Braveheart' who had helped my mother find and buy her home (even if he did want his money back later). His son and I said we were 'cousins'. My mother clearly had a relationship with him going back years, probably before I was born.

But I had 'Torquemada's' colouring and hair and he – or, more likely, his fellow Knights – had paid for my College education, even if there were considerable strings attached. However he was short – and I'm tall.

Finally, there was 'Jack the Lad'. Maybe I was making too much of the weird way my family had censored his character out of existence? Perhaps there was an innocent explanation after all?

All three were strong contenders. The jury was still out. I took a deep breath and looked at the results, which were shown in map form. At last I would discover my Celtic roots, which had always been my motivation for writing *Sláine*.

The results were a shock. I was only 50% Irish.

To be precise: 45% Irish. 1% Northern Ireland. 4% Liverpool. That was definitely from my mother, with her family's known, strong Irish-Liverpool connection. There was not a Viking in sight, which is not that surprising because I believe the percentage breakdown is more recent. Possibly covering the last two hundred years, or less.

And the rest? Various areas were marked in percentage terms elsewhere in Britain, but all I could see, all I could pay attention to at that moment, was a series of percentages in the south of England: 23%.

And one in particular jumped out at me: 9.1% East Anglia.

So it *had* to be 'Jack the Lad'.

I'd got it all hopelessly wrong. He was my dad, after all. I was surprised, but delighted. I had been clearly affected by confirmation bias in so desperately wanting it to be 'Braveheart'. I went to bed reassured and pleased that my dark suspicions about family secrets were unfounded. I couldn't have been happier.

Mystery solved.

I was woken abruptly in the middle of the night. It was the ancestors calling.

Check the percentages again.

They could have left it to the next morning, but ancestors tend to call you in the middle of the night, when they have your undivided attention.

The next morning, I duly checked.

I guess I was in such a state of shock, and so focused on Ireland and East Anglia, I paid no attention to the large percentage in Scotland and the north of England. Perhaps because I didn't want it to be true. It totalled 22%.

And the biggest chunk of that 22% was 9.4%: *Glasgow*.

I checked with the Mills family and they have no known Scottish branch or connection.

So it *was* 'Torquemada', after all.

Well, I told myself, it could have been worse – It could have been Darth Vader.

More confirmation may well come through from subsequent DNA matches who bear his surname, but this data, combined with other evidence, is good enough for me. So 'Torque' is my dad. I'm hardly affected by confirmation bias this time! No wonder I wrote so many stories about him.

Actually, there's a clue in Roth's appearance in the Wickerman all those decades ago. I only realised it as I wrote this chapter. I went back to check and, sure enough, I had subconsciously written Roth's dialogue with a *Glasgow* accent. I remembered that I was trying for a Rab C. Nesbitt character, and it's far from perfect – but then I am a Southerner. The clincher is when Roth says, 'Aye! That's right, son. You and me together – eh? We'll take the Drunes on... *Nae bother!*' 'Nae bother!' is of course a Glasgow expression.

In some ways, Roth was a fusion of all three possible dads, so dimly remembered after a lifetime. He was the outcast that was 'Jack the Lad'. The hard drinker that was 'Braveheart'. And the Glaswegian that was 'Torquemada'.

However, anyone 'cast out' from the family tree is likely to cause problems for those who did the casting out, or their descendants. Cast outs, unfortunately for me, include 'illegitimate dads'.

And, like Sláine, I had most emphatically cast out my father. Cast him out from my mind, my memory and my heart. I last saw him in a pub in Ipswich – at least it wasn't the Milk Bar this time. I was sixteen, and I'd just successfully left home to escape him and his creepy, entitled fellow Knights, so they no longer had coercive control over me. He knew it was over for him and this was goodbye. 'I did the best I could for you, Paddy,' he whined. I imagine Darth said something similar to Luke!

We went our separate ways, and I swore I would forget this man ever existed. I would erase every single memory I had of him. Including his Glasgow accent. He was *history*. And I did so successfully for most of my life. I cast him out.

This wretched character died a long time ago, but in magical terms he's still in the Otherworld, raging because he's cast out from his rightful and non-negotiable place in the family tree. Cast out from being my father. Doubtless it hasn't helped that – to his Catholic eyes – I must seem like Damian to him. Good. Perhaps he should have thought about that at the time of my conception.

So in order to restore balance, he has to be properly acknowledged, and that is one of the purposes of this book. I can't ignore or escape my connection to my family tree, much as I might like to. Just as Sláine can't escape his family or his tribe and has to return to them.

In esoteric terms, without over-egging it, I need to exorcise The Curse of 'Torquemada'. Otherwise, the 'injured' party finds suitable surrogates to unconsciously act as his mouthpiece, reflecting his egotistic character or venting his spleen through them, in addition to their own. And 'Torquemada' had a whole lot of spleen. He was an angry individual when he was alive, and doubtless being dead hasn't improved his temper.

Unlikely as it may seem, magic can – and really *does* – work like that. I've been on the receiving end of it at least three times. It can be scientifically described and explained in psychoanalytical (transference) or epigenetic terms if that feels more comfortable for you. But, long before Freud, it was the basis of ancestral curses that pass down through the generations from excluded family members. Again, consider numerous famous dysfunctional families and the impact of past wrongs that still affect them today.

Anyone who has done ancestral work, such as Family Constellations, knows how an ancestor will look for a surrogate to vent their feelings and it doesn't have to be a blood relative. On the contrary. It's quite astonishing to witness or take part in the process. I'm being rather coy here. It's actually spooky. But it's their bid to be finally acknowledged. It's also possible to make a connection with them alone, just by quietly focussing on the troubled ancestor, but it is not a parlour game or a séance, and they are not all as unsympathetic as 'Torquemada'.

Sometimes the ancestors' troubles can be very moving and it is possible to feel at first-hand just what they went through and how they survived, albeit at a cost that resonates through the generations. Ancestor worship – or more accurately 'ancestor veneration' – is, after all, the earliest religion, long before the religions of the book, and is still a powerful force in many cultures today. To conclude that they are primitive and deluded for believing in the power of their ancestors is to dismiss an important strata of human behaviour that affects every single one of us, whether we accept it or not.

Tony Skinner and I wrote a horror story exploring this form of 'possession' with malevolent gangster 'Liquid Lennie' finding and controlling a suitably malevolent surrogate, the teenager Lily the Fink, in *PsychoKiller* (illustrated by Dave Kendall, available from Millsverse). So I understand and take the whole process seriously.

Therefore, as Roth says to Sláine, 'You and me *together* – eh?' Reluctantly, just like Sláine, I have to agree. Okay. If you insist. *Together*.

Sigh!

A public acknowledgement is powerful magic and it acts as the necessary antidote, as well as releasing all that pent-up psychic energy. It's the same motive behind all public ceremonies. The ceremony is real because it is witnessed by an audience. Thankfully, I don't have to *like* or forgive 'Torquemada'. Forgiveness is for Christians. It's not one of the requirements of the ancestors. In fact it's not within the remit of a son to forgive a father, because the father came first. Instead, it's about restoring balance, which is similar in its effect, but rather more profound.

So now he's done with.

And it's not all bad – I absolutely *love* Glasgow and Glaswegians, so it's good to know I have that connection to the city.

My battle with 'Torquemada's' Knights continues to this day. I've recently won two important victories relating to them and I hope more will follow. But that story lies outside this book. If you're interested, it can be found on patmills.wordpress.com, a site I run for Old Boys of my old college. It's encouraging how speaking out makes an important difference in this modern era where most people keep their heads down and their mouths shut.

Leaving *Sláine* behind will still be a wrench, especially because it was finally drawn to such absolute perfection by Leo Manco. I can't sing his praises highly enough. Some words from Leo himself reveal his total dedication to the saga:

'Regarding *Sláine*, all of this was magical and strange to me, and it still seems so. When this character came into my hands for the first time, I was 19 or 20 years old, and at that time I was jumping from one temporary low-tow job to another. One night after coming back from one of those jobs, I looked at this comic and I said to myself, "How lucky is this artist, to be able to draw this book". I liked it so much that I gave one of my cats the name of Cuchulain, although its character would have been more appropriate to Ukko. Forty years later, you say goodbye to your own creation, and I could be the final artist. I don't care too much about being the best, those things are subjective, without having disappointed your fans, that's enough for me. You know now why so much love in this project, and how much I appreciate your support and Matt as well during all this time.'

Thank you, Leo.

Final words from *Sláine* fan Andrew McIlwaine. Andrew is *very* Glaswegian, so that is important for me esoterically. It helps restore balance.

'There is no finer artist for the last *Sláine*, his work in color is every bit as breathtaking as *The Horned God*. For the purists there was *The Book of Scars*. I don't have a favourite *Sláine* artist, they all brought something to the table, maybe Fabry. The joy of *2000AD* was the eye being used to changing artists. The dance goes on.'

Sláinte!

ACKNOWLEDGMENTS

Thanks for reading *Sláine* and *Kiss My Axe*, his Secret History. It's been a privilege sharing Sláine's quest with you. Special thanks to the following: to Angela Kincaid, for co-creating *Sláine*, a fantastic but truly thankless task, created against all the odds, an achievement that is greatly valued by the readers, myself, and all those who believe in *the truth* in comics; to *all* the incredible *Sláine* artists who followed her – I dare not single one of you out above the others! You *all* brought something very special to the series; to Geoff Gilbertson, co-author of *The Dark Gods* whose powerful work pointed me in the right magical direction; to Matt Smith, editor of *2000AD*, for his valuable support, encouragement, and for *two decades* of editorial peace on *Sláine*! To Tony Skinner, whose pagan insights have played such an important magical role in *Sláine* from *The Horned God* onwards. To Lisa, my publisher, for bringing a fresh and objective pair of eyes to the *Sláine* saga. And, above all, to you the readers, for your great enthusiasm, support, and for staying with the series through good times and bad.

APPENDIX
SLÁINE – A TIMELINE OF SKULLDUGGERY

The order of events is based on my recollections, but I kept no records or diary on actual dates. So I've based my dates on those historian Dave Bishop used in *Future Shock*, the official history of *2000AD*. However some of his dates and details are vague and there are noticeable gaps in his record.

JANUARY 1981 ONWARDS

Angela and I talk about producing a new *2000 AD* strip together.

After discussing doing a dinosaur serial first, maybe a *Flesh* sequel, we eventually decide to create a barbarian hero together.

I spend some months thinking about and trying out different story versions of the barbarian.

During this period I read heroic fantasy novels and research Celtic and other myths and legends to inspire me.

Finally, I decide to break with traditional fantasy heroes and make Sláine rather different: a teenage rebel with a crooked side-kick, Ukko, who involves him in endless skullduggery.

SUMMER 1981

Based on our creative 'jam sessions' together, Angela designs Sláine, Ukko, the Time Monster, the Drune Lords and the Skull Swords. She produces various black and white full page images which show her inking style.

She sends these concept art pages to *2000 AD*, who respond positively. These images will be used extensively in her episode one and provide a reference source for subsequent artists.

(The images she sent to *2000 AD* do not include Sláine wearing his original rusty, battered helmet.)

JULY 1981

Inspired by her concept art pages, I write the first version of *Sláine* episode one, which features Ukko as a Russo-Finnish dwarf.

AUTUMN – DECEMBER 1981

I'm aware Angela's creation will need to be shared with other artists: Belardinelli because of his illustrative qualities and McMahon because of his strong desire to draw heroic fantasy.

I discuss and choose these two artists with Tharg McManus.

I write some *Sláine* stories for Belardinelli first, including *the Bride of Crom* (Wickerman). I then write *Sky Chariots* for Mike.

JANUARY/FEBRUARY 1982

Mike would have been shown Angela's concept art. So it's probably at this stage, rather than later, he asks for Sláine's 'Brainbiter' to be changed to a single-headed axe, which he felt was more realistic. He tightens up her logo and tweaks Sláine's 'waist mat'.

Mike must have done a sketch to show how he wanted his version of the axe and the 'waist mat' to look and sent it to Angela.

MARCH 1982

After taking a break to work on other art projects for other companies, Angela pencils her episode one.

I intend to write an additional *Sláine* saga for Angela when she has completed episode one.

Angela submits her pencil pages of episode one to *2000 AD*. This probably included the changes Mike wanted: namely her double-headed axe was replaced by his single-headed axe.

Robin Smith asks Angela for just *one* art change, for unstated censorship reasons. Namely, no axe to be embedded in Sláine's victim's head. Robin redraws her picture to show what he has in mind.

It was an important but actually straightforward change although Bishop seems to think otherwise, relating in his typically crude way: 'Kincaid battled to satisfy Smith.'

This was not the case. If there had been any to-ing and fro-ing and further changes required, I would remember. We were actually pleasantly surprised Robin Smith didn't ask Angela for further major changes.

The same applies to her subsequent cover.

APRIL 1982

Angela decides not to continue with *Sláine* after she's completed episode one.

MAY 1982

According to Bishop, Mike delivers episode one of *Sky Chariots* – although Angela and I did not see this art until many months later.

DECEMBER 1982

Mike does his brilliant version of Angela's character as the dummy cover for *Zarjaz,* an adult/more sophisticated version of *2000 AD.*

The date is unclear, but it's probable it was the end of the year.

This Sláine is handsome and thus follows Angela's version of Sláine much closer than Mike's *Sky Chariots* black and white 'rugged-looking' Sláine.

It's 'publicly displayed at a comics event', according to Bishop, who also says Mike is talking about *Sláine* in a fan interview.

It's thus produced *ahead* of Angela's episode one appearing in print. Or indeed before she'd even completed inking *her* creation.

I protest vehemently to Tharg about the *Zarjaz* cover, because I was not consulted, because of the insensitive timing, and because I do not believe his excuse that it's 'only a dummy'.

Fortunately, the publisher, John Sanders, dislikes *Zarjaz,* so the dummy dies.

JANUARY 1983?

Angela sends in her episode one by this date. Her inked pages are accepted without a word of comment by *2000 AD.*

This date is assuming Bishop's dates are actually accurate. Because he notes Angela was 'battling with the pencils' in 1982. Once she had finished her alleged battling, there would be no reason for her to delay. She was a fast and confident inker and, like all freelance artists, she would want to get her invoice in and finally be paid.

The long subsequent delay to publication date seems most unlikely.

As Bishop is the comic historian, I have reluctantly deferred to his dates, but I think they're at least six months too long. I believe some events must have taken place over a shorter period of time.

However, it doesn't really matter.

The *order* of events is the important thing and this is correct, with the possible exception of Mike drawing the *Zarjaz* cover *after* he had started *Sky Chariots*.

SPRING 1983

I write the final draft of *Sláine* episode one, editing it against a copy of the artwork. In this version, I delete all references to Ukko being a Russo-Finnish dwarf who calls Sláine 'a Bogatyr' (A 'God Warrior'). This change applies, of course, to all my subsequent episodes, including *Sky Chariots*.

SUMMER 1983

Mike completes *Sky Chariots*. Angela and I only asked for and saw the pages some time after she had completed her episode one.

Although I had some reservations about Mike's work, I put them to one side because of Angela's enthusiasm for *Sky Chariots*.

Accordingly, I decided to write some extra stories leading up to it to make *Sky Chariots* a mega-event, the equivalent of Dredd *The Cursed Earth*.

These shorter stories are *Warriors Dawn*, *Beltain Giant*, *Hero's Blood* and *The Shoggey Beast*.

20TH AUGUST 1983

Angela's episode one appears in print.

It's a number one hit story with the readers, an astonishing and unique achievement, but is ignored by my peers and a minority of purist fans.

Tharg McManus tells me of *Sláine's* huge success.

He does not phone Angela to congratulate her.

AUGUST-NOVEMBER 1983

Subsequent *Sláine* episodes drawn by Belardinelli are popular but only reach number two in the vote charts, directly after *Dredd*.

OCTOBER 1983 ONWARDS

Mike's prequel episodes appear in *2000AD* and flop with the readers, because they are more rugged, minimalist, and downbeat in art style compared to *Sky Chariots*.

This minimalist style is possibly influenced by all the tensions surrounding *Sláine*, which must have taken its toll on Mike, too.

AUTUMN/WINTER 1983

Sky Chariots also, sadly, flops with the readers, primarily because the prequels sent out a negative vibe to readers.

But all Mike's episodes are still hailed by a purist minority and my peers as the right way forward for *Sláine*, despite all the commercial evidence to the contrary.

Thus Titan Books, publishes Mike's *Sláine* stories soon after, but Angela's and Belardinelli's *Sláines* are not published *for two decades*, until Rebellion take over *2000AD*.

Current recollections from readers have been exampled in Part I.

They confirm the feedback and readers' opinions *2000AD* received at the time is correct.

Namely, that they still rate the artists in the same way and in the same order.

They still have a huge regard for Angela's work, the first story to beat *Judge Dredd* .

The readers votes show *Sláine* losing a little of its popularity with Belardinelli, which is further evidence that the success of *Sláine* in episode one was *more* Angela's achievement than mine.

A comic writer is only as good as his artist.

It would take Glenn Fabry's brilliant interpretation of the character to undo the damage caused by Tharg McManus and co. and restore *Sláine* to its original popularity.

Be Pure! Be Vigilant! Behave! 2000AD & Judge Dredd: The Secret History

As *2000AD* and *Judge Dredd* celebrate their 40th birthday, Pat at last writes the definitive history of the Galaxy's Greatest Comic, and the turbulent, extraordinary and exciting events that shaped it.

Everything you've always wanted to know about *Judge Dredd*, *Sláine*, *Nemesis*, *ABC Warriors*, *Flesh*, *Bill Savage* and more, is in this book.

The writers and artists who created them and the real-life people and events they drew on for inspiration. The scandals, the back-stabbing and the shocking story that was regarded as too sensitive to ever see the light of day is finally told.

Funny, sad, angry, defiant, and outrageous: it's the Comic Book memoir of the year!

SPACEWARP

From the **Sfeer**, beyond Space and Time, the **Warp Lords** have launched a **SPACEWARP** on an unsuspecting Earth, splintering the planet into infinite realities:

Hellbreaker: A Prisoner escapes the fires of Hell to punish the Living and becomes the coolest Influencer on Earth!

SF1: A Special Force of elite Human, Robot and Alien soldiers battle monstrous Invaders!

Fu-tant: At the Warpstar Academy, a teenage boy must use his mutant powers for evil. If he disobeys – his friends die!

Jurassic Punx: Time-travelling shoplifter Dada and Joe Megiddo, a scientist searching for his family, fight Dinosaurs in post-apocalyptic Liverpool!

Xecutioners: Future Cops hunt and terminate the Aliens who walk among us!

Slayer: One rebel Robot stands against a million Space Knights enslaving the Galaxy!

And all the while, the Warp Lords **WATCH...**

Action-packed, heroic, humorous, and fast-paced!

SERIAL KILLER (Read Em And Weep: 1)

A rotten childhood. A comic book crime spree. One last chance to get his killer reputation...

London, 1975. Dave Maudling escaped his rotten childhood by losing himself in comic books. Now an editor for the same comics that served as his escape, he uses his window into the minds of youth to hide dangerous clues in his most popular strip. But when his pipe bomb instructions reach the wrong demographic, Dave takes his plot to a whole new audience...

But when a suspicious reporter gets in the way of his sweet retribution and the fur-draped phantom of his dead mom nags him from beyond the grave, he has no choice but to think outside the panels. If he fails, he'll never salvage his reputation as a comic genius and a killer.

GOODNIGHT, JOHN-BOY (Read Em And Weep: 2)

The Geek Detective is back! In book two of the *Read Em And Weep* series, comic book editor and armchair serial killer, Dave Maudling, takes on a Masonic order of Knights in a bid to solve his mother's murder.

And to save kids from the Knights' Grand Master, depraved TV celebrity and charity fundraiser 'Fabulous' Keen, who is getting away with worse than murder. The 'national treasure' believes he is above the law, but not Dave's law.

But Dave, the 'lard-arse assassin', can't murder him by proxy like his other victims; he has to face and kill Keen himself.

And his *femme fatale* mother, a 'ghost in mink', is there to help him.

Psychokiller by Pat Mills & Tony Skinner, illustrated by Dave Kendall

ARE YOU READY FOR YOUR DEMONIC IRRIGATION?

A Ouija board session to summon 1950s gangster Liquid Lenny goes horribly right. Lily the Fink starts acting weirder than usual. Mary Anne's boyfriend is brutally murdered in his own bathroom, and she develops a sudden penchant for doo-wop music and beehive hairdo's.

Timid Jamie Anderson saw something that night. He knows Mary Anne needs urgent medical help. And there's only one doctor qualified to give it...

56 pages of full colour strip art, and a bonus 9-page, beautifully gruesome art gallery from Dave Kendall.

Carlos Ezquerra's 2000AD & Judge Dredd Colouring Book

COLOUR LIKE CARLOS!

The late, great, Carlos Ezquerra was one of the best-loved and most successful sci-fi fantasy creators in the world. Collected here are 50 superb drawings of his top characters in a colouring book guaranteed to get your creative and law-giving juices flowing.

IT'S THE LAW

Go wild with colour as Dredd arrests perps, chases mutants on his Lawmaster Bike, and fights zombies! Strontium Dog, Durham Red, Judge Anderson, The Dark Judges, The Fatties, and many more beloved 2000AD characters join Dredd in this epic collection of Carlos's stunning creations.

Unleash your creativity and lose yourself in the sci-fi world of Carlos Ezquerra!

Includes special introduction by John Wagner, Judge Dredd writer-creator!

MORE GRAPHIC NOVELS BY PAT MILLS

Accident Man, by Pat Mills & Tony Skinner, illustrated by Martin Emond,
Duke Mighten, John Erasmus (Now a film starring Scott Adkins)

Marshal Law, by Pat Mills & Kevin O'Neill

Requiem: Vampire Knight, by Pat Mills & Olivier Ledroit

Claudia: Vampire Knight, by Pat Mills & Franck Tacito

2000AD COLLECTIONS

Sláine

ABC Warriors

Nemesis The Warlock

Defoe

Flesh

Greysuit

Savage

Third World War

BRITISH TREASURY OF COMICS

Charley's War, by Pat Mills & Joe Colquhoun

Sugar Jones

Concrete Surfer

FREE STORIES FROM PAT!

While Pat's working on his next tale, why not join our mailing lists and download some stories from him while you're waiting?

Six-page comic strip Future Shlock, BRANDED! from the **SPACEWARP** universe. Art by Cliff Cumber. Sign up to our newsletter at spacewarpcomic.com to download your copy!

And head over to www.millsverse.com to grab two text stories:

RELIEVING MR MAFEKING

A 7000-word story from the *Read Em And Weep* universe.

What is the dark secret of Mafeking & Jones? What's waiting for Dave Maudling in the basement of their caning emporium? And what does Mr Jones really mean when he tells Dave that Mr Mafeking is 'no longer with us'?

Dave's tough new comic *Aaagh!* – known to the press as the 'eightpenny nightmare' – is so controversial, questions are asked in Parliament. Yet Dave naively believes all publicity is good publicity.

He's invited to visit Mafeking and Jones of St James's, the famous cane-makers. Lured by the prospect of a bottle of ten-year-old malt whisky, he accepts, and is shown an awesome array of swagger sticks, swordsticks, bullwhips, riding crops and school canes.

But there is a nightmare waiting for him in the basement.

A tale of revenge, treachery and treason, with even more blood and gore than *Aaagh!*

THE ARTISTS' DEBT COLLECTION PARTY (Being an account of how the Toxic! artists, led by Pat Mills, did recover their unfairly withheld wages from the Publisher)

This true story short (just under 3000 words), written with Pat's trademark acerbic wit, is a companion piece to Pat's *Be Pure! Be Vigilant! Behave! 2000AD & Judge Dredd: The Secret History*. Can definitely be enjoyed on its own.

ABOUT THE AUTHOR

Pat Mills created Britain's most successful comic *2000AD* and it is the subject of his autobiography *Be Pure! Be Vigilant! Behave! 2000AD and Judge Dredd: The Secret History*. He also co-created the girls' mystery comic *Misty*, now enjoying new success in collected editions.

He was the key writer on *Crisis* with his political thriller, *Third World War*, illustrated by the late Carlos Ezquerra. Some of his well-loved and long-running British series are the anti-war saga *Charley's War*, the Celtic barbarian *Sláine* and *ABC Warriors*.

He developed and wrote *Judge Dredd*, as well as *Doctor Who* audio plays and comics, *Dan Dare*, and series for Marvel and DC Comics. His *Marshal Law* – co-created with Kevin O'Neill – now published by DC Comics, was a New York Times Best Seller.

Pat continues to write all manner of challenging stories today, including the French graphic novel series *Requiem: Vampire Knight*, illustrated by Olivier Ledroit, which is also available in English as a digital release on Amazon.

His most recent title is the sci-fi comic *Spacewarp*, suitable for all ages. *Spacewarp* is available in all good comic shops and online bookstores.

Pat's crime series *Accident Man* – co-created with Tony Skinner – is now a movie starring Scott Adkins. His future cop sci-fi thriller *American Reaper*, produced by Repeat Offenders Ltd, has been optioned by Amblin Partners.

Pat has also written two text novels in a dark comedy thriller series called *Read Em and Weep*: *Serial Killer* and *Goodnight, John-Boy*. The third book in the series, *The Grim Reader*, got a little delayed by *Spacewarp* – and this book – but Pat swears it's his next writing project!

For Pat's full bibliography, see his Wiki page.

facebook.com/PatMillsComics
twitter.com/PatMillsComics
instagram.com/patmillswriter

Printed in Great Britain
by Amazon

49569969R00196